Ethics

An Overview

Robin Attfield

Continuum International Publishing Group

The Tower Building	80 Maiden Lane
11 York Road	Suite 704
London SE1 7NX	New York NY 10038

www.continuumbooks.com

British Library Cataloguing-in-Publication Data
A catalog record for this book is available from the Library of Congress.

ISBN: HB: 978-1-4411-4403-4
PB: 978-1-4411-8205-0

Library of Congress Cataloging-in-Publication Data
Attfield, Robin.
Ethics : an overview / Robin Attfield.
p. cm.
Includes index.
ISBN 978-1-4411-4403-4 (hardcover) – ISBN 978-1-4411-8205-0 (pbk.)
1. Ethics. I. Title.

BJ1012.A845 2012
170–dc23

2011031700.

Typeset by Newgen Imaging Systems Pvt Ltd, Chennai, India
Printed and bound in India

Contents

Preface

I was both surprised and delighted to be invited by Continuum to write this textbook on ethics. An earlier textbook of mine, *Environmental Ethics* (Cambridge: Polity, 2003), has been well received, and a second edition is due to appear within a couple of years. But it was still encouraging to be considered capable of explaining and conveying the central ideas and issues of the whole field of ethics to a broad international student audience, and of offering readers the opportunity to think through these ideas and issues for themselves.

Students and former students of Cardiff University have often expressed personal thanks for interesting modules (taught undergraduate courses, that is) in Ethics or in Applied Ethics. Some of the same people have kindly agreed to comment on particular sections of this book and on their suitability for second- and third-year undergraduates and for magistral students. This book, then, is based on two kinds of experience: mine as a lecturer and seminar-tutor and that of students of mine as once apprentice philosophers, and now as shrewd connoisseurs, and as philosophers and ethicists themselves.

Within its covers the whole field of ethics is studied in outline, with chapters dedicated to six specific areas. These are: history of ethics; value-theory and the good life; normative ethics; applied ethics; meta-ethics; and free will and responsibility.

The chapter on the history of ethics presents key contributions from the thought of five leading historical figures: Aristotle, Hobbes, Hume, Kant and John Stuart Mill. It does not pretend to supply a continuous history of this area of thought; suggestions are given for finding such histories elsewhere. Rather it seeks to clarify key themes of these thinkers, which are related to contemporary ethical thinking both in this chapter and in the following ones. Thus the thought of Aristotle is related to virtue ethics in Chapter 3, and that of Hobbes to the problem later raised by Hume of how we (or anyone) can derive an 'ought' from an 'is', and also, in Chapter 2, to whether we all need virtue. Hume's views on motivation are returned to in (for example) the debate about internalism and externalism in the chapter on meta-ethics. Kant's cosmopolitanism has been a major contribution to contemporary thought, while his 'categorical imperative' is revisited in the chapter on normative ethics. So is Mill's utilitarianism, studied later in the revised form of practice-consequentialism.

In this chapter, as in every section of the book, study questions and reading-lists are supplied, while the accompanying website (http://philosophy.attfield.continuumbooks.com) carries bullet-point summaries, sets of learning objectives and essay titles plus related lists of reading, together with powerpoint slides devised so as to be usable by instructors in presenting the relevant material. For some sections it also offers case studies, charts and, for the Aristotle Section, Multiple Choice Questions (MCQs), allowing instructors to select forms of teaching and learning appropriate to their situation. The four sections of the history of ethics chapter could be used either separately or as part of a longer course including the two chapters that follow, or the chapter on meta-ethics.

The chapter on the good life and value-theory opens these issues with a section on pleasure, happiness and flourishing, and then proceeds to one on moral standing, value and intrinsic value, in each case inviting readers to develop their own stance. The section on worthwhile life, self-respect and meaningful work takes matters further, and then the final section (on 'The Good Life, Needs, Virtue and Morality') considers explicitly a range of issues, such as the nature of needs, and whether virtue is needed for the good life, implicitly raised previously. Some students and instructors may prefer to begin their study of ethics with this chapter, reserving their study of history for a subsequent occasion. In this and the following chapter, there are several references to my more detailed book on these matters, *Value, Obligation and Meta-Ethics* (1995), which delves into the relevant issues more thoroughly and systematically.

The chapter on Normative Ethics builds on the insights about moral standing and intrinsic value of the previous chapter, opening with a section on 'Moral Standing, Value, Rights and Rightness'. This discussion of concepts such as rightness prepares the way for the coming sections on 'Consequentialism and Its Critics', while the following section considers other theories of normative ethics such as deontology and contractarianism. The Section on 'Virtue Ethics' opens with a consideration of whether theories and principles are needed at all, and proceeds to consider virtue ethics, sometimes regarded as a move away from principles towards prioritizing practical dispositions. But it goes on to argue that principles of rightness and of obligation remain crucial all the same. The final section introduces the possibility that the advocacy of virtue (such as the advocacy by environmentalists of green virtues) can be fruitfully integrated with practice-consequentialism.

The Chapter on Applied Ethics cross-refers to the previous chapters, but does not assume their conclusions, and instead discusses the implications of a range of normative theories (including Kantian and other forms of deontology, contract-theory and virtue ethics, as well as consequentialism) for specific practical fields. It opens with coverage of 'The Re-emergence of Applied Ethics', since applied ethics was in abeyance in the English-speaking world for approximately the first six decades of the twentieth century, and then of factors explaining its near-disappearance and its subsequent resurrection. This section also introduces inter-generational ethics and population ethics. The following five sections introduce Medical Ethics, Animal Ethics, Development Ethics, Environmental Ethics and the Ethics of War, and explain their origins (ancient in some cases, recent in others), together with recent issues and contributions, and with related comments and appraisals. Their bearing on matters of ethical theory is also raised, not least in connection with the wider scope of ethical concern brought to the fore by recent work in Environmental Ethics.

Some instructors and students may prefer to begin their use of the book either with this chapter as a whole, or with one or more of its sections. If used together with the powerpoint slides available from the website, it could form the core of a short course on applied ethics, or (with Chapter 3) part of a longer course on normative ethics and its applications.

The next chapter explains key positions and developments in Meta-ethics. While some students sometimes feel apprehensive about this area of ethics, experience suggests that University and College students are well capable of grasping (and writing good essays or papers about) the material presented here. Issues about the meaning and status of moral discourse (and thus of the metaphysics of ethics) are philosophically important ones, including issues about whether moral claims have any kind of objectivity and can be known; and such issues are introduced in the five sections of this chapter. The first section introduces and considers theories that deny the possibility of such knowledge, while the second reviews attempts to throw light on how claims about 'good' and about 'ought' can be grounded. The third appraises the case for moral realism and cognitivism, while the fourth considers arguments (originating with Hume) against these stances based on the motivating capacity (or 'practicality') of moral language. The final section introduces ethical naturalism, and at the same time theories about the grounds of moral claims, in ways that cohere with stances presented in previous parts of the book.

This chapter could be studied alone, forming the basis of a short course, or could be combined with the first chapter, or the first three chapters, in a longer one. Here the website is likely to be of help, particularly to those not previously trained in meta-ethics. The later chapters of my book *Value, Obligation and Meta-Ethics* may also be found to serve as an amplification of this chapter, alongside the many other works referenced here.

Chapter 6, on Free Will and Responsibility, has been given an historical structure to make these issues more accessible. The first of the four sections introduces the treatment of related issues by Aristotle, the original discovery of the problematic implications of determinism by Epicurus, and the attempt to reconcile this stance and belief in human freedom made by the Stoics. This approach supplies a followable entry into the central problem and also into issues surrounding compatibilism and incompatibilism. The second section brings in belief in laws of nature (newly introduced in the Early Modern period), together with related understandings of determinism, the stances of Hume and Kant and the theory of agency of Reid (all of which have contemporary followers). The third covers more recent thought about these matters, including the implications of Darwinism and of quantum indeterminacy, and compatibilist attempts to analyse the key phrase 'could have done otherwise'. The final section, 'The Future is Open', embodies arguments against compatibilism and determinism, and a suggested account of how human evolution makes libertarian freedom possible.

Once again, this chapter could be used for a short, self-standing course. (The powerpoint slides of the website will prove particularly useful to instructors.) Alternatively it could be used in conjunction with the first chapter in a course on the History of Ethics, or with chapters such as the ones on the Good Life and on Normative Ethics, to which issues of the nature of character and of degrees of responsibility are also relevant. Or it could be used with the rest of the book as a whole, so as to cover all the key areas of ethics.

This book is not, of course, comprehensive. For example, it omits important tracts of the history of ethics and of moral psychology, and its chapter on applied ethics omits business ethics. Also there are gaps in its coverage of continental ethicists, with much more attention being paid to ethicists from the analytic tradition. But selectiveness has been the price of breadth and of focus on stimulating and (particularly in the field of applied ethics) ongoing debates by which people are currently exercised. Studying this book will confer on its readers a good grounding in the rudiments of ethics, and will offer numerous ways of taking this study further, of progressing into work of a more advanced and ramified nature and generally of doing ethics for yourself.

Acknowledgements

I would like to express thanks for their helpful suggestions to the publishers' referees, Nigel Dower and Clark Wolf, and to others who contributed ideas that have enhanced this book: Julian Bennett, Ruth Chadwick, Patricia Clark, Rebekah Humphreys, Simon Waltho and Jonathan Webber. Patricia Clark was website assistant until her untimely death in September 2010, and I want to pay tribute to her encouragement, her checking of sections and her supplying of diagrams such as the one in the website illustrating Aristotle's doctrine of the mean. I would also like to pay tribute to Rebekah Humphreys, who took over as website assistant, checked many sections, cheerfully persevered with the project while busy with job applications, and skilfully (and crucially) supplied all the powerpoint slides. Also to Christopher Norris, to Cardiff University and to Continuum for making it possible for there to be a website assistant.

Thanks are also due to students or former students who checked particular sections: Julian Bennett, Sally Cosgrove, Clare Pusey, Lucinda Stewart and Helen Taylor. I am also grateful to Sarah Campbell of Continuum, and to her replacement during her leave, David Avital, for their unfailing cooperation and helpful responses to queries and problems. I give particular thanks, however, to my wife, Leela Dutt, for checking the Preface and for sustaining both myself and this project throughout; but for her this book would not exist.

List of Abbreviations

BCE	Before the Common Era
BU	Crisp's criterion of Biographical Utilitarianism
CE	Common Era
FAO	United Nations Food and Agriculture Organization
MCQs	Multiple Choice Questions (in website only)
MDGs	Millennium Development Goals
WCED	World Commission on Environment and Development

1

History of Ethics

Chapter Outline

Section 1: Aristotle on eudaemonia and virtue

1. Aristotle on the good

Aristotle's best-known book on ethics, the *Nicomachean Ethics* (see below), was intended to give practical guidance for life in the real world. His world was different from ours, for he had been the tutor of Alexander the Great, and lived and lectured in classical Athens. Yet he wrote to help people reason reflectively about the good life and the good community, and what is attainable within them. He wanted to avoid abstract theories such as those of his teacher, Plato, about ideals like the form of the good (or 'the Good Itself'), something which was supposed to embody what was common to everything that is good. Such theories, even if they made sense, were in his view of no practical help; they gave no clues about what kind of life is worth pursuing. What he put forward instead is widely considered highly relevant to the modern world and to all varieties of human society, so much so that he is currently one of the more influential of historical philosophers and ethicists. See Table 1.1.

Table 1.1

ARISTOTLE TIMELINE
Plato, Aristotle's teacher (429–347 BCE)
Aristotle (384–322 BCE)
Alexander the Great, whom Aristotle tutored (356–323 BCE)
Thomas Aquinas (1225–74 CE) called Aristotle 'THE philosopher'.
Aristotle returned to philosophical prominence in the writings of Peter Geach, Elizabeth Anscombe, Philippa Foot and Martha Nussbaum (late twentieth century CE: 1950–2000).

Aristotle opens Book I by declaring that 'the good' is what everyone and every action and enterprise aims at. There is a deep truth here, for there does seem to be some necessary (or non-contingent) connection between 'what is aimed at' and 'good'. He proceeds to explore what this good consists in, both for individuals and for communities. After considering and sifting opinions, he presents two criteria or requirements for successful specifications of the good. Nothing will be the good unless it is 'final'; that is to say, it is always chosen for its own sake and never for the sake of something else. There again, nothing will be the good unless it is self-sufficient; that is to say, it is in no way incomplete or lacking, and unable to be supplemented in point of desirability by anything else, as if it were just one good among others. These requirements eliminate most of the usual particular candidates for being the good, such as wealth or reputation or pleasure (see Book I, chapters 1 to 7).

Aristotle deduces in chapter 7 that the good for human beings consists in 'eudaemonia' (literally 'blessedness') or human flourishing or fulfilment (sometimes inaccurately translated as 'happiness'), for eudaemonia uniquely satisfies these requirements. Further, his conclusion about what actually comprises eudaemonia, reached through an argument to be mentioned shortly, is that it consists in activity of the soul (i.e. psychological or mental activities) in accordance with excellence, or, if there are a number of excellences or virtues, then with the best or most perfect of them; and indeed in a lifetime of such activity, for 'one swallow does not make a summer'. For eudaemonia, the liver of such a life must also have friends and a modicum of resources, or we would not say that he or she is flourishing. (Aristotle probably had just males in mind, for the activities of women were severely limited in Greek society.)

His argument for this conclusion runs as follows. Each kind of person has a final end, specific activity or function ('ergon' in Greek); thus that of a harp-player is to play well, just as that of a shoe-maker is to make good shoes. So it would be surprising if human beings did not have a function as such, which belongs to them simply as humans. This function will not be any of the capacities shared with other species, such as that of growth (shared with plants), or mobility (shared with other animals). The capacity which is exclusively human is rationality, and so it is in the exercise of their rational powers that the specific activity of human beings consists, and that is where human excellence is to be found. We can now see how Aristotle reaches his account of 'eudaemonia' as 'activity (of the soul) in accordance with excellence'. (The word for excellence, 'arete', is sometimes translated 'virtue', but his concept of excellence, as we shall see, is broader than what we usually mean by 'virtue', qualities of *moral* excellence, including as it does *intellectual* excellences too. In any case it is now apparent that the concept he needs is not a specifically moral one, but rather one involving high-quality functioning of distinctively human capacities.)

While Aristotle's conclusion is far from absurd, his argument is widely held to be defective and inconclusive. The most striking problem is that on many views humans simply do not have a function, and so it is futile to go in search of one. Aristotle, for his part, believed that every distinct entity has a function, but this metaphysical view is not one that most of us share in. So his reliance on the premise that all humans have a function is misplaced. Yet maybe the argument can be repaired. For perhaps he was right to hold that human beings have certain essential capacities (including rationality), capacities in the absence of which they would not be human, and could go on to locate human excellence in the exercise of these capacities; if so, something like his conclusion could be reached without appeal to humans having a specific or characteristic function.

Another objection to Aristotle's reasoning is that he appeals to distinctive capacities (and to psychological ones at that), whereas the essential capacities of human beings include many that are not distinctive, but are shared with other animals, such as sensory perception, mobility and reproduction. If the argument is to turn on essential capacities, then these non-distinctive ones should be recognized too, despite being in some cases physical rather than psychological ones. Indeed all of these capacities can contribute to human well-being, as they can to that of other animal species. Aristotle's appeal to what is distinctive about human beings can beneficially be superseded and his theory broadened to include those other capacities in the absence of which we would not be recognizably human. (While Aristotle might well have resisted the modifications of this and the previous paragraph, they rest on a very Aristotelian basis, the importance of essential qualities.)

Another objection may now be raised. Well-being does not involve exercising every one of the essential human capacities. Thus we would not say that blind people or childless people cannot have a good quality of life just because they are blind or childless. To claim that human flourishing depends on exercising all the essential human capacities would be an insensitive exaggeration. Yet it remains plausible that quality of life depends on exercising most (or at any rate enough) of them. So Aristotle could still be substantially right.

One final criticism remains to be considered. In Book I, chapter 7, Aristotle makes the following addition to his conclusion that eudaemonia consists in 'an activity of soul in accordance with excellence': if there is more than one form of excellence, it will consist in 'activity in accordance with the best and most complete form of excellence'. Subsequently, in Book X, he infers that this is in fact theoretical or contemplative reason. So, although most of the intervening books focus on excellences of character and also on practical reason (the kind of reason on which they all depend), he concludes in Book X that human flourishing really consists in a life of contemplation (such as the life of the philosopher) *instead*. But this makes him open to the criticism that his account of human flourishing is too exclusive, and should admit other excellences (such as virtues of character), and friendship too. (See the articles of Hardie and Ackrill, listed under 'Further Reading'.)

This criticism can be expressed in Aristotle's own terms. In Book X, he claims that a life of contemplation is self-sufficient because it is relatively immune to life's vicissitudes. But this reasoning changes the meaning of 'self-sufficient' from that of Book I. 'Self-sufficiency' there meant that a self-sufficient good cannot be enhanced through any form of supplementation, and any account of it would have to be an inclusive one. But a life of contemplation *can* be enhanced through being supplemented by the presence of other excellences (such as courage and prudence) and with the inclusion rather than the omission of friendship. (These examples are ones Aristotle acknowledges in earlier books; you can probably suggest others.) So Aristotle's eventual conclusion infringes his own self-sufficiency requirement. To put things another way, his addition mentioned at the start of the previous paragraph was misguided, and he would have done better to leave his account of 'eudaemonia' unqualified. See Table 1.2.

Table 1.2

KEY TERMS
'eudaemonia' = flourishing or fulfilment
Literally, the state of someone blessed by the gods.
Often translated 'happiness', but not about a state of mind.
More about a life of achievement, like being 'happy' in:
'happy the man who achieved discovery of the causes of things'
(Virgil, *Georgics*, II, 493).
'ergon' = work, task, role or function
'arete' = excellence or (in that sense) virtue
NB There are *intellectual* excellences as well as excellences of *character*.

2. Aristotle on virtue

But this suggests that what Aristotle has to say about other excellences, such as excellences of character, is worth studying. (Many of his analyses of concepts have proved to be of lasting value; for his account of pleasure, see J. O. Urmson, 'Aristotle on Pleasure'.) In Book II, Aristotle analyses virtues as dispositions to choose in accordance with reason (or a principle), dispositions which have been acquired through past choices. Practical or ethical virtues differ from intellectual ones in concerning actions or emotions, and involving practical wisdom, which Aristotle distinguishes from theoretical wisdom (Book VI, chapters 5 to 13). This is gradually developed through making practical choices. Aristotle's account of the virtues in terms of dispositions, choices and reason has survived the test of time, and stands in marked contrast with accounts like that of David Hume which are indifferent to the role of choices and sceptical about the relevance of practical reason (see the part of the next section on Hume).

On the way to explaining the virtues, Aristotle analyses what we mean by 'voluntary' and by 'choice'. Voluntary actions are ones that are neither coerced nor due to ignorance, and it is only voluntary actions that qualify for praise or blame (Book III, chapter 1; if only Aristotle's incisive findings had been heeded across the centuries). But not all voluntary actions are chosen; for choices are accompanied by deliberation, in which people reflect on matters within their control in the light of goals or principles (Book III, chapters 2 and 3). Aristotle's notion of choice or deliberate action is narrower than ours, involving the presence of deliberative reasoning. Yet while we might object that not all choices involve such deliberation, A. C. MacIntyre is right to comment that all choices can be appraised by the decisions that deliberation would have issued in (*Short History*, p. 74), and therefore that, as Aristotle holds, principles or understandings of the good are always relevant to them. So the development of character and of the virtues of character involves coming to behave as a person with such principles would do. (Can we help forming the characters that we do? Aristotle believes that we are answerable for them, but his discussion will be returned to in the chapter on Free Will.)

Yet how can we act virtuously (bravely or temperately, for example) at all, given that we do not begin life with settled characters? According to Aristotle, to act virtuously is to act as the virtuous person would act. But if so, how can we ever begin to be brave or to act with moderation? We can begin, Aristotle replies, if we are well brought up, and are led through rewards and deterrents to face problems, dangers or enticements as the virtuous person would do. By choosing to act in a virtuous manner not just once but recurrently, we acquire the related virtuous disposition (Book II, chapter 4). Whether or not moral education always follows this course (and despite there being some evidence of sudden changes of character), Aristotle's dispositional view of the nature of virtue has continued to command widespread assent. His theory of virtue, however, as the mean between pairs of extremes (Book II, chapter 6), courage (for example) being a mean between cowardice and rashness, has proved more controversial. Indeed some commentators suggest that he is driven to invent extremes for the virtues to fit between, that his theory is a contrived rationalization of the virtues of his own society, and that some of his 'virtues' such as that of the self-important 'great-souled' man (Book IV, chapter 3) seem to bear out this criticism.

Problems include the difficulty of finding pairs of extremes (attitudes of excess and of defect) to match every virtue (as the mean between them). While a term for excessive indulgence in pleasures does not need to be invented, insensitivity to pleasure, as Aristotle acknowledges, is seldom to be found. And as he also concedes, some matters do not admit of moderation (adultery is a good example). Besides, Aristotle modifies his own theory: the mean is not a mathematical median, but 'the mean relative to us'; just as the needs and circumstances of the average person and of heavy-weight wrestlers are different (and thus their diets too), so the doctrine of the mean must likewise take circumstances into account (Book II, chapters 6 to 8). But this betokens that the mean is in any case a matter of judgement.

This retreat, however, need not suggest that Aristotle's whole theory of virtue is beyond redemption. For his virtues (or rather many of his virtues) answer to problems that recur in virtually every society, and some to problems in all, and arguably most of his virtues are qualities that are needed by everyone. As Martha Nussbaum has argued, people in all societies have in common problems such as facing situations of danger and opportunities for pleasure, and thus need virtuous dispositions like courage and self-control to cope with these recurrent spheres of experience, as much for their own good as for that of others.[1] So (subject to certain exceptional instances, such as 'greatness of soul') we should not regard Aristotle's theory as a mere rationalization of the parochial code of his own society; in part, we can treat it as speaking to the universal condition of humanity (see Nussbaum; also Crisp[2]). Besides, even if doing what is right is an elusive achievement, people can be brought up to behave as a decent or virtuous person would, and this makes his account of the virtues of character (courage, temperance, generosity, truthfulness, justice and the rest: see Books II to V) all the more important.

The importance of Aristotle's study of the virtues has given rise in recent years to a revival of his moral philosophy under the title of 'virtue ethics'. Virtue ethics can be followed either in a weaker or in a stronger form. In its weaker (or less demanding) form, it affirms the centrality of the virtues in the moral life and in moral education. Without adhering to Aristotle's entire catalogue of virtues of character, let alone to his theory of the mean, it encourages us to focus on developing qualities like fairness, trustworthiness and kindness (not itself an Aristotelian virtue), rather than focusing primarily either on our various obligations or duties, or on the impacts of our actions. In its stronger form, it asserts either that right action simply consists in doing what the virtuous person would do, or that there is no criterion of rightness beyond that of doing just this (one of Aristotle's own themes).

There is much to be said for the weaker version. Thus even if it is the impacts of action that ultimately make right actions right, the best guarantee of right actions and thus of beneficial impacts might well consist in our adoption of habitual qualities or virtues with overall beneficial tendencies. (Dale Jamieson defends this kind of approach, and thus the importance of certain 'green virtues': see the chapter of this book on Normative Ethics.) But this kind of rationale for the centrality of the virtues could well count against the stronger version of virtue ethics. For if there were to be a rationale such as this for fostering the virtues, then it could be important on occasion to appeal beyond what the virtuous person would do, and consider the actual impacts of actions, decisions or policies, because of the crucial difference that they are prone to make. In a technological world, it is unlikely that the upbringing of the virtuous person would enable them to identify the right course of action on all occasions as such, without reflecting on the circumstances and the impacts of their actions.

So there is a stronger case for supporting the weaker version of Aristotle's ethics than the stronger version. His analysis of voluntariness, choice and virtue is incisive, and many of his substantive conclusions continue to stand up (see the section on Responsibility). But it remains an open question whether his view that, once people behave as the virtuous person would behave, nothing more can be expected, itself carries conviction. At the same time, the account that he implicitly gives of human flourishing, for example in Book I, and implicitly of the flourishing of other species as well, has itself inspired many recent ethicists to make such flourishing a central element in ethics; whenever the theme of human flourishing appears in other chapters, it will have been Aristotle's thinking that ultimately gave rise to it.

Study questions

1. To what extent is Aristotle's account of what is good for human beings acceptable?
2. How far does Aristotle's account of virtue suggest or support 'virtue ethics'?

Notes

1 Martha Nussbaum, 'Non-Relative Virtues: An Aristotelian Approach', in Martha Nussbaum and Amartya Sen (eds), *The Quality of Life*, Oxford: Clarendon Press, 1993, pp. 242–76.

2 Aristotle, *Nicomachean Ethics*, Roger Crisp (trans. and ed.), Cambridge, UK and New York: Cambridge University Press, 2000, p. xix.

Priority reading

For Aristotle's *Nicomachean Ethics*, any of the following three translations is recommended:

Aristotle, *The Ethics of Aristotle*, J. A. K. Thomson (trans.), Harmondsworth, UK; Baltimore, USA and Mitcham, Australia: Penguin Books, 1953, OR.

—, *Nicomachean Ethics*, Roger Crisp (trans. and ed.), Cambridge, UK and New York: Cambridge University Press, 2000.

For H. Rackham's translation of the *Nicomachean Ethics*, see: http://old.perseus.tufts.edu/cgibin/ptext?doc=Perseus:text:1999.01.0054&query=section%3D%2347.

For present purposes, the most central parts are Books I, II, III, chapters 1 to 7, VI and X.

For readers of Greek, the text is available in Aristotle, *Ethica Nicomachea*, I. Bywater (ed.), Oxford: Clarendon Press, 1894.

Further reading

Ackrill, John, 'Aristotle on *Eudaemonia*', in Nancy Sherman (ed.), *Aristotle's Ethics: Critical Essays*, Lanham: Rowman & Littlefield, 1999, pp. 57–77.

Crisp, Roger (ed.), *How Should One Live?: Essays on the Virtues*, Oxford: Clarendon Press and New York: Oxford University Press, 1996.

Gottlieb, Anthony, *The Dream of Reason: A History of Western Philosophy from the Greeks to the Renaissance*, London: Penguin, 2001; see chapter 12, 'The Master of Those Who Know: Aristotle', pp. 220–79.

Hardie, W. F. R., 'The Final Good in Aristotle's *Ethics*', in J. M. E. Moravscik (ed.), *Aristotle: A Collection of Critical Essays*, London: Macmillan, 1968, pp. 297–322.

Jamieson, Dale, 'Why Utilitarians Should Be Virtue Theorists', *Utilitas*, 19.2, 2007, 160–83.

Kraut, Richard, 'Aristotle's *Ethics*', *Stanford Encyclopedia of Philosophy*; see: http://www.seop.leeds.ac.uk/entries/aristotle-ethics/.

MacIntyre, A. C., *A Short History of Ethics*, London: Routledge, 1967, chapter 7, 'Aristotle's *Ethics*', pp. 57–83.

Nussbaum, Martha, 'Non-Relative Virtues: An Aristotelian Approach', in Martha Nussbaum and Amartya Sen (eds), *The Quality of Life*, Oxford: Clarendon Press, 1993, pp. 242–76.

Urmson, J. O., 'Aristotle on Pleasure', in J. M. E. Moravscik (ed.), *Aristotle: A Collection of Critical Essays*, London: Macmillan, 1968, pp. 323–33.

Section 2: Some themes from Hobbes and Hume

1. Introduction

Thomas Hobbes (1588–1679) and David Hume (1711–76) made substantial contributions to ethical thinking in the Early Modern period. For this reason their thought figures in most courses on ethics, as it does in this section.

Hobbes is best known for his theory that morality and society both originate as a social contract, into which self-interested individuals freely enter to avoid the 'war of all against all' that otherwise prevails. This kind of theory originated with Plato (in *Republic*, Book 2); a further, but rather different, contract theory has recently been defended by John Rawls in *A Theory of Justice* (discussed here in 'The Re-Emergence of Applied Ethics'). Hobbes' own version was presented in his famous work *Leviathan* (1651).[1] One problem for

Hobbes' variety of contract theory concerns the promises these individuals make (promises to obey the sovereign, etc.) when they enter society; if morality originates with the contract, how are pre-social people supposed to understand (and be bound by) the morality of the promises they make when society does not yet exist? Another problem concerns their grasp of language; for if language is essentially social, how could pre-social people understand it, and use it to reason about society and to make promises to comply with its rules?

2. Hobbes' egoism

Rather than discuss Hobbes' version of contractarianism, this section will address two other themes from *Leviathan*, Hobbes' egoism and his derivation of 'oughts' from facts.

Delving beneath the surface of people's moral assumptions, Hobbes claimed that everyone pursues nothing but their own self-interest as they understand it (psychological egoism), and also that this is what they have every reason to pursue and thus ought to pursue (ethical egoism). Indeed his conclusion about what people *ought* to pursue is based on his understanding of what they inevitably *do* pursue. These claims have generated much reflection, both across the three hundred and fifty years after they were made by Hobbes, and in the present, which is why they receive attention here.

Hobbes believed that we are so made as to seek our own survival and self-aggrandizment (or self-advancement). Our bodies are (supposedly) so structured as to make these tendencies inbuilt goals. Besides, all our behaviour can (supposedly) be interpreted on this basis. Apparent exceptions, such as acts of generosity or sanctity, are really performed with a view to enhancing our fame or our reputations. And of course if Hobbes is right about society embodying a tacit contract between self-interested individuals, then the social bond itself is also to be interpreted along these lines.

There are, of course, many apparent exceptions to psychological egoism, as when Hobbes himself gave alms to a beggar. His reply (that he did it because it pleased him to see the poor man pleased)[2] would only work if the good of Hobbes' pleasure (a second-order good) did not depend on the good of the poor man's pleasure (a first-order good), which Hobbes clearly assumes to be an independent good. Similarly, egoistic accounts of (say) pride in one's children's achievements actually depend on those achievements being independently good. Indeed it would be hard for Hobbes to explain why people care for their children in the first place.

In any case, psychological egoism has a problem in showing that the huge diversity of human motives always conforms to one single pattern. People desire (for example) fun, football and also the health of their friends, chocolate, travel and also world peace; and some seem to desire the moon. How can it be known that all these desires turn entirely on just one common element?

The egoist, however, can always try to reinterpret any action as wholly self-interested. But such interpretations amount not to interesting and testable claims, but to hidden appeals to a supposedly necessary truth, such as that all wanting is necessarily a seeking of what is in one's own interests. But if this is the basis, then the egoist is simply redefining 'wanting' or 'desire'; the rest of us, however, remain at liberty to disregard this hidden stipulation, and continue using these terms in their ordinary sense, in which wanting is sometimes for goods other than our own.

This is where an egoist like Hobbes can try suggesting that egoism, rather than being directly applicable to motivations in current society, applies to the desires of the pre-social people whose agreement formed society, desires which still lurk beneath the veneer of civilization. But this is also the moment to raise the problems for his contract theory outlined above, such as how pre-social people could discuss forming a social contract, language being essentially social itself, and how they could understand promises or their binding force before morality was (supposedly) instituted by that contract. It is far more plausible that the existence of society opens up possibilities for being cooperative and uncooperative alike than that the advantages of cooperation were imagined and contrived by isolated people with no previous experience of those advantages, as part of a plan for self-protection.

3. Hobbes' derivation of 'oughts' from facts

While Hobbes' defence of psychological egoism is less than convincing, his derivation of 'oughts' from facts is more impressive. While many later philosophers (following Hume: see below) have held that no such derivation from facts alone, or from facts plus necessary truths, is possible, Hobbes appears to have been successful here.

From the premise that everyone desires their own security more than anything else, Hobbes derives (indeed deduces) the conclusion that they ought to adopt the most efficient means to that end.[3] This conclusion amounts to ethical egoism, which is implausible if his premise is rejected (see above). But if his premise is granted as factual (for the sake of argument), then his conclusion really seems to follow.

The other premise that he implicitly appeals to runs as follows: Whoever desires a given end more than any other ought to adopt the most efficient means to that end. If challenged to defend this further premise, Hobbes could say that it is a necessary truth which simply spells out what 'ought' means; the very meaning of 'ought' is what makes it true. And where 'ought' is short for 'prudentially ought', he would seem to be right. Hence, if the initial premise is also granted, then his conclusion follows validly, from a supposed fact (the initial premise) and this necessary truth. (The only reason why it is an unsound conclusion is that the initial premise should not be granted.)

Hobbes gets as far as he does because 'ought to do X' is an incomplete expression, short for something like: 'has reasons of a particular sort to do X', and Hobbes is able to rely on what it is short for. The particular sort of reasons that Hobbes has in mind consist of prudential ones (the only sort that Hobbes credits). Once the particular sort of reasons is made clear, it is equally clear why the conclusion follows. But if so, then an 'ought' can be validly derived from a would-be fact and a necessary truth alone, contrary to the claims of Hume and his followers.

There are, however, other sorts of reasons, because 'ought' is sometimes short (instead) for 'legally ought' or 'technically ought' or 'aesthetically ought' or 'morally ought', which may itself mean something like: 'ought insofar as contributing to the wellbeing of all the affected parties is concerned'. (Can you give examples of people like judges, mechanics or artists being subjects of the other kinds of 'ought'?) Hobbes, of course, would reject this interpretation of 'morally ought', since his psychological egoism inclines him to the view that all moral 'oughts' are prudential 'oughts' (in disguise).

But this does not vitiate his reasoning. Indeed his reasoning suggests that it may be possible validly to reach other sorts of 'ought' (and even moral 'oughts') by some parallel reasoning from facts and necessary truths that spell out the meaning of 'morally ought', without appeal to 'oughts' of a controversial nature. This is roughly the view of (meta-ethical) naturalists: see Section 5 of Chapter 5, on naturalism.

4. Hume on reason and passion

Hume, by contrast, held that there is no process of reasoning by which we can move from an 'is' to an 'ought'. Understanding why he held this involves grasping his view of the role of reason. Hume was a great philosopher, who did important work on the basis of our ideas, including our ideas about identity, causation and religion. Here, however, his views on the role and scope of reason are what we need to study.

According to Hume, reason is confined to reasoning of either a deductive or an inductive nature. Valid *deductions* with true premises establish their conclusions; this is how people can, for example, prove Pythagoras' theorem just from definitions and axioms about the areas of triangles. *Inductive* reasoning, however, does not prove its conclusions, but infers them as probably true on a basis of observations and experience. If reason is restricted to deduction and induction, then its scope is limited to matters of fact, the definitions of terms (or what Hume called 'the relations of ideas') and whatever can be shown to follow from all this. Thus maintaining that decisions or actions are reasonable or unreasonable actually goes beyond the scope of reason, and the same applies to judgements intended to guide such decisions.

So reason is impotent in practical matters. Hume famously expresses this view by asserting that 'Reason is and ought only to be the slave of the passions'.[4] The passions include desires, and without desires and other emotions, no actions are possible, nor judgements either. Neither judgements nor actions can be explained without the explanation introducing desires (and thus passions), and so reason cannot generate either of them. It can serve to supply information (as a Roman slave might once have done), but the final judgement or decision depends not on reason but on the passions, to which this slave can only be subservient.

However (Hume adds), not all the passions are violent ones; some reflect our sentiments becoming adjusted and attuned to those of others, and these 'calm' passions (ones like sympathy and tolerance) are sometimes called 'reasonable' ones, albeit (according to Hume) improperly.[5] This usage in turn accounts for people thinking that reason has a wider scope than it really has.

Many philosophers endorse either some or all of the above theories. However, Hume's stance diverges from Aristotle's view that one kind of reasoning is practical reasoning,[6] and that a judgement or even an action can be the conclusion of such reasoning.[7] And whether or not Aristotle is right, we certainly can reason about whether actions are desirable. So there can be reasoning about the desirability (and thus the justification) of actions (and for and against judgements relating to actions), even if Hume is right that actions cannot be *explained* in the absence of desires, and judgements in the absence of feelings.

But this already shows that reason is not entirely impotent in practical matters; and certain further possibilities suggest that its scope is greater still in this regard. Thus moral principles can be appraised by reason, and particular ones shown by reasoning to apply to some cases and not to others; and yet, on some views, holding moral principles involves of itself enough commitment to spur us to action (at least some of the time). If we add that there could be principles relevant to sympathy and tolerance, we can also see that these too are matters about which reasoning is possible, and thus that sympathy and tolerance might turn out to be 'reasonable' after all (without any improper use of that term).

Even our 'passions' turn out to have a logic of their own. No one can sympathize with something inanimate, or resent entities not regarded as responsible, or be proud of what is not regarded as their own (either individually or through some group to which they belong). So we can reason about whether and when these emotions or attitudes are in place, and, if so, then also about what we can approve. The scope of reason, then, seems much broader than Hume was prepared to allow. And this brings us back to the issue of whether 'oughts' are really beyond its scope.

5. Hume on the non-derivability of 'ought'

In a celebrated passage of his *Treatise*,[8] Hume wrote that it seems inconceivable that we can reason from what we take to be facts to 'ought' conclusions, even though people often speak otherwise. To judge by what he wrote elsewhere,[9] his thinking probably went along these lines. 'Oughts' are practical language, capable of stirring either the speaker or the hearers to action. But reason is incapable of motivating action or stirring us towards it. Nothing but passions have this capacity (see above). Therefore 'ought'-language, rather than being based on reason, must express passions. (Fortunately we are so made, according to Hume, as to feel much the same passions as each other, at least where approval and disapproval are concerned. This makes possible some degree of agreement between different users of 'ought'-language.)

But as we have seen, there is reason to resist the view that reason and its conclusions cannot motivate action; for reasoning about what is desirable can do just this. It is true that we sometimes believe we ought to do something but fail to do it; but this only shows that 'oughts' sometimes fail to motivate (although sometimes they succeed), and not that they cannot be derived by means of reasoning. Incidentally, not all 'ought'-language is practical in the sense just mentioned; for much of it relates either to the past (see the example of Nero below), or to hypothetical or imaginary situations, as when I reflect on what I ought to do if I were in your position. So we should not assume that all uses of 'ought' are related to action in the immediate future as suggested in the previous paragraph.

Hume's view, it should be noted, does not say that 'ought'-language reports or states our feelings; if he thought this, then he could accept that it is either true or false, depending on whether we have the relevant feelings or not. Instead, he claims that 'ought'-language *expresses* our passions, rather as 'hurray!' or 'alas!' do, and thus that this language is neither true nor false, but is not the kind of talk that can be either of these (not truth-apt, that is). This kind of stance was later called 'emotivism', and is discussed in the section on 'Non-cognitivism'. But it would be undermined if, as was claimed above in discussion of Hobbes, we can reason validly from facts and necessary truths to 'ought'-conclusions, for if such reasoning is valid and its premises are true, then its conclusion must also be true. So maybe we should hold that 'ought'-language can sometimes both be true and motivate; for example, when its user is committed to acting accordingly, then it usually will motivate (as when someone says to herself in all sincerity 'I ought to keep my promise').

Hume has an interesting example of the relation of moral judgements both to facts about the world and to our own feelings. Compare what we say about the Roman Emperor Nero, who murdered his mother Agrippina, and about a sapling that supplants and kills its parent tree.[10] The facts of the relations involved are surely the same in each case, and yet we condemn Nero (saying that of course he ought not to have done what he did), but not the sapling. But there is, according to Hume, no objective difference, from which we could reason to our moral judgements (as conclusions). Hence the difference must lie simply in our feelings, which we can express in 'ought'-language or other language of disapproval, such as 'Murder!'.

However, just as there is a logic to emotions and attitudes, so there is to disapproval. It does not make sense to disapprove of the behaviour of a tree, or of any being incapable of responsible action. But it makes excellent sense to disapprove of Nero, who (if ancient historians are to be trusted) acted both voluntarily and knowingly, and could have done otherwise. Thus the logic of approval and disapproval both explains the difference in our reactions, and shows how we can reason from facts and principles to the judgements that we form. So there is no need to adopt Hume's views about either the limits of reason or the non-derivability of 'ought' to explain either our feelings or our judgements. (We should further note that Hume does not regard virtues as essentially arising from voluntary choices, unlike Aristotle, but as akin to talents or gifts of nature;[11] here Aristotle seems to hold the stronger ground.)

6. Hume on utility and justice

Hume held that we are so constituted as to approve what is either useful or agreeable to ourselves or to others.[12] Since what is useful is conducive to what is agreeable (or to what makes people and other creatures happy), we can interpret him as introducing an early version of utilitarianism, the normative theory that what is right is what promotes the general happiness. The *name* 'utilitarianism' was devised later, but no matter. (For present purposes, we can disregard Hume's relating all this to our feelings or passions.)

Hume also held that under specific circumstances, justice promotes the general happiness or good. Justice involves whole practices which are beneficial overall. The inheritance of property is given as an example of such a system. In particular cases, when great wealth is inherited by a young wastrel, this seems bad for society, but the overall system is beneficial, and should for this reason be approved and preserved.[13] (Hume's understanding of justice confined it to the spheres of property and of promises, which strikes many people as unduly narrow.)

Some of the virtues, Hume held, resemble a wall, in that each additional brick (or act) adds to the overall benefit to society. But justice is not like this, but more like what he calls 'a vault' (or arch).[14] Before the arch is complete, individual bricks seem to contribute little, but once the coping-stone at the top is in place, the whole arch carries a great weight of advantage, of immense benefit to the community. Thus Hume's version of utilitarianism turns on the overall benefits of entire practices, and not on the benefits of individual acts, thus supplying a normative theory that remains of continuing interest. Hume's particular theory of justice (or rather the way he deploys it) is also a conservative one; it could serve to justify existing institutions, but is unsuited to revising or changing them.

The particular circumstances in which Hume claims that justice arises and is beneficial help explain this. He holds that justice applies to conditions in which resources are neither plentiful (like air) nor inaccessible (like snow in summer), but rather in restricted supply (like money and land); only here are rules of distribution beneficial. There again, justice applies neither where there is universal goodwill, nor where there is no trust at all, but in communities where trust exists, but is limited. Finally he holds that justice applies only among parties approximately equal in strength.[15]

Maybe rules of justice arise more readily in the above circumstances than in others. But that does not show that there are no rights in situations of extreme scarcity or extreme distrust, nor that no rights can belong to those whose relative strength is slight or non-existent. Brian Barry points out that Hume's theory would imply that justice does not apply to relations between generations, as future generations have no power over previous ones; but this is an unacceptable conclusion.[16] Thus Hume's theory about the limits to the circumstances in which justice has a point should be rejected. Yet this does not mean that his utilitarianism of practices must be rejected at the same time.

Study questions

1. Do you agree that, when Thomas Hobbes writes in *Leviathan*, chapter 14: 'A law of nature . . . is a precept or general rule, found out by reason, by which a man is forbidden to do that, which is destructive of his life, or taketh away the means of preserving the same; and to omit that, by which he thinketh it may best be preserved', he was endorsing the view that everyone ought to adopt the most efficient means to the end that (in his view) everyone desires more than anything else, their own security?
2. Is sympathy reasonable only if we speak improperly, as David Hume holds, or literally speaking?
3. Consider the view that reason is more like a family solicitor (attorney) than (as David Hume suggests) a slave.

Notes

1 Thomas Hobbes, *Leviathan*, ed. Michael Oakeshott, Oxford: Basil Blackwell, 1955; see chapters 6–15, pp. 31–105. Also available at www.earlymoderntexts.com.

2 A. C. MacIntyre, *A Short History of Ethics*, London: Routledge, 1967, p. 135.

3 *Leviathan*, chs 14–15 (see Oakeshott, pp. 84–105, particularly 85 and 104).

4 David Hume, *A Treatise of Human Nature*, ed. Ernest C. Mossner, Harmondsworth and New York: Penguin, 1969 and 1985, 2. III. 3. Also available at www.earlymoderntexts.com.

5 *Treatise*, 2. III. 3.

6 Aristotle, *Nicomachean Ethics*, Book VI, chapter 2.

7 *Nicomachean Ethics*, Book VII, chapter 3.

8 *Treatise*, 3. I. 1.

9 David Hume, *An Inquiry Concerning the Principles of Morals*, Section 1 and Appendix 1; available in David Hume, *Enquiries Concerning Human Understanding and Concerning the Principles of Morals*, ed. P. H. Nidditch, 3rd edn, Oxford: Clarendon Press, 1975. Also available at www.earlymoderntexts.com.

10 *Inquiry*, Appendix I.

11 *Inquiry*, Appendix IV.

12 *Inquiry*, Section V.

13 *Inquiry*, Section III.

14 *Inquiry*, Appendix III.

15 *Inquiry*, Section III.

16 Brian Barry, 'Hume and the Circumstances of Justice', in R. I. Sikora and B. Barry (eds), *Obligations to Future Generations*, Philadelphia: Temple University Press, 1978; reissued, Cambridge, UK: White Horse Press, 1996.

References

Aristotle, *Nicomachean Ethics*, Roger Crisp (trans. and ed.), Cambridge, UK and New York: Cambridge University Press, 2000.

Barry, Brian, 'Hume and the Circumstances of Justice', in R. I. Sikora and B. Barry (eds), *Obligations to Future Generations*, Philadelphia: Temple University Press, 1978.

—, 'Hume and the Circumstances of Justice', in R. I. Sikora and B. Barry (eds), *Obligations to Future Generations*, Cambridge, UK: White Horse Press, 1996.

Hobbes, Thomas, *Leviathan*, ed. Michael Oakeshott, Oxford: Basil Blackwell, 1955.

—, *Leviathan*, available at www.earlymoderntexts.com.

Hume, David, *A Treatise of Human Nature*, ed. Ernest C. Mossner, Harmondsworth and New York: Penguin, 1969 and 1985.

—, *A Treatise of Human Nature*, available at www.earlymoderntexts.com.

—, *An Inquiry Concerning the Principles of Morals*, in David Hume, *Enquiries Concerning Human Understanding and Concerning the Principles of Morals*, ed. P. H. Nidditch, 3rd edn, Oxford: Clarendon Press, 1975.

—, *An Inquiry Concerning the Principles of Morals*, available at www.earlymoderntexts.com.

MacIntyre, A. C., *A Short History of Ethics*, London: Routledge, 1967.

Section 3: Some Kantian themes

1. Kant and the moral law

Immanuel Kant (1724–1804) contributed to normative ethics his influential theory of the Categorical Imperative, widely held to capture and encapsulate the demands of morality. Whether or not we can endorse his conclusions, his thought is indisputably central to ethical theory, and so students of ethics need to grasp his message. His ethical thought was itself informed by his findings about metaphysics (concerned with the nature of reality) and about epistemology (the study of knowledge and its basis), but these aspects of his work can receive no more than perfunctory treatment here. For present purposes, however, the key text is Kant's *Groundwork for the Metaphysic of Morals*; references will be to Lara Denis' recent edition of the translation by Thomas K. Abbott.

When introducing his answer to the question what makes anything moral, Kant opens by asserting that nothing is unconditionally good except a good will (Denis, p. 55). Here he is using 'good' of what is 'morally good', for he discounts several goods like health and intellect because they can be used badly. Rather he has in mind what merits moral praise, and rightly directs us to the region of character and intentions. (Right acts, it might be held, also merit moral approval, but can still, as Kant later remarks, be performed for the wrong reasons.) However, he has in mind not a will directed by emotion or inclination (which would in his view make it unfree, because it would be determined by factors beyond the agent's control, and therefore not responsible), but a rational will. So the next issue for Kant concerns what is the motive of such a good will.

Since motives such as emotions and inclinations (however generous) have to be excluded, the one remaining motive is acting for the sake of doing one's duty (Denis, pp. 58–9). Inclinations (sympathy and love included) confer no worth, for the agent is invariably causally determined. The only way to be free is thus to choose duty rather than inclination, and act for duty's sake. (Kant does not require this to be one's only motive, and so it could co-exist with motives like love or sympathy, but he is convinced that in its absence moral worth is absent too.)

Acting from duty, however, involves respect for a universal moral law, binding on all rational beings (Denis, pp. 61–2); it is through such respect alone that rational beings can be true to their rational nature, rather than being deflected by partiality or human weakness. Such respect brings in its train respect for all other beings capable of a similar rationality. Kant's approach may by now appear unpromising, and grounded in questionable assumptions about inclinations, emotions (implicitly human relationships too) and their relations to freedom of action; and certainly few modern philosophers writing about agency or character begin from where he begins. However, as soon as Kant turns to the moral law itself, and thus to moral rightness (such as the rightness of actions and policies) rather than moral goodness (and issues of character and of sense of duty), what he has to say has a much wider appeal.

The content of the moral law is to be discovered from its rational and universal nature. Moral precepts are ones that can be obeyed by all rational beings. So the test of a moral imperative is that I can consistently will that it should be a universal law, or be acted on universally (Denis, p. 63). We should notice that Kant's position in normative ethics is not based on the consequences of actions or practices (indeed Kant rejects consequentialist theories), but by contrast is based on the intrinsic nature of duty (a deontological or anti-consequentialist stance; 'deontological' comes from the Greek for 'duty' and literally means 'duty-based').

2. Kant's first formulation

Kant calls this requirement to act in accordance with universal law 'The Categorical Imperative' (Denis, pp. 74–6), contrasting it with imperatives conditional on inclination (like 'Be honest if you want to be well regarded'), which he calls 'Hypothetical Imperatives', and regards as less than moral. We are now ready to grasp his first formulation of the Categorical Imperative: 'Act only on that maxim through which you can at the same time will that it should become a universal law' (Denis, p. 81). Maxims are descriptions of actions of the form 'I will do X,' and 'will' means 'rationally and consistently will'. So he is saying that permissible actions are confined to ones that we can consistently and rationally desire to be universally adopted. This is sometimes called the test of 'universalization'.

Universalization serves to preclude from permissibility two kinds of action. First, there are actions that could not conceivably be acted on by everyone. These include (Kant's own example: Denis, p. 82) lying promises, where the agent's maxim is 'I will make a promise that I intend not to keep.' But the very idea of everyone acting on this maxim is contradictory, because no one would trust promises, and so the practice of promising would break down, as would the possibility of breaking them. (This kind of contradiction is sometimes called 'contradiction in concept'.)

Secondly, there are actions that could be adopted universally, but whose universal adoption no one could rationally desire. Kant's example (Denis, p. 83) is 'I will accept help from others, without myself helping others in need of help'. While this maxim could prevail across the world, no one could rationally desire that it should, since their own purpose of receiving help would be frustrated. (This kind of contradiction is sometimes called 'contradiction in will'.) Kant had other examples of both kinds of contradiction, but they concern duties to oneself (a kind whose existence some philosophers deny altogether), and in any case they seem not to work as well as the ones selected here.

By way of a variant on the first formulation, Kant suggests that the Categorical Imperative is equivalent to 'Act as if the maxim of your action were to become through your will a universal law of nature' (Denis, p. 81). (Kant went on to present yet further formulations which he also regarded as equivalent; but let us stick to this one for the present.) Laws of nature are obeyed everywhere by everything to which they apply, and at all times too; so the suggestion here is that we should only perform acts which we would be willing to make the invariable practice of everyone in our situation (past, present and future). This supplementary version might seem to reinforce the previous examples; for promises would have died out long before my plan to break one could be devised, and, since no one would ever help others by now, my hope of receiving help would be non-existent in the first place. So far, then, Kant's Categorical Imperative seems to be generating acceptable verdicts about which maxims are acceptable, or rather unacceptable.

Before appraising these formulations, we should notice that they concern everyone in a society or in the world acting in the same way; such is universalization. Some commentators speak instead of 'universalizability', but this term is best reserved for a quite different idea, the claim of the twentieth-century British ethicist Richard Hare that what it is right for me to do is also right for any relevantly similar agent in relevantly similar circumstances. This cogent universalizability thesis, however, is about what *anyone should do singly*, and not a test about what *could be done by everyone simultaneously*, and so it should not be confused with Kant's claim (even though Hare sometimes claimed that he was influenced by or even echoing Kant). Kant's universalization claim relates, although he does not acknowledge that it does, to human solidarity, and to this (as we shall see) some of its strengths and its weaknesses are closely attached.

3. Some appraisals

One of the objections to Kant's approach is that it is purely formal; it omits mention of human or animal well-being and harm, and thus tells us nothing of substance; another is that it is purely negative, and tells us nothing positive.

Let us consider these objections together. Kant's approach must be agreed to work by eliminating maxims that are unacceptable, and in this regard to be negative. But in many situations the rejection of a number of options leaves only one, and if this one passes Kant's test, then this one will be permissible (and in this sense right, and perhaps a duty). For example, if not helping someone is rejected as impermissible, then helping them is obligatory. Hence Kant's test can supply positive verdicts for practical situations, and at the same time substantive guidance too.

But does Kant's test supply cogent verdicts? Consider acts of racial discrimination. They pass the 'contradiction in concept' hurdle, but could be held to fail that of 'contradiction in will', because our underlying but pervasive purpose of not being discriminated against would be frustrated if everyone adopted discriminatory behaviour against people with a different pigmentation including ourselves. (Just say such behaviour became a universal 'law of nature': this conclusion becomes all the clearer.) But what if the maxim were 'I will discriminate on a racial basis once every year'? Unfortunately this maxim passes both versions of the universalization test. Yet such behaviour is obviously unacceptable. The same applies to occasional promise-breaking and occasional lying. So there seem to be unacceptable actions that Kant's test lets through.

However, maybe Kant's test can be relied on whenever it rejects behaviour as impermissible, and can thus at least be used as a screening device. But consider acts that could not be performed in the same society or the same world by everyone. These include driving along a particular named road at a certain time of day; not everyone could do this, and yet it is not normally considered wrong for one or another of us to do this. But in case it is suggested that Kant managed to foresee the harm done by the cumulative impact of carbon emissions and was implicitly but perhaps rightly rejecting all driving of automobiles, let us change the example to *walking* along a particular named road at a certain time of day. It would be impossible for all 7 billion of us to do this either. But that fact does not make it wrong for a few of us to do so. (No doubt if it were at all likely that everyone would try to do this, matters would change; but that is not remotely likely.) So Kant's test apparently rejects walking along a named road at a given time of day, and many other entirely innocuous actions, and accordingly cannot be relied on when it declares a maxim unacceptable.

Besides, there is a deeper problem. Let us consider voting in an election, and ask which is the relevant maxim. The same act could be described indifferently as 'exercising one's rights as a citizen', 'taking revenge on the current elected representatives', 'protecting one's interests' and 'blackballing upstart candidates'. But only some of these descriptions can be universalized without contradictions ensuing (of one kind or another), and so the same action turns out, according to Kant, to be right under some descriptions and wrong under others. What is more, almost every action exemplifies this problem. Even lethal acts of stabbing become acceptable if described as 'wielding a knife'. Besides, deeds however nefarious are likely to admit of universalization when the relevant maxim is so worded as to apply to people matching the agent's personal details only ('I will cheat in exams but only if I am six feet seven inches tall and have a triangular scar on my left ear'), since the idea of everyone acting in this way will actually involve no change of behaviour on the part of anyone else.

Kant's supporters could attempt to reply by introducing second-order rules about the maxims to be considered. Maxims, it might be suggested, must exclude avoidable details such as 'once per year' (as in the discrimination case), proper names (as in the example of the named road) and irrelevant personal details (as in the cheating example). But this still leaves us to choose between an infinity of possible maxims for each action, and risks people being allowed to choose their own description of their action, and thus to excuse almost anything through disregarding what others would regard as the salient details. So, despite such defences, the problems about identifying maxims still turn out to render the universalization test unsatisfactory. (For an attempt to overcome such problems, see Christine Korsgaard, *Self-Constitution: Agency, Identity and Integrity*.)

4. Kant's other formulations

Kant, however, presents three further formulations of the Categorical Imperative, holding that while diverging in expression they are effectively equivalent. The most famous is usually regarded as his second (provided that we regard the 'law of nature' formulation, discussed above, as simply a variation on the first). It runs: 'So act as to treat humanity, whether in your own person or in that of any other, in every case at the same time as an end, never as a means only' (Denis, p. 88). This formulation bans exploitation, because exploitative treatment fails to recognize the humanity of the person exploited. At the same time it apparently rejects racial discrimination, including discrimination on an occasional basis, and other kinds of arbitrary discrimination (whether or not occasional) too, and thus seems to fare better than the first formulation.

Kant's third formulation implicitly runs as follows: 'So act that your will can regard itself at the same time as making universal law through its maxim' (Denis, pp. 90–2). This formulation stresses that each individual is to see herself as legislating for the whole of humanity. No one can hide behind the authority of others, no matter how esteemed or authoritative they may be; such a posture Kant calls 'heteronomy' (or being ruled by others), with which he contrasts 'autonomy' (Denis, p. 91) or taking responsibility for oneself and one's own decisions and actions. (This idea of legislating for humanity was later made central to ethics by Jean-Paul Sartre in *Existentialism is a Humanism*.) This said, the third formulation is very close to the first, and thus fits the same examples, and labours under the same difficulties.

However, Kant also supplies a variant of the third formulation (Denis, p. 92), along these lines: So act as if you were through your maxims a law-making member of a kingdom of ends. This variant retains the idea of the individual agent as legislator, but adds that each should see herself as a member of a community in which everyone is recognized to be an end (rather than a means), and to warrant the appropriate respect. This variant, then, incorporates the key elements of the second formulation into the framework of the first and the third. Incidentally, Kant's choice of the term 'kingdom' should not be interpreted as support from Kant for monarchy. He is borrowing and adjusting the New Testament idea of 'the kingdom of heaven' or the realm where righteousness prevails, but using it in a secular context, without implying any particular religious (or equally any particular political) assumptions.

This said, it should be acknowledged that in the final section of the *Groundwork* (Denis, pp. 103–18) Kant argues that the ethical consciousness presupposes a certain metaphysic: belief in God, in human freedom and in immortality. The first and third of these beliefs lie beyond the scope of this book, while aspects of the second are discussed in Chapter 6.

5. Some related appraisals

Kant's themes of autonomy and of treating people as ends chime with the sentiments of many of his readers. In stressing that the individual is ultimately responsible for all her judgements, whether or not they include endorsements of traditions, religious figures or the structures of current society

(Denis, pp. 98–9), he seems right, although he may be representing the individual as unduly isolated and not embedded in her family, circle of friends or community. Certainly there is room for some correctives in this matter; nevertheless we should avoid going to the opposite extreme and holding that all obligations stem from communities and that none exist outside them. Indeed Kant's own belief that each moral agent has obligations with regard to all others, regardless of their location or community (his *cosmopolitanism*: Denis, p. 89) is arguably one of his most important contributions to ethics.

We should return, however, to his advocacy of treating humanity as an end and not a means (as in his second formulation: Denis, p. 88). Here, the objection that what he says is formalistic and lacking in substance is just as inappropriate as the recurrent objection that it is negative and fails to give positive guidance. Nor is he open to the objection that life becomes impossible if we can never treat others as means, for example by employing them. For what he condemns is not treating people as means (period), but treating them as means only. Thus if I employ someone but recognize her as a human being having purposes of her own, paying her a fair wage and supplying fair conditions of employment, then my behaviour is not an infringement of this formulation. It is infringed only if I fail to treat someone else (or myself) as an end.

But what does this mean? Robin Downie and Elizabeth Telfer suggest that it involves recognizing the capacities of human beings for rule-following, for self-determination and for emotional sensitivity, and respecting them accordingly. However, not all humans exhibit these capacities (leaving a problem about the treatment of the others), and some non-humans manifest these capacities in some degree (presenting a problem when Kant draws the line at humanity). So Kant's suggestion that all and only human beings deserve respect, relevant as it is to many cases, raises problems of both these kinds. (However, some of his followers have modified his position so as to allow of respect for other possibly rational animals such as dolphins and gorillas.) Nor is the idea of respecting people unproblematic, as it could involve a variety of forms of treatment. (Some people have held that nothing short of punishment shows respect for criminals.)

As for treating humanity as an end and not only as a means, it is less than clear what it means in practice. Just say a man with an infectious disease enters a country from which it is immune. He could be placed in quarantine in an isolated location for a number of months; yet this would be treating him not as an end at all, but as a means (to the health of others). But if we avoid doing this, we are equally treating those now exposed to the infection as means (to his freedom). The point of this example, taken from C. D. Broad, is that quite often we treat someone or other as a means whatever we do. It follows that Kant's second formulation gives no guidance in such cases. Guidance is only to be gained from a theory of some other kind, such as rights theory (but this faces the same problem as Kant's) or consequentialism.

But if Kant's Categorical Imperative fails as a comprehensive guide to the rightness of actions, what accounts for the success of his examples about promises and about accepting help? The answer, I suggest, is that there are certain practices which depend on widespread compliance and thus human solidarity, practices of which promising and helping are instances. Universal (or even widespread) non-compliance would render them null and void, and so Kant's universalization test readily generates the contradictions that he seeks. Many other kinds of harmless actions, however, do not depend on such solidarity (walking along a road, say, or eating anchovies), and so the fact that their universal adoption would be disastrous has no tendency to make them right or wrong. Some of Kant's examples, then, seem to support his theory, but only because we are prone to ignore the difference made by the background of the practices concerned. This difference, however, returns to attention the centrality of the consequences of compliance and non-compliance in moral practices, and thus reintroduces the need for the very consequentialism that Kant rejects (in the name of deontology) from start to finish.

Study questions

1. Which of Immanuel Kant's formulations of the Categorical Imperative is the most plausible?
2. Does Kant's advocacy of treating people as ends and never only as means capture or fail to capture the core of morality?
3. What is it about persons which makes respect for persons possible?

Priority reading

Kant, Immanuel, *Groundwork for the Metaphysic of Morals*, trans. Thomas K. Abbott, ed. Lara Denis, Peterborough, Ontario: Broadview, 2005.

Thomas K. Abbott's 1949 translation of the *Groundwork* (as *Fundamental Principles of the Metaphysic of Morals*) is available in HTML at: http://ebooks.adelaide.edu.au/k.kant/immanuel/k16prm/index.html, and in several formats at: http://www.gutenberg.org/etext/5682.

Further reading

Broad, C. D., *Five Types of Ethical Theory*, London: Routledge & Kegan Paul, 1930.

Cummiskey, D., *Kantian Consequentialism*, Oxford: Oxford University Press, 1996.

Downie, R. S. and Elizabeth Telfer, *Respect for Persons*, London: Allen & Unwin, 1970.

Korsgaard, Christine M., *Self-Constitution: Agency, Identity and Integrity*, Oxford: Oxford University Press, 2009.

MacIntyre, A. C., *A Short History of Ethics*, London: Routledge & Kegan Paul, 1967.

Paton, H. J. (ed.), *The Moral Law: Kant's Groundwork of the Metaphysic of Morals*, trans. H. J. Paton, London: Hutchinson University Library, 1948.

Sartre, Jean-Paul, *Existentialism and Humanism*, trans. Philip Mairet, London: Eyre Methuen, 1948.

References

Broad, C. D., *Five Types of Ethical Theory*, London: Routledge & Kegan Paul, 1930.

Cummiskey, D., *Kantian Consequentialism*, Oxford: Oxford University Press, 1996.

Downie, R. S. and Elizabeth Telfer, *Respect for Persons*, London: Allen & Unwin, 1970.

Kant, Immanuel, *Groundwork for the Metaphysic of Morals*, trans. Thomas K. Abbott, ed. Lara Denis, Peterborough, Ontario: Broadview, 2005.

—, *Fundamental Principles of the Metaphysic of Morals*, trans. Thomas K. Abbott (1949) is available at: http://ebooks.adelaide.edu.au/k.kant/immanuel/k16prm/index.html, and at: http://www.gutenberg.org/etext/5682.

Korsgaard, Christine M., *Self-Constitution: Agency, Identity and Integrity*, Oxford: Oxford University Press, 2009.

MacIntyre, A. C., *A Short History of Ethics*, London: Routledge & Kegan Paul, 1967.

Paton, H. J. (ed.), *The Moral Law: Kant's Groundwork of the Metaphysic of Morals*, trans. H. J. Paton, London: Hutchinson University Library, 1948.

Sartre, Jean-Paul, *Existentialism and Humanism*, trans. Philip Mairet, London: Eyre Methuen, 1948.

Section 4: John Stuart Mill's utilitarianism

1. Mill's utilitarianism

John Stuart Mill (1806–73) held that the end (or goal) of life and also the standard of morality are lives of happiness, lives, that is, as exempt as possible from pain and as rich as possible in enjoyments. Since the happiness of others is no less desirable or valuable than one's own happiness, 'actions are right in proportion as they tend to promote happiness, wrong as they tend to produce the reverse of happiness'; and this is the core of his ethic of utilitarianism, as expounded in his book *Utilitarianism* (1861) (p. 6; references in this section are to the Everyman edition). And since it is not single actions that can be said to *tend* to promote anything, but rather types of actions, this account of rightness is best interpreted as saying that it is *types* of actions, such as actions complying with a rule or practice, which are made right or wrong by what they tend to promote. (We shall return to this interpretation shortly.)

A life can be rich in enjoyments, according to Mill, both with respect to their quantity and to their quality. Here, Mill diverged from his predecessor, the first explicit Utilitarian, Jeremy Bentham (1748–1832), who had compared pleasures in quantitative terms only (intensity, duration, proximity, prospect of generating further pleasures, etc.). To these measures, Mill added the superiority of higher pleasures (pleasures of culture and of cultivated tastes, for example) to lower, more sensual pleasures, on the basis that those who have experience of both (and thus comprise the only competent judges) invariably prefer higher pleasures. So some pleasures can be preferable to others even when both kinds are quantitatively alike (chapter 2, pp. 7–10). But even if Mill were right about what competent judges choose, he seems here to introduce a supplementary criterion of value independent of pleasantness, since preferability and pleasantness need not coincide, and so, given his view that enjoyment is, together with the absence of pain, the sole criterion of happiness, he seems entrammeled in inconsistency. However, since happiness includes not only performing enjoyable activities but also having an attitude of satisfaction towards one's activities as a whole (whatever their nature), this apparent inconsistency effectively allows him to have a deeper understanding of happiness than Bentham's.

Mill makes better progress towards defending utilitarianism when he replies to objectors who accuse utilitarians of neglecting motives, and distinguishes between the rightness of actions and the worth of agents and their characters. The criterion of maximizing happiness relates to the morality (and thus the rightness) of actions, rather than to the worth of agents, for right actions can be performed from motives good or bad; what the motives tell us about is the character (and sometimes the worth) of the agent, he holds (p. 17), and not whether the action in question is right or not. (This is an important distinction, as it allows him to appraise actions by their causal tendencies, without needing to disregard other moral questions such as the importance of motives.) Mill does in fact have views about what makes motives and traits of character virtuous or otherwise, views which relate the motive or trait to its overall tendency to promote happiness (sometimes, as with self-sacrifice, the happiness of others), and these views are consistent with his utilitarianism. The relation between traits and impacts on happiness is just a rather indirect one.

But this brings us back to the question of how promotion of the greatest happiness makes right actions right. Mill has often been interpreted as holding that to discover whether an action is right or not we should appeal, whenever time permits, directly to the greatest happiness criterion (act-utilitarianism). However, passages such as the one about the impacts that actions tend to produce (mentioned above) indicate that a different interpretation should be preferred. In fact Mill explicitly rejects act-utilitarianism when he says:

> In the case of . . . things which people forbear to do from moral considerations, though the consequences in the particular case might be beneficial – it would be unworthy of an intelligent agent not to be consciously aware that the action is of a class which, if practised generally, would be generally injurious, and that this is the ground of the obligation to abstain from it. (chapter 2, pp. 17–18)

Or rather, this is a significant part of the ground, alongside other factors. These other factors include the influence of such deeds on the character of the agents performing them, and the value of having a code of moral rules which, if generally followed, would maximize happiness and whatever conduces to it (utility). This makes Mill a *rule*-utilitarian, adhering to moral rules not as mere generalizations of beneficial deeds but as an ideal moral code. It also fits some of his other themes. Thus actions are justified through compliance with one of these rules, principles which are shown to be correct by showing that general compliance with them would promote the greatest happiness (but only where the difference made is more than marginal). Among these principles are strict rules guaranteeing individual liberty, necessary, at least in Mill's belief, for enhancing the happiness of society (see his *On Liberty* (1859)). In practice, then, decision-makers seldom need to refer to the end of morality; they should refer to the rules instead.

This leaves the problem of cases where rules clash. To cite an example considered by Mill, the rule against lying could clash with the duty to protect innocent lives (e.g. by withholding and concealing bad news from someone who is dangerously ill and in danger of death) (chapter 2, p. 21). For such cases Mill's view seems to be that the greatest happiness criterion is to be used to limit the scope of one or other of the rules; in the case of this example, the rule against lying does not apply to cases where an innocent life is at stake, because of the difference to utility involved. (We may contrast here Kant's view that the rule against lying admits of no exceptions.) So Mill can take credit both for upholding recognition of moral rules (a central feature of most people's moral consciousness), and for being consistently able to justify one of them taking preference over another when they conflict, something that few if any other systems of ethics can claim. He can also consistently defend adherence both to the greatest happiness criterion (his first principle) and to 'secondary principles', commenting that: 'To inform the traveller respecting the place of his ultimate destination is not to forbid the use of landmarks and direction-posts on the way' (p. 22).

2. Mill's proof

Thus, if the unique desirability of the general happiness can be taken for granted, Mill presents a convincing case for his form of utilitarianism. However, he was not willing to take its desirability for granted, and in chapter 4 he attempted to prove it, or rather to explain (as the title of this chapter runs) 'Of what sort of proof the principle of utility is susceptible' (despite recognizing earlier that 'questions of ultimate ends do not admit of proof' (p. 32)). His would-be proof appeals to the faculty of desire, and runs as follows.

Just as the only proof that an object is visible is that people actually see it, the only proof that anything is desirable is that people actually desire it. But each person desires their own happiness, and so happiness is a good; accordingly the general happiness is a good for people in general (pp. 32–3). Besides, happiness is the sole object of desire, for nothing is desired which is not either a means to happiness or a part of happiness. Happiness must then be the sole end of human action, and so its promotion is the test of conduct and the criterion of morality (p. 36).

However, there are several apparently glaring weaknesses in this reasoning. First, 'desirable' is not comparable to 'visible', as 'visible' just means 'able to be seen', whereas 'desirable' means 'fit to be desired', and is used of what there is reason to desire. So his argument seems to move fallaciously from facts about desire to value-claims about desirability. Secondly, even if each person desires his or her own happiness, it does not follow that everyone desires the general happiness, let alone that the general happiness is desirable. Thirdly, Mill's attempt to show that virtue (in particular) is desired as a part of happiness, because it is desired for the pleasurable experiences that it involves (pp. 33–6), is unconvincing. Fourthly, if only one thing could be desired, it would not follow that we ought to pursue it, but rather that we would have no alternative but to pursue it.

But to these criticisms replies can be made. Thus (on the first point) being able to be desired is at least a necessary condition of being desirable. Further, if, as Mill thinks he can show, only one thing is actually desired, and if, as nearly everyone assumes, something or other is desirable, then this will have to be the one thing that can be desired (for nothing else is eligible) and is desired. So his opening move need not be construed as a fallacy at all, although it depends on the vulnerable claim that only one thing is actually desired.

As for the second criticism, the relation of the general happiness of society to society could be regarded as parallel or analogous to the relation of the happiness of one person to that person. Since what is desirable is what there is reason to desire, the happiness of society will be even more desirable for society than individual happiness is for that individual. (Mill disclosed in a letter that he was not arguing in this passage that the general happiness will be desirable *to* each person, but rather that since happiness is desirable and can be multiplied as the number of happy people increases, the aggregate happiness is also desirable, and multiply so.)

On the third criticism, while virtue is not plausibly part of happiness in Mill's sense of a life of pleasure and of the absence of pain, it is widely contended (as it was, for example, by Aristotle) that virtue is itself constitutive of well-being, with which some people identify happiness (but in a broader sense than Mill's). Mill could perhaps agree, if he were to enlarge his understanding and definition of happiness (as he seems half-inclined to do: see above), beyond a life of pleasure to a life in which (alongside other goods) certain human capacities are developed and fulfilled.

And on the fourth criticism, Mill does seem to argue from what we must seek to what we ought to seek. But if happiness were understood in this enlarged manner, then it would include dispositions (the virtues) which, if Aristotle is right, can only be acquired through repeated choices which all admit of alternatives. So alternative dispositions could have been acquired instead, if a different understanding of well-being had been pursued, and thus the voluntariness of virtue could be restored.

However, the claim that only one thing is or can be desired is a relic of the psychological hedonism (the claim that pleasure alone is desired) that Mill inherited from Bentham and (before him) from the ancient Epicureans. This claim (which attempts to represent all desire as necessarily desire for pleasure) is no more convincing than the psychological egoism of Hobbes (see Section 2 of this chapter), and should surely be discarded. So too, as I have already suggested, should be Mill's hedonistic view of happiness as comprising a life of pleasure and the absence of pain. And by the time these moves have been made, Mill would need both to drop his would-be proof, and also to adopt an understanding of well-being less like that of Bentham and more like that of Aristotle. At the same time, his defence of the greatest happiness principle as the criterion of morality would fare better if it were based on its succeeding in tracking our convictions about morality better than its rivals (such as Kant's approach), rather than on his claims about human nature and desires. Presented like this, his ethical system would emerge as much more credible than Mill's attempts at proof make it appear.

3. Utilitarianism, supererogation and justice

In chapter 5 of *Utilitarianism*, Mill attempts to reconcile utilitarianism with our convictions about justice, and at the same time reveals some distinctions that further clarify his overall position. For while some moral obligations turn out to concern respecting rights and are requirements of justice, others, while remaining duties, and contributing significantly to the general happiness, do not turn in this way on rights, and no one is wronged when they are not performed. Mill represents this distinction as one between duties of perfect obligation and of imperfect obligation. In the former case, there is always an 'assignable individual' to whom the duty is owed, and who has a right which is infringed by its non-delivery (p. 46). In the latter case, the agent has a duty but (as with duties of charity) can choose when and where to discharge it, and there is no such assignable individual who is wronged if it is not discharged or if he or she is not the beneficiary.

Perfect obligations apply where the interests at stake are so vital, and thus the impact on the general happiness so great, that they can justifiably be enforced, and this is the realm of justice. Mill's example of such a vital interest is a person's interest in their security, a precondition of their other interests (p. 50). Imperfect obligations also concern important interests, but in these cases the interests are not crucial enough to justify enforcement, except by the sanction of the agent's own conscience.

While these two classes both involve moral obligations, and in one sense exhaust the realm of morality, Mill does not deny that some other actions are morally desirable without being obligatory at all, even though (in Mill's view) they contribute to the general happiness. These are praiseworthy deeds that cannot in any sense be required or expected of an agent; as such, contemporary ethicists call them 'supererogatory'. Mill termed many such actions 'expedient', not intending to underplay their utility, but holding that converting them into expectations would be too costly to be appropriate. Others he termed 'aesthetic', because of the amiability or nobility of the qualities of character that they expressed, qualities that no one would dream of making morally compulsory.

While some recent writers have suggested that utilitarianism cannot cope with supererogation, since the general happiness either requires an action or regards it as either indifferent or wrong, Mill seems here to present a cogent distinction between deeds the impacts of which make them desirable but are not crucial enough for them to be expected, and ones of which the characteristic impacts are great enough to justify a moral rule, and the expectations that go with such a rule. But there is greater scope for debate about whether Mill's other distinction (between the requirements of justice and other moral rules) allows him to reconcile utilitarianism and justice successfully.

4. Utilitarianism, impartiality and equality

As Mill recognizes, one of the requirements of justice is impartiality. Here he claims that impartiality is 'involved in the very meaning of Utility', for the Greatest Happiness Principle is meaningless 'unless one person's happiness . . . is counted for exactly as much as another's'. This, he holds, echoes Bentham's dictum, 'everybody to count for one, nobody for more than one' (p. 58). What Mill says here is consistent with his application of arithmetic to happiness, and with his claims about desirability, although it would make it harder still to argue that the general happiness, thus understood, is desirable simply on the basis of what people desire. But while impartiality is thus reconciled with utilitarianism, there are now tensions with some other areas of morality.

One problem is with special obligations to family and friends. If nobody counts for more than one, there is a problem with prioritizing those close to you, even in situations where only one person can be rescued (say, from a blazing inferno). Utilitarianism appears to require agents to save whoever would benefit society most, and not your own children, spouse or best friend. However, here Mill can appeal to secondary principles, governing friendship and family life; these practices, he can say, involve special obligations to one's nearest and dearest, and are themselves conducive to the general happiness, which would not be served nearly so well in their absence.

The apparent problem arises only if we are to appeal direct to the greatest happiness principle, impartially understood, when making decisions, instead of adhering to beneficial practices grounded in that principle. But Mill clearly advocates the latter approach. Meanwhile the same principle also supports other practices, such as procedures for appointing to public offices and procedures in law courts, where the requirements of impartiality have to be fully observed, because such practices benefit society and deviations from them (including ones favouring our nearest and dearest) would seriously disrupt it.

Another problem is with equality, something which Mill claims to support. While 'everybody to count for one' sounds egalitarian, this principle also appears to mean that it does not matter who is benefited as long as the total happiness is increased. But this could support very unequal distributions of wealth or other resources, as long as there is an overall gain to society as a whole, even if relative poverty for some is implicated in the outcome. Thus Bentham's dictum apparently does too little to entrench equality.

Here it is open to Mill to reply that the poor should be prioritized because one dollar or pound spent on someone at the margin of poverty makes far more difference to the general good than the same money spent on someone wealthy ('diminishing marginal utility' in the language of economists). He can also appeal to the social benefits of equality, like respect, trust and cooperation, as he does in the matter of equality of the sexes in *The Subjection of Women* (1869).

But these arguments do not sit easily with his view that units of happiness count alike irrespective of circumstances. Equality is best defended, I suggest, if the satisfaction of needs is prioritized over making already happy people happier, and the satisfaction of basic needs over that of other needs; and this could be accepted by someone who (like Mill) holds that it is the outcomes of actions or practices that render them right or obligatory (consequentialism). But to accept this is also to move away from the greatest happiness principle, and thus from utilitarianism.[1]

5. Mill's harm principle and paternalism

Closely allied to Mill's treatment of justice is his claim (in *On Liberty*) that nothing but the prevention of harm to others justifies interference with an adult's freedom (p. 73). This stance precludes interference for the sake of the good of the individual coerced (paternalism). Mill upholds it partly on the grounds that the individual knows best where his or her happiness lies (in some cases a vulnerable claim), and partly because of the importance of people governing their own lives, or of autonomy (a view which, interestingly, may recognize a value independent of happiness).

Yet it does not seem wrong to intervene to prevent attempts at suicide, even on the part of strangers. For people are sometimes wrong about where their happiness lies, and the survivors of suicide attempts often thank those who saved them. Supporters of Mill can claim that such intervention is justified by the value of the would-be suicide's future autonomy, which would be precluded by his or her death; and they can add that if the person is determined to commit suicide, maybe on a rational basis, they will have other opportunities. So there can be libertarian defences of paternalistic intervention. Plausibly, though, there are other defences, just as there are values other than happiness and autonomy. Thus concern for the person's health seems a consideration independent of both of these, but significant enough to justify intervention on some occasions. (See the section on Medical Ethics.)

In any case we can harm others by inaction as well as action, as Mill also recognizes in *On Liberty* (p. 74), holding that people can rightly be compelled to save someone's life or protect defenceless people from harm. Thus failure to help can count as harm. Mill probably intended this interpretation to apply only where serious interests were at stake, or he would have risked bringing the whole of morality into the province of justice. Yet it raises issues such as whether actions and omissions with the same outcomes are really morally different, and whether we are responsible for what we allow to happen as well as what we make to happen. These are among the issues that figure in ongoing debates about consequentialism, and thus about Mill's legacy.

Study questions

1. Can you distinguish between act-utilitarianism and rule-utilitarianism? What do they each say when keeping a promise conflicts with saving a life?
2. Is Mill's 'proof' of the greatest happiness principle fatally flawed?
3. What is at issue when paternalism is pitted against autonomy?

Priority reading

Mill, J. S., *Utilitarianism, On Liberty and Representative Government*, London: J.M. Dent & Sons, and New York: E.P. Dutton & Co (Everyman's Library), 1910.

The seventh edition (of 1879) is also available in several formats at http://www.gutenberg.org/etext/11224.

Further reading

Attfield, Robin, *Value, Obligation and Meta-Ethics*, Amsterdam and Atlanta, GA: Éditions Rodopi, 1995.

Crisp, Roger, *Mill on Utilitarianism*, London and New York: Routledge, 1997.

Lyons, David (ed.), *Mill's Utilitarianism: Critical Essays*, Lanham, MD: Rowman & Littlefield, 1997.

MacIntyre, Alasdair, *A Short History of Ethics*, London: Routledge & Kegan Paul, 1967.

Mill, J. S., *Collected Works of John Stuart Mill*, J. M. Robson (ed.) (33 vols), Toronto: University of Toronto Press, 1963–91.

Urmson, J. O., 'The Interpretation of the Moral Philosophy of J.S. Mill', in *The Philosophical Quarterly*, 3, 1953, 33–9; reprinted in Philippa Foot (ed.), *Theories of Ethics*, Oxford: Oxford University Press, 1967, pp. 128–36.

West, Henry R. (ed.), *The Blackwell Guide to Mill's Utilitarianism*, Malden, MA: Blackwell, 2006.

Note

1 Robin Attfield, *Value, Obligation and Meta-Ethics*, Amsterdam and Atlanta, GA: Éditions Rodopi, 1995, pp. 133–48 (on justice and giving priority to basic needs) and pp. 97–131 (on non-utilitarian consequentialism).

References

Attfield, Robin, *Value, Obligation and Meta-Ethics*, Amsterdam and Atlanta, GA: Éditions Rodopi, 1995.

Crisp, Roger, *Mill on Utilitarianism*, London and New York: Routledge, 1997.

Lyons, David (ed.), *Mill's Utilitarianism: Critical Essays*, Lanham, MD: Rowman & Littlefield, 1997.

MacIntyre, Alasdair, *A Short History of Ethics*, London: Routledge & Kegan Paul, 1967.

Mill, J. S., *Utilitarianism, On Liberty and Representative Government*, London: J.M. Dent & Sons, and New York: E.P. Dutton & Co. (Everyman's Library), 1910.

—, *Collected Works of John Stuart Mill*, J. M. Robson (ed.) (33 vols), Toronto: University of Toronto Press, 1963–91.

—, *Utilitarianism* (the seventh edition of 1879), available in several formats at http://www.gutenberg.org/etext/11224.

Urmson, J. O., 'The Interpretation of the Moral Philosophy of J.S. Mill', in *The Philosophical Quarterly*, 3, 1953, pp. 33–9; reprinted in Philippa Foot (ed.), *Theories of Ethics*, Oxford: Oxford University Press, 1967, pp. 128–36.

West, Henry R. (ed.), *The Blackwell Guide to Mill's Utilitarianism*, Malden, MA: Blackwell, 2006.

2
Value-Theory and the Good Life

Chapter Outline

Section 1: Pleasure, happiness and flourishing

1. Pleasure

This chapter concerns what is desirable or valuable. As we have already seen in Chapter 1, some people believe that this is nothing but pleasure, while Mill took it to be happiness, and Aristotle claimed that it was 'eudaemonia' or flourishing. These views, and related ones, will be further discussed in this section.

Pleasure or enjoyment seems undeniably desirable. If someone is told that an activity is enjoyable but still goes on to ask what is good about it, what they say is difficult to comprehend, to say the least. It may, of course, be a dangerous or harmful activity, and that could count against it, but the fact that it is enjoyable can hardly be denied to count in its favour. If so, we already have part of the answer to the question, 'What is desirable?' There are certainly some problems about this: see Robin Attfield, *Value, Obligation and*

Meta-ethics.[1] For example, some say that pleasure in others' discomfiture has nothing desirable about it at all. But it can be said in reply that the pleasure involved remains a good, but one that is outweighed by the undesirability of behaviour of that kind and of its social impacts. Thus, though all pleasure is good, some pleasures should be avoided.

It may also seem obvious what pleasure is: pleasant experiences. While this answer is not wrong, for some pleasures really do consist in pleasant sensory experiences (like enjoying the smell of hyacinths), it is far from the whole story. Aristotle conveyed this well in his discussion of pleasure in Book X of his *Nicomachean Ethics.*[2] Much pleasure is enjoying *doing* something, whether perceiving, thinking, working or playing. The pleasure and the activity can scarcely be distinguished, for the pleasure is not a consequence of the activity, but part and parcel of it, particularly when the activity is not impeded by defective faculties or defective circumstances. (Enjoying doing something is simply doing it in favourable circumstances without impediment: a fine piece of analysis on Aristotle's part.) Each activity has its own kind of pleasure, and absorption in one can detract from performing another. Aristotle appears to suggest in Book X that all pleasure is of this kind (enjoying doing), but (as J. O. Urmson has argued[3]) he makes it clear in Book VII that this account does not apply to pleasant sensory experiences such as those of food, drink and sex. So pleasure is of two kinds: pleasant experience and enjoying doing.

Ethical hedonism is the theory that nothing but pleasure is desirable, and nothing but pain undesirable. As we saw in Chapter 1, Mill defended a version of this view. Now that we have a clearer grasp of what pleasure is, we can investigate the cogency of hedonism. To hedonists such as Bentham, who take pleasure to consist simply in pleasant experiences, one obvious reply is that enjoyable activities are desirable as well. Similarly to any hedonists who defend the view that nothing but the enjoyment of activities is desirable, one reply is that pleasant experiences too are desirable. (Fred Feldman has recently defended a version of this view, and has replies to this reply[4]; some further replies, however, can be found in what follows.) However, there is nothing to prevent a hedonist arguing that nothing is desirable but pleasant experiences *plus* the enjoyment of activities; to this stance some different replies are in place.

One of these replies comes from Aristotle (who here acknowledges Plato as the source of his argument). If pleasure alone were desirable, then it could not be enhanced through the addition of something else, such as understanding or accomplishment. But lives are widely held to go better when pleasure (however widely construed) is supplemented in one of these ways. Therefore something other than pleasure must be desirable (*Nicomachean Ethics*, Book X, chapter 2). Hedonists could reply that what seems to supplement pleasure is really the enjoyment of understanding or accomplishment. To this their opponents can counter by saying that this is unconvincing where this enjoyment is grounded in illusory impressions, rather than in true achievements. Objective realities, they can add, would have to be involved for the desirability of the pleasure to be enhanced, and not just further forms of enjoyment.

This counter-reply echoes in part an impressive contemporary reply to hedonism from Robert Nozick. Imagine that you are offered the opportunity to be wired up for the next few years to an Experience Machine, which will give you whatever blend of experiences you care to select beforehand, however futuristic or fantastical. The experiences will be convincingly lifelike in their vividness, but you will not really be having them, because you will be wired up to electrodes while floating in a tank. Most people, as Nozick says, would refuse to go on the Experience Machine; for there is something that they value and that would be missing. But if hedonism were true, then there would be no reason not to accept the offer of a few years on the Machine.[5] What we miss might be the exercise of our faculties, or control of our own life (autonomy), or it might be genuine accomplishments as opposed to the illusory impression of achieving them. (It might be both.)

Fred Feldman suggests in reply that hedonism be modified to limit it to those enjoyments which correspond to reality rather than illusion. But this suggestion seems to pave the way for acceptance of something other than enjoyment as desirable. Admittedly such an acceptance would depend on agreement that (say) the exercise of one's faculties is desirable whether they are enjoyed or not (like someone all but discovering a cure for cancer but not living to know and rejoice that they have done so). But many people would readily agree to this view. The thought-experiment of the Experience Machine thus suggests that much is desirable other than enjoyment.

One other objection to hedonism should be mentioned here. If pleasure alone is desirable, and the undiluted gratification of everyone's pleasure makes actions or practices morally right, if not mandatory (as Mill seems to suggest), then committing atrocities is at least justified, and possibly obligatory. For if a large majority would enjoy watching a small minority being tortured to death (as when Christians were thrown to the lions for entertainment), then the majority's pleasure would outweigh the pains of the persecuted few, and make this practice justified (and maybe a duty).[6] While there could be other replies to this objection, such as adoption of a version of rule-utilitarianism that entrenches rights (as in Mill's chapter on justice), it is difficult to avoid such implications while accepting hedonism as presented above. Adherents of a broader value-theory, such as one that acknowledged enjoyment but prioritized the satisfaction of basic needs, could consistently resist the implication just drawn, but only through rejecting hedonism in unmodified form.

2. Happiness

'Happiness' has a range of different meanings. Sometimes it relates not to feelings or attitudes at all, but to good fortune or a life of blessedness, or one favoured by the gods. Virgil probably meant this when he wrote of his fellow-poet, Lucretius, 'Happy the man who was able to discern the causes of things', and then to add, about himself and his own variety of poetry, 'Fortunate too is he who knows the deities of the countryside'.[7] But this is not the kind of happiness intended by advocates of the greatest happiness principle, or by most current speakers of English; in modern usage, happiness consists either of feelings or of attitudes.

Mill, as we have seen, regarded a life of happiness as one as full as possible of pleasure and as free as possible from pain. However, his recognition of higher pleasures meant that he found room within his understanding of happiness for various satisfactions, including satisfaction towards one's activities as a whole, and this seems to be a component of what we usually mean by 'happiness'.

Maybe 'satisfaction' understates what is involved in happiness. Thus Joel Feinberg writes: 'to flourish is to glory in the advancement of one's interests, in short, to be happy'.[8] But while happiness can take this form, happiness does not always involve this kind of pride or self-satisfaction. Happiness, after all, is possible for people whose active life is largely behind them, for babies, and (to all appearances) for many non-human creatures too.

Elizabeth Telfer is more on target in holding that human happiness involves being pleased both with our circumstances and with ourselves, our character and our feelings.[9] Granted human self-consciousness, this holds good of most happy adults, although it is possible to be happy but bed-ridden, and happy but poor. The happiness of babies and of non-human animals would not, of course, involve feelings about one's character or course in life.

Happiness is in almost all circumstances a blessing, although our reservations about drug-induced happiness and illusory happiness in general already suggest that it is not uniquely desirable. Indeed if we ask how credible is the view that nothing but happiness is desirable, many of the objections to hedonism turn out to be objections to this view as well. This is clearest where happiness is taken simply to consist in pleasure and the relative absence of pain; for a life of this kind need not involve autonomy, achievement or even good health. But this conclusion is almost as clear where happiness is acknowledged to include various attitudes of satisfaction or enjoyment. For autonomy, achievement and good health could each still be absent from such a life, particularly as such attitudes could be illusory. And if, to escape the problem about illusions, we stipulate that happiness is uniquely desirable only when attitudes are veridical (or capture reality), we are effectively recognizing that happiness can be enhanced by the presence of other goods, and is not the full story about a good life.

3. Flourishing

To attain a broader account of the good life for human beings than the ones considered so far, we need to introduce the development of various human capacities, among which autonomy could readily be included. This returns us to an argument considered in Section 1 on Aristotle, where Aristotle's reasoning about the good life was reconstructed like this. Human beings have certain essential capacities (including rationality), capacities in the absence of which they would not be human. Implicitly (Aristotle held), the flourishing (or well-being) of any kind of creature involves the development of its essential capacities. Hence human flourishing involves the development of these capacities.[10]

We should recognize that this was not Aristotle's own argument; that was the one discussed in Section 1. Yet this argument has been reconstructed out of Aristotelian materials, and he would almost certainly accept both the premises and the conclusion. One bonus of this argument is that the premise about flourishing would allow parallel conclusions to be drawn about the flourishing of other species, from gorillas to gnus; but in those cases the relevant capacities would be different, and would probably not include rationality or autonomy (unless this underestimates the rationality and autonomy of gorillas).

Another strength of this argument is that it does not require us to focus on distinctive human capacities, as Aristotle eventually did, but allows us to include among essential capacities not only distinctive ones, such as reasoning about the future and ability to use language to arrive at universal truths, but also non-distinctive ones, such as the capacities for self-motion, for perception, for forming friendships and for reproduction. As was pointed out in the section on Aristotle, these capacities can contribute to human well-being, just as they also can to that of other animal species. If so, we should not exclude them from an account of human flourishing. To flourish is simply to live well (or fare well) as a member of one's own species, and we need not a narrow conception of flourishing (as W. F. R. Hardie points out that Aristotle's conception in *Ethics*, Book X turns out to be), but an inclusive one, not tailored to locating the good life in just one kind of life, such as the life of speculative thinking.[11] This being so, all the relevant capacities should be included, because omitting any of them would be to fail to recognize one of the standard ways in which human life can go well.

At the same time, we should not require that, for human well-being, all essential human capacities have to be developed to the stage of being exercised. As was further remarked in the same section, well-being does not involve exercising every single essential human capacity; to quote that section, 'we would not say that blind people or childless people cannot have a good quality of life just because they are blind or childless'. However, accepting this is consistent with holding that the good life for any species (human beings included) depends on exercising most of these capacities, or at any rate of a fair number of them; for where this does not happen, lives will be truncated, but where it does happen, lives will be fulfilled, whether the persons concerned realize this or not.

Accordingly health, autonomy and accomplishment will usually be present in a good life, although occasionally one or other of them may not be. For health involves developing or exercising capacities for mobility (etc.); autonomy involves developing the capacity to think and decide for oneself;[12] and accomplishment involves the development of a range of capacities, plus doing so to some good effect or purpose.

Here it may be asked whether happiness (in any of the senses discussed above) figures as a constituent of human well-being, and indeed whether pleasure does. The presence of pleasure manifestly enhances well-being, and its absence may be an indication that well-being is at least diminished. Yet a failure to enjoy what one is doing need not betoken the absence of well-being, because the person could still be leading a life of autonomy and of considerable achievement, perhaps in circumstances too adverse to allow these facts to be relished or even noticed.

Parallel comments are in place about the relation of happiness to well-being. Where 'happiness' is taken as meaning a life of pleasure relatively free from pain (Mill's interpretation), happiness clearly contributes to well-being, but, for the reasons just given about pleasure, its absence need not imply lack of well-being. Where it is understood to involve an attitude of satisfaction with one's life, as well as the presence of enjoyable experiences and activities, its absence is harder to reconcile with well-being or flourishing, and yet a person who is discontented with their life (and therefore not happy in this sense) could still exemplify well-being through leading a life of autonomy and accomplishment.

4. Autonomy

It should also be asked how important or central autonomy is within well-being. The section on Medical Ethics considers a principle of autonomy that is often considered independent of the principles of Beneficence and of Non-Maleficence, which are of course both aimed at well-being (the first by promoting it and the second by not undermining it). But it would be at least as reasonable to regard autonomy as a constituent of well-being, and respecting it as not comprising an independent principle, but as fostering a different dimension of a person's interest in well-being, one that can be compared to other dimensions of well-being or flourishing. However, if we take this approach, we need to recognize how crucial autonomy is to well-being, and how it cannot rightly be overruled except in some life-threatening situations where there is genuine uncertainty about the autonomy of a person's decision that her or his life should be ended. As that section also maintains, respecting autonomy depends on people's expressions of their wishes not only being informed and voluntary, but also being made by someone competent to make decisions, that is, having full possession of their mental faculties.

Given the centrality of autonomy within well-being (and of respecting it as a requirement of normative ethics), it is also worth asking whether it can ever rightly be overridden. John Stuart Mill, as we have seen in Section 4, held that no one should be coerced except to prevent harm to others; he regarded constraining people for their own good as paternalism, and objectionable as such. Mill was rightly emphasizing the importance for a person's well-being of her moulding her own life. But as is illustrated in the section on Medical Ethics, some expressions of wishes may fail to be properly informed, or may diverge from the person's underlying values (or be inauthentic) through force of circumstance. There again, sometimes a decision, such as that of a would-be suicide, would, if not frustrated, undermine that person's future autonomy. Besides, if we really believed that autonomy overrides all other considerations, then we would accede to autonomous requests to end the life of a person making such a request; our reluctance to do so suggests that autonomy does not override everything else. Thus the centrality of autonomy within well-being does not show that all apparently autonomous decisions should always be respected; this does not apply, for example, to decisions that are ill-informed, or ones that would deprive the person concerned of powers of self-determination in the future. Autonomy, then, can be weighed up against other dimensions of well-being (even that of competent adults), and occasionally paternalistic intervention should be preferred to inaction or acquiescence.

Study questions

1. How cogent is EITHER psychological OR ethical hedonism?
2. Can a person's autonomy ever rightly be overridden?

Notes

1 Robin Attfield, *Value, Obligation and Meta-ethics*, Amsterdam and Atlanta: Éditions Rodopi, 1995, pp. 33–4.

2 Aristotle, *Nicomachean Ethics*, Book X, chapter 5 (any translation).

3 J. O. Urmson, 'Aristotle on Pleasure', in J. M. E. Moravcsik (ed.), *Aristotle: A Collection of Critical Essays*, London: Macmillan, 1968, pp. 323–33.

4 Fred Feldman, 'The Good Life: A Defense of Attitudinal Hedonism', *Philosophy and Phenomenological Research*, 65.3, 2002, pp. 605–27.

5 Robert Nozick, *Anarchy, State and Utopia*, New York: Basic Books, 1974, pp. 42–5; see Attfield's discussion at *Value, Obligation and Meta-ethics*, pp. 38–9.

6 See Attfield, *Value, Obligation and Meta-ethics*, p. 38.

7 Virgil, *Georgics* 2, 490 and 493 (my translation); for the original Latin text, see F. A. Hirtzel (ed.), *P. Vergili Maronis Opera*, Oxford: Clarendon Press, 1900.

8 Joel Feinberg, 'The Rights of Animals and Unborn Generations', in William T. Blackstone (ed.), *Philosophy & Environmental Crisis*, Athens, GA: University of Georgia Press, 1974, pp. 43–68, 55.

9 Elizabeth Telfer, *Happiness*, London and Basingstoke: Macmillan, 1980, p. 36.

10 This argument is further discussed in Attfield, *Value, Obligation and Meta-ethics*, pp. 45–56.

11 W. F. R. Hardie, 'The Final Good in Aristotle's *Ethics*', in J. M. E. Moravcsik (ed.), *Aristotle: A Collection of Critical Essays*, London: Macmillan, 1968, pp. 297–322.

12 See Attfield, *Value, Obligation and Meta-ethics*, pp. 63–5.

References

Aristotle, *Nicomachean Ethics*, Roger Crisp (trans. and ed.), Cambridge, UK and New York: Cambridge University Press, 2000.

Attfield, Robin, *Value, Obligation and Meta-ethics*, Amsterdam and Atlanta: Éditions Rodopi, 1995.

Feinberg, Joel, 'The Rights of Animals and Unborn Generations', in William T. Blackstone (ed.), *Philosophy & Environmental Crisis*, Athens, GA: University of Georgia Press, 1974, pp. 43–68.

Feldman, Fred, 'The Good Life: A Defense of Attitudinal Hedonism', *Philosophy and Phenomenological Research*, 65.3, 2002, pp. 605–27.

Hardie, W. F. R., 'The Final Good in Aristotle's *Ethics*', in J. M. E. Moravscik (ed.), *Aristotle: A Collection of Critical Essays*, London: Macmillan, 1968, pp. 297–322.

Nozick, Robert, *Anarchy, State and Utopia*, New York: Basic Books, 1974.

Telfer, Elizabeth, *Happiness*, London and Basingstoke: Macmillan, 1980.

Urmson, J. O., 'Aristotle on Pleasure', in J. M. E. Moravcsik (ed.), *Aristotle: A Collection of Critical Essays*, London: Macmillan, 1968, pp. 323–33.

Section 2: Moral standing, value and intrinsic value

1. Moral standing

The findings of Section 1 and of previous sections allow us to answer some important questions about ethics. One of these is the question 'Which things matter, morally speaking, and should be taken into account when decisions are being made?' This is a question about the scope of moral standing, or, in Kenneth Goodpaster's terms, of 'moral considerability' (by which he meant the issue of which things ought to be taken into consideration).[1]

The philosophers considered in earlier sections would give different answers to this question. Thus Kant would give the answer 'rational beings', having human beings primarily in mind, because these alone qualify for (his kind of) respect. Aristotle might well have agreed (with some reservations about slaves), while recognizing that all creatures have a good. But Hume, who often argued from the emotions (or passions) of animals, would probably have included all sentient creatures as well; while Mill would probably agree, since sentient creatures are capable of feeling pleasure and pain.

While Kant's answer continues to receive much support, because certain kinds of respect are possible only towards autonomous, self-determining creatures, there is a strong case against drawing the line, in answer to the question of moral standing, at human beings. Thus if we are to include all human beings, and give some reason by way of qualities that qualify them for moral standing, we may well have to resort to feelings (whether sensations or emotions or both) which in fact belong to most non-human animals too. Besides, if we include pleasure and enjoyment in our answer to the question of what is desirable, it makes good sense to include the full range of creatures capable of enjoyment, and thus to include sentient non-humans rather than human beings alone. Indeed the belief that all sentient beings have moral standing now enjoys widespread support among philosophers. Here the writings of Peter Singer[2] have had a wide influence.

However, it is unclear that having feelings is a prerequisite for moral standing. The reason for the moral standing of both human beings and of sentient animals in general could be their ability to be benefited or be beneficiaries (e.g. of benevolence or kindness); and what is required for this is having interests or a good of one's own. For this reason, Goodpaster includes in his own answer to the question about moral standing everything that satisfies this requirement, or, in other words, all living creatures. His conclusion tallies with many people's intuitions, such as regret about the unnecessary felling of a tree. This conclusion also tallies with the findings of the previous section, which included in its account of the good the development of essential capacities. But the bearers of such capacities are not only human beings or sentient creatures, but living creatures in general. Besides, since future ones will have a good of their own and are liable to be affected by current actions, they should be included too; in fact, to include future generations, we need to include all the possible creatures that could be brought into being.[3]

When asked to explain why he stops short at living creatures and does not include rocks, cliffs and rivers, Goodpaster went on to explain that these things lack a good of their own, and for that reason cannot be benefited.[4] We could add that things with a good of their own, as living creatures are, can be harmed, injured, helped and healed, whereas other things cannot (even if, as in the case of artefacts like cars, they can be damaged). It is also worth noticing that he is not saying that all living creatures have high moral significance, but just that they count; how much they count remains an open question, at least until we reflect on their value. (Moral standing, in other words, is different from moral significance.) Similarly he is not saying that living creatures are sacrosanct, or that they must never be killed or injured. That, as he explains, would make life unlivable, but is no part of his claim.

Having moral standing is sometimes confused with having one or another kind of value. There is likely to be some connection between moral standing and having value, since what has a good of its own (and thus moral standing) can be benefited and such benefit is likely to be valuable (in one sense or another). But it is not, strictly speaking, creatures or things that are valuable or desirable, but their states or activities, for those are what it makes sense to have reason to promote or cherish, which is the core of the meaning of 'being valuable'. It is to the subject of value that we should now turn.

2. Value, valuation and valuers

Something has value if there is reason to value it, or if it is fit to be valued. Likely examples of valuable states or conditions are pleasure, happiness and flourishing (all discussed in the previous section). These are also examples of states valuable not because of what they cause or facilitate, but for themselves. Such non-derivative value is known as 'intrinsic value', and will be further discussed below.[5] So once again the previous section puts us in a position to consider important questions, this time ones about value.

Yet many philosophers write as if having value depends on being valued by someone or other, and would say that there is no value without actual valuation (past, present or future). What people value really does give some indication of what is valuable; similarly Mill was not entirely wrong to hold that what people desire supplies evidence of what is desirable. But just as neither he nor we can reason from what is desired to what is desirable, we cannot reason either from what is valued to what is valuable. This is because what is valuable is what there is reason to value; and instead of valuing that, people often value something else. In fact, there could be valuable states of affairs that are never valued, such as perhaps the flourishing of species that are and remain undiscovered. There again, things could be much valued that have little or no value; the rise and fall of fashions supply many likely examples.

This may make it seem difficult to reason about value and recognize what is valuable; and there are sceptics who think that we cannot without great difficulty manage either. However, we have come across examples of such reasoning in the last section, or of appeals to it. That section began with the desirability of pleasure or enjoyment. If a sceptic were to ask why enjoyment should be held desirable, there is a ready reply: if enjoyableness does not count as a reason for choosing something, then nothing counts as such a reason, because there are no other reasons as clear as this one. (This does not mean that nothing but enjoyment is desirable or valuable, but it does undermine the claim that it is not desirable or valuable at all.)

To take another example from the last section, people's reactions to Nozick's Experience Machine thought-experiment[6] strongly suggest not only that people do not value life on the Machine above everything else, but also that there is something lacking in such a life, pleasant as it might well be, and some reason for choosing to stay in control of one's life. If so, then there must be something desirable other than pleasure (and so we should reject the view that nothing but enjoyment is valuable). The something else could be autonomy, self-determination, or the exercise of one's faculties; further reflection would be needed to discover which of these is valuable, if they are not all such. But the present point is that progress can be made in discovering what is valuable through thought-experiments such as Nozick's, and therefore that scepticism about what is valuable should be rejected.

3. Intrinsic value and value of other kinds

By now it is clear that at least something is valuable; we should reject the nihilist view that nothing is. But clearly there are different kinds of value, for some things are valuable because they facilitate or bring about others, while others are valuable simply because of what they are, or because of their own nature. (I am not denying that something could be valuable in both these ways; it is often suggested that a good example is education. Do you agree?)

As was mentioned above, those states of affairs that are valuable because of their own nature, independently of whether they are valuable for any reason extending beyond themselves, are said to be valuable intrinsically or to have intrinsic value. Happiness is one example. Other kinds of value (such as the value of money) will be derivative, but this kind is non-derivative.

Some things are valuable because they are conducive to valuable outcomes (such as flourishing). Examples are knives, forks, spoons and chop-sticks. Their value is instrumental value. But not everything with instrumental value has been made as an artefact or instrument. Ecosystems (such as rivers, forests and mountains) are valuable (at least on one view) because they make possible valuable and flourishing lives. So they form the preconditions that facilitate value. Some people give their value the distinctive name of 'systemic value' (the value they have as valuable *systems*). But because their value turns on that of what they facilitate, it is in any case instrumental value, although this does not mean that we can or should treat them as instruments (as if they were made by us, or exist to serve our purposes).

Another kind of value is inherent value, the value that something has when it enhances human life through its presence, such as anything which is interesting to study or beautiful to contemplate. The aesthetic value of works of art like paintings or music is (I suggest) of this kind; here the value depends not on the existence of the work of art but on its appreciation by a conscious subject. Natural items such as lakes and waterfalls can often have this kind of value, but only if they are appreciated. Inherent value should be distinguished both from intrinsic value and from instrumental value.

Another kind of non-instrumental value is contributive value, as when the character of a friend contributes to the value of a friendship, making the friendship more valuable overall. Character can of course be valuable in other ways, but here it adds to (or possibly multiplies) the value of the whole (friendship) of which it forms part.

Imagine that someone now suggests that while value is truly to be found in the world, it is always derivative, being either instrumental or inherent or contributive. (This kind of view is sometimes advanced by philosophers sceptical about intrinsic value.) By now, we can reply as follows. If all value were derivative, there would be nothing to confer value on what is derivatively valuable, or to make them valuable, and so nothing would be valuable either instrumentally or inherently or in any other way. So everyone who accepts that something is valuable must also accept that something or other is intrinsically valuable. (This argument is an adjusted version of one supplied by Aristotle early in Book I of *Nicomachean Ethics*.[7]) The only way to escape this conclusion is to adopt nihilism and deny that anything is valuable in the first place. But no one who places value on argument can be a consistent nihilist. Effectively, everyone grants that there is intrinsic value – including those who claim to deny this.

4. Some theories of value

We do not need to start from scratch to produce a theory of value, because that is what we were already studying in the previous section. What was under discussion there could be re-expressed as whether pleasure or happiness or flourishing is intrinsically valuable, or whether perhaps they all are. But by now we can trace how one or another answer to questions about moral standing goes well (or coheres) with one or another account of intrinsic value, and at the same time review possible answers to these various questions and issues.

Before investigating this, it should be stressed that having intrinsic value does not involve a thing having rights or being off-limits in one way or another. Occasionally philosophers use the language of 'intrinsic value' with one of these meanings, but that is a different way of using this language from that of this book, and of most discussion of intrinsic value. Thus to say that an animal's health has intrinsic value is not to say anything about the animal's rights, nor to say that it could not rightly be killed. It is only to say that there are reasons to protect its health for what it is; but there could well be other reasons for acting otherwise (such as the need of a person for food), turning on the intrinsic value of the continued flourishing of that person. When someone uses the vocabulary of intrinsic value, it is wise to check in what sense they are using it, to avoid discussion being at cross-purposes. The presence of value (intrinsic or otherwise) is understood here to convey there being reasons for action such as protection, rather than there being overwhelming or overriding reasons for or against some deed.

Let us return to the way that some theories cohere with others. Let us first imagine someone taking the view that human beings alone have moral standing. Such a person cannot consistently adopt the view that all pleasure (let alone all flourishing) has intrinsic value, for much pleasure is enjoyed by non-human creatures, and many such creatures flourish, but this person does not regard that as a reason for taking their interests into account. Hence they are likely to restrict intrinsic value to the development or exercise of human faculties such as reasoning or self-determination, or activities involving them. (This is a position likely to be held by traditionalist Kantians.) Such a stance, however, has to understand all concern for animals' well-being as covert concern for the well-being of human beings.

Others hold that all sentient creatures have moral standing (sentientism). Theorists of this kind cannot hold that health always has intrinsic value, as many non-sentient creatures are healthy. But they are likely to go on to hold that pleasure has intrinsic value and pain intrinsic disvalue (hedonism), since it is precisely sentient creatures that can enjoy pleasure and undergo pain. So sentientism about moral standing goes with hedonism about intrinsic value. Or rather, it does except where a broader theory of intrinsic value is held, one for which something other than pleasure (such as understanding, perhaps) contributes to the good of a conscious mind. Thus hedonists have reason to be sentientists, although not all sentientists will be hedonists. But if there can be value that is not dependent on minds or on consciousness, and there was value in the world before minds or consciousness evolved (perhaps in the flourishing of non-conscious creatures), then a yet broader view is needed.

People who accept that the flourishing of creatures has intrinsic value (without restricting the relevant creatures to ones that are conscious) are likely to adhere to biocentrism about moral standing, the view that all living creatures are morally considerable. Conversely, biocentrists are likely to be sympathetic to a value-theory recognizing the intrinsic value of flourishing (including the development of the various capacities, distinctive and non-distinctive, which make each kind of creature the kind that they are).

Yet others adopt a holistic view of moral standing, and ascribe moral standing not only to living creatures but also to ecosystems, species and the biosphere (ecocentrism). Such people are likely to locate intrinsic value in these same entities. But they are likely to find difficulty in explaining how the non-living components of ecosystems or of the biosphere can have their interests heeded or taken into consideration (for they do not have interests at all), and how the interests of species diverge from and supplement those of their present and future members. For if moral standing and intrinsic value are located simply where there are living creatures, then it is simpler to stick to biocentrism about moral standing, and a theory of intrinsic value which locates it in creatures' flourishing, or the development of creatures' capacities plus their pleasure and happiness (where creatures are capable of them).

Such a value-theory is sometimes known as 'perfectionism', which is a useful label unless it is confused with the other main meaning of this term (that of setting oneself unduly high or demanding standards). As long as we remember that there is no connection between perfectionism in the sense just introduced and perfectionism in the other, then there is no harm in adherence to a perfectionist view (in the first sense) of intrinsic value.

5. Degrees of value

One thing can be more valuable than another, and not only from one person's perspective. Thus there can be interpersonal reasons to value freedom of speech more than doughnuts. So in normal circumstances freedom of speech has greater value than doughnuts not just from one or another perspective, but unqualifiedly. It would be different if someone were starving, and the only available food consisted in doughnuts; but that would hardly be a normal circumstance.

Peter Singer has wisely advocated that like interests should receive equal consideration,[8] and this implies that the satisfaction of like interests has equal value (and of greater interests, greater value). But he also distinguishes equal consideration from equal treatment, because different people have different needs, which would make equal treatment (irrespective of these differences) inappropriate. The same holds for different creatures. For some have interests (e.g. in not being made to suffer) that are absent from others (such as plants). Because of their different interests, it will often be right to prioritize the interests of sentient creatures over those of non-sentient ones, because the satisfaction of these interests has greater value.

Generally, the satisfaction of the good of creatures with more complex and sophisticated capacities is more valuable than that of the good of other creatures. This does not mean that all human beings should be prioritized over all non-humans; for some non-humans have capacities equal to those of a number of human beings. Also, much will depend on which interests are at stake. In a clash between the interests of a human diner and a veal-calf which has scarcely begun to live its life, much more is at stake for the veal-calf than for the human being, even though the human being will probably have ampler intellectual and emotional capacities. But it is reasonable to prioritize needs over gratifications that do not correspond to needs, and the needs of creatures with sophisticated capacities over the needs of other creatures.

For these reasons, we should avoid the view that all creatures should be given equal consideration, let alone be treated equally. The biocentrist says that they all have moral standing, but need not go on to say that the good of each and every one of them has *equal* intrinsic value. (Here, I diverge from egalitarian biocentrists such as Paul Taylor.[9]) As was mentioned earlier, how much a creature counts depends on the value of its good or its flourishing, and to this the considerations mentioned in the previous two paragraphs will be relevant. This topic is discussed in greater detail in *Value, Obligation and Meta-Ethics*, chapter 6, where I have tried to explain how grasp of degrees of value can give practical guidance for action.[10]

Study questions

1. Which things have moral standing (or moral considerability)?
2. What, if anything, is valuable intrinsically?

Notes

1 Kenneth Goodpaster, 'On Being Morally Considerable', *Journal of Philosophy*, 75, 1978, pp. 308–25.

2 See Peter Singer, *Practical Ethics*, 2nd edn, Cambridge: Cambridge University Press, 1993.

3 See Robin Attfield, *Value, Obligation and Meta-Ethics*, Amsterdam and Atlanta, GA: Éditions Rodopi, 1995, pp. 7–27.
4 Kenneth Goodpaster, 'On Stopping at Everything: A Reply to W.M. Hunt', *Environmental Ethics*, 2, 1980, pp. 281–4.
5 See pp. 48–50 (below).
6 Robert Nozick, *Anarchy, State and Utopia*, New York: Basic Books, 1974, pp. 42–5.
7 Aristotle, *Nicomachean Ethics*, Roger Crisp (trans. and ed.), Cambridge, UK and New York: Cambridge University Press, 2000.
8 Singer, *Practical Ethics.*
9 Paul Taylor, *Respect for Nature: A Theory of Environmental Ethics*, Princeton: Princeton University Press, 1986.
10 See Attfield, *Value, Obligation and Meta-Ethics*, pp. 79–94.

References

Aristotle, *Nicomachean Ethics*, Roger Crisp (trans. and ed.), Cambridge, UK and New York: Cambridge University Press, 2000.
Attfield, Robin, *Value, Obligation and Meta-Ethics*, Amsterdam and Atlanta, GA: Éditions Rodopi, 1995.
Goodpaster, Kenneth E., 'On Being Morally Considerable', *Journal of Philosophy*, 75, 1978, pp. 308–25.
—, 'On Stopping at Everything: A Reply to W.M. Hunt', *Environmental Ethics*, 2, 1980, pp. 281–4.
Nozick, Robert, *Anarchy, State and Utopia*, New York: Basic Books, 1974.
Singer, Peter, *Practical Ethics*, 2nd edn, Cambridge: Cambridge University Press, 1993.
Taylor, Paul, *Respect for Nature: A Theory of Environmental Ethics*, Princeton: Princeton University Press, 1986.

Section 3: Worthwhile life, self-respect and meaningful work

1. The concept of a worthwhile life

A worthwhile life is a life worth living, as opposed to a life that falls short of being worth living. It is the kind of life that kindly people wish one another, and that pantomime fairy-godmothers used to wave magic wands to bestow.

For the sake of clarity, we should distinguish a worthwhile life from a worthy life or a life of virtue. While a worthwhile life would often be one rich in virtue, and praiseworthy as such, morally praiseworthy lives are unfortunately not always worth living, while lives worth living (and even lives well worth living) are sometimes morally flawed or fall short of moral rectitude; and those who live them are not always paragons of virtue. This is because flourishing lives (or lives of well-being) necessarily involve many fulfilments, but not necessarily moral ones; a person can develop their capacities for understanding, aesthetic appreciation, physical fitness and friendship, and combine all this with health, happiness and self-respect, without exhibiting conscientiousness or modesty or generosity. Aristotle wrote otherwise, as if a life of flourishing involved having all the virtues of character; but even he ended up, in the final book of the *Nicomachean Ethics*, claiming self-sufficiency for a life of contemplation, whether it was morally virtuous or not.[1]

Later in this section, the relation of a good life for a human being (considered in the opening section of this chapter) to states that have intrinsic value is discussed, together with the relation of self-respect and of meaningful work to a worthwhile life. But first it is worth reflecting on conditions of life that might fall below the level at which life is worth living.

The great majority of human lives are worth living to some degree. But occasionally people fall into a coma that proves irreversible, and arguably nothing of value remains in their lives. As one philosopher has put it, they have biological lives, but no longer lead biographical lives. New research suggests that even people apparently in a coma can in some cases understand what is going on around them, and can convey responses by imagining an activity (playing tennis, in some recently publicized research), a thought which registers on a brain-scanning machine. But in many cases there are no such responses, and conscious life has ceased. This is, I suggest, an example of a life not worth living. In such a case, it would arguably be justified to switch off the respirator on which such a life depended.

There are also cases of the quality of a conscious person's life falling below the level at which live is worth living. Imagine a life of considerable and unremitting pain, able to be countermanded only through drugs inducing unconsciousness. Such a life could still be worth living if there are prospects of this being a temporary phase, and if there are likely to be worthwhile experiences and activities, or perhaps the enjoyment of relationships, after it is over. But we could imagine a case in which there were no such prospects, and where failing faculties meant that whatever had previously made life worth living was no longer available (whether sensory experiences, communication with friends or family or memories of happier days). This seems a reasonable description of a life not only not worth living, but actually worth *not* living; and many people would like to be able to authorize that in the event of their being certified by competent experts to be in such a condition they should be painlessly killed.

Safeguards would be needed to ensure that such wishes were fully autonomous, and involved informed consent; but to refuse people this entitlement could involve condemning them to a condition of life worse than death.

If such a life would be not worth living, then there will probably be other cases of lives that people should be spared from having to live. For example, babies born with severe anencephaly (without a brain, that is), should arguably not be required to live out a life of pain and indignity, even if it were medically possible to keep them alive for weeks or months. In such cases, there is no possibility of the consent of the infant concerned; consent would need to be given by parents or guardians, while safeguards would be needed to ensure that the medical condition was irremediable and that the consent was not given from self-interested motives. Yet allowing such infants to die is widely accepted. Indeed there is a strong case for the view that, rather than our waiting for such an infant to die (a form of passive euthanasia), it would be kinder to kill them (a form of active euthanasia).[2] Euthanasia means killing someone in their own interests. In the case of infants, such killing or letting-die would also amount to infanticide.

So considerations relating to the absence of worthwhile life can be relevant in rare cases to the ethics of life and death, cases where quality of life has become negative. (This is all relevant to the lives of non-human animals as well as to those of human beings.) Largely, however, ethics is concerned with promoting and enhancing positive qualities of life, or lives that are worth living; where there is suffering or sorrow, they can usually be overcome not by death but by fostering more satisfactory states of life. Besides, when a life is worth living, or even capable of becoming so, that forms a very strong reason against extinguishing that life. As we have seen, it cannot be assumed that life will always be worth living, let alone that life as such is what is intrinsically valuable. But this makes it all the more important to reflect on what *makes* life worth living, and gives the great majority of people a positive quality of life.

2. What makes life worth living?

Jonathan Glover persuasively writes: 'If a list could be made of all the things that are valuable for their own sake, these things would be the ingredients of a "life worth living"'.[3] The 'things' of which he writes are of course states, activities and experiences of human beings. So a life worth living could be understood as a life in which states, activities and experiences of positive intrinsic value outweigh whatever states, activities and experiences the person concerned has reason to avoid or regret (things of negative intrinsic value, such as pain and anguish. For the concept of intrinsic value, see the previous section). Normally the person will also have a favourable attitude towards (or be pleased with) the way in which their life is unfolding, or be happy; but as we have seen in the first section of this chapter, a person could be flourishing (or in that sense leading a good life) even if happiness were absent.

Which, then, are these states, activities and experiences? It is sometimes suggested that it is simply being alive and conscious that has intrinsic value and makes life worth living. But this would mean that any and every kind of consciousness has intrinsic value, pain and unremitting boredom included. As Glover maintains, this is simply not what we believe[4]; and we certainly do not believe that a life of such boredom would be a life well lived. Where conscious states have intrinsic value then, the reason will not consist in consciousness alone. (Indeed where there is intrinsic value in the lives of non-conscious creatures, it will not turn on consciousness at all.) And this tallies with what was argued in the previous section about intrinsic value.

We should turn instead to those states, activities and experiences that constitute flourishing, and human flourishing in particular. As was argued in the first section of this chapter, there is intrinsic value in the development of essential human capacities in general. Here are some examples of such capacities: the capacities for growth and self-motion; for perception; for linguistic communication; for practical reasoning; for self-determination; for understanding and theoretical reasoning; for taking responsibility for one's beliefs, attitudes and actions; for memory; and for experiencing a wide range of emotions. This is not an exhaustive list, and others will be added later in this section. Further, there are many ways in which the development of these capacities can be expressed. But they have in common being essential human capacities, ones in the absence of which a species of creatures would not be recognizable as human beings; and this means, if the argument developed earlier in the chapter is valid, that their development is in each case intrinsically valuable, and that the development of most (but not necessarily all) of them is involved in a flourishing life and accordingly in a life worth living.[5]

Other states have also been argued to have intrinsic value, including enjoyment (or 'having fun') and happiness. While their absence does not mean that a life is not worth living, their presence will enhance the quality of a life, sometimes to that of a life *well* worth living.

The quality of a life can also be enhanced if the development of relevant capacities is harmonious. For it is possible for the development of one capacity to take a form that actually frustrates or prevents the development of another, as when the development of someone's gustatory capacities (one form of their capacity for perception) produces obesity which prevents the development of athletic ones. By contrast with this, harmonious capacity-development would involve the development of each capacity taking a form consonant with that of the others. Thus the harmonious development of capacities can contribute to human well-being and to the living of a worthwhile life.

Another factor that can supplement life's worthwhileness is length of life, although, since capacities can be developed in its absence, it is not strictly a requirement for a life to be worthwhile. But where activities have intrinsic value, then the longer they continue the better.[6] Certainly it is an evil for someone to be deprived of the continuation of worthwhile activities, or of the completion of autonomously chosen projects in which their faculties were being exercised.

Someone might say, by way of objection, that what makes life worthwhile varies with conceptions of life, and that these conceptions are constituted by the values of one's society. So, the objector might continue, conceptions of a good life are so shaped by particular societies that considerations such as the above, which seem not to take social contexts into account, fall short through excessive abstraction and abstractness. To this it can be replied that the position presented above is compatible with numerous conceptions of what makes life worthwhile (where 'conceptions' consist in sets of beliefs about the application of the key concepts, such as flourishing and worthwhileness). The existing diversity of beliefs about the worthwhileness of particular practices, pastimes and relationships is not a problem for what is argued here. Nor have social contexts been disregarded; rather, we have looked beyond them to common human capabilities and fulfilments, embodied in a variety of actual social forms, and capable of embodiment in others. Indeed this approach makes it possible to compare different conceptions of what makes life worthwhile, and occasionally put forward suggestions for how provision for worthwhile lives could be changed for the better.[7]

3. Self-respect

If self-respect has intrinsic value, then it too will enhance the worthwhileness of a life. And if so, and if meaningful work characteristically involves self-respect, then this will be one good reason for including meaningful work among the constituents of a worthwhile life. So it is worth asking what is self-respect.

According to John Rawls, self-respect combines two ingredients: 'a person's sense of his own value, his secure conviction that his conception of the good, his plan of life, is worth carrying out' (let us read 'his or her' where Rawls wrote 'his') and 'a confidence in one's ability, so far as it is within one's power, to fulfill one's intentions'. He adds that without self-respect, either nothing may seem worth doing, or people lack the desire to strive even for what they regard as valuable. He classifies self-respect as 'a primary good', something which all rational people want, whatever else they want.[8] But is it also valuable for itself?

Before this question is addressed, a slight corrective to Rawls' view that self-respect involves having a plan of life is in place. For people with no plan of life can still have self-respect, as long as they have standards about which they care, related to the central practice or practices of their life, and thus have a set of implicit priorities. This helps explain why meaningful work (discussed further below) normally facilitates self-respect. For people whose work is meaningful comply with their own standards of skill or judgement, and are typically aware of doing so. So we already have one reason for including meaningful work in most accounts of a worthwhile life.[9]

To return to the question of the intrinsic value of self-respect, when people care about standards relating to their activities in this way, they necessarily want to comply with them; and so the awareness that they are achieving this will necessarily be rewarding, even if they remain dissatisfied with their achievements to some degree. This is already one reason why self-respect has intrinsic value. But there is another. For to understand and comply with standards in our activities is thereby to exercise several essential human capacities, including autonomy, being in control of our actions and guiding our behaviour by rules. So if the argument from essential capacities (see above) is valid, then self-respect has intrinsic value for this reason too. (Besides, what is true of self-respect in the ordinary sense must also hold good for Rawls' more demanding sense, introduced above.) It follows that the worthwhileness of a life will be enhanced by the presence of self-respect.

4. Meaningful work

Meaningful work, as understood here, consists in free and creative productive activity. Here creativeness need not involve originality or innovation, as opposed to the activity being autonomous (in that the worker endorses its point and its standards), depending on skill and judgement, and taking its shape from the worker's conception of the operation. Production includes the generation of theories and of works of art as well as of services and of material goods. Where work is meaningful, the worker cares to some degree about its standards. Besides, the worker will not be likely to endorse the point of allotted tasks or the standards required for good workmanship unless he or she is enabled to have some say in deciding how their work is to be executed. Thus meaningful work involves autonomy in several ways.[10]

This means that quite a lot of work is not meaningful at all, although it could often be made meaningful without too much effort or too drastic a change of working methods. It also means that there is much meaningful work outside paid employment, in forms varying from subsistence farming, through gardening, unpaid care of the young or the elderly, to the studies of a student. Yet paid employment probably remains the best prospect of meaningful work for most people in contemporary society.

Here we should reflect on whether the capacity for meaningful work is one of the capacities or potentials essential to being human. Is it a capacity in the absence of which from most members of a species it would not be recognizable as the human species? There might, certainly, be sub-sets of humanity lacking this capacity, and if they were fortunate enough to be located on a very fruitful island with a benign climate they might well survive for a time. But it is implausible that humanity in general could survive in the absence of this capacity from most human beings, and in the absence of this capacity in any generation either; indeed a species most of whose members lacked this capacity would not be recognizably human.[11] If so, then this will be an essential human capacity, and thus (granted that the development of a creature's essential capacities has intrinsic value) its development will be an intrinsically valuable constituent of human well-being or flourishing, the presence of which enhances the worthwhileness of a life.

So there are two arguments for including meaningful work in accounts of a worthwhile life, the argument from self-respect and the argument just presented from essential human capacities. The latter argument also illustrates how parallel arguments concerning other essential human capacities reach their conclusions. The outcome is a richer-than-usual understanding of states and activities of intrinsic value and a correspondingly rich account of a worthwhile human life.

The strong but contingent connection between meaningful work and paid employment also has practical implications. It means that there is a strong case for policies of full employment not only in the developed world, but also in the policies of development agencies and Third World governments. For unemployment and under-employment are widely prevalent in the Third World (where the majority of humanity lead their lives), and conclusions about the importance of meaningful work matter not only in the abstract, but also in the context of policies to promote human well-being where the need is greatest.

Study questions

1. Is euthanasia ever morally acceptable?
2. Does meaningful work have intrinsic value?

Notes

1 Aristotle, *Nicomachean Ethics*, Roger Crisp (trans. and ed.), Cambridge, UK and New York: Cambridge University Press, 2000.

2 See James Rachels, *The End of Life: Euthanasia and Morality*, Oxford: Oxford University Press, 1986; Jonathan Glover, *Causing Death and Saving Lives*, Harmondsworth, UK: Penguin, 1977.

3 Glover, ibid., p. 51.

4 Glover, ibid., pp. 46–50.

5 See further Robin Attfield, *Value, Obligation and Meta-Ethics*, Amsterdam and Atlanta, GA: Éditions Rodopi, 1995, chapters 4 and 5.

6 See Glover, ibid., pp. 54–7; also Thomas Nagel, 'Death', *Noûs*, 4, 1970, pp. 73–80, at p. 74.

7 For a fuller expression of the themes of this paragraph, see Attfield, *Value, Obligation and Meta-Ethics*, p. 78.

8 John Rawls, *A Theory of Justice*, Cambridge, MA: Harvard University Press, 1971, p. 440.

9 See further Robin Attfield, 'Work and the Human Essence', *Journal of Applied Philosophy*, 1, 1984, pp. 141–50.

10 Robin Attfield, 'Meaningful Work and Full Employment', *Reason in Practice*, 1.1, 2001, pp. 41–8.

11 For a fuller exposition of this argument, see Attfield, *Value, Obligation and Meta-Ethics*, pp. 57–9.

References

Aristotle, *Nicomachean Ethics*, Roger Crisp (trans. and ed.), Cambridge, UK and New York: Cambridge University Press, 2000.

Attfield, Robin, 'Work and the Human Essence', *Journal of Applied Philosophy*, 1, 1984, pp. 141–50.

—, *Value, Obligation and Meta-Ethics*, Amsterdam and Atlanta, GA: Éditions Rodopi, 1995.

—, 'Meaningful Work and Full Employment', *Reason in Practice* (now *Philosophy of Management*), 1.1, 2001, pp. 41–8.

Glover, Jonathan, *Causing Death and Saving Lives*, Harmondsworth, UK: Penguin, 1977.
Nagel, Thomas, 'Death', *Noûs*, 4, 1970, pp. 73–80.
Rachels, James, *The End of Life: Euthanasia and Morality*, Oxford: Oxford University Press, 1986.
Rawls, John, *A Theory of Justice*, Cambridge, MA: Harvard University Press, 1971.

Section 4: The good life, needs, virtue and morality

1. Human needs

This section addresses several issues raised by the previous three, and by the previous chapter. What are human needs, and how are they related to well-being and morality? Are there reasons for being moral, and how is morality related to a worthwhile life? How does virtue contribute to such a life, and is virtue a need or practical necessity? We begin with human needs.

Needs are whatever is necessary for well-being, and are not to be identified with wants. As Elizabeth Anscombe wrote: 'To say that [an organism] needs an environment is not to say, e.g. that you want it to have that environment, but that it won't flourish unless it has it'.[1] So needs are to be distinguished from desires or motivations. Human needs are whatever is necessary for a human being to live and to live well (or flourish) as a human being. (Thus I am not using 'human needs' in the same sense as Abraham Maslow does, when putting forward his well-known hierarchy of human needs, considered as motivations[2]; even so, his findings still coincide with some of those reached below.)

There are two kinds of needs. Some needs have instrumental value, and are needed either for survival (such as food, clothing and shelter) or for flourishing (such as the friendship or support of others). Others have intrinsic value, and are constituents of human flourishing (such as self-respect, discussed in the previous section or autonomy, the development of which is needed for a life moulded to some degree by the person living that life).

Some needs are of both kinds. Health is one example. People may need health as a means to carrying out the plans that contribute to their lives being worthwhile; at the same time, health consists in the unimpeded functioning of our faculties, and is thus itself a constituent of our well-being. The same can be said of skills of practical reasoning, needed both as a means to tackle and overcome problems that might impede our flourishing, and for themselves, as instances of the successful functioning constitutive of a worthwhile life.

The ways in which friendship is needed are more subtle. As we have seen, your friendship may give me the support and sympathy that I need, and in this regard it has instrumental value. But at the same time you may be developing your capacity to understand and relate to other people, something constitutive of your well-being and thus valuable intrinsically. So it may be a need (under one description or another) for you as well as for me, as a constituent of your own flourishing. (Later it will be suggested that some of the virtues work in parallel ways.)

Some needs are more basic than others (as well as being needed more than wants that are not needs at all), and as such will have greater value. One obvious suggestion is that people's survival-needs are basic needs; and this can hardly be denied, since if they are not satisfied, a life is lost, and what would be needed for that person's well-being has no remaining place. Yet there is a strong case for regarding self-respect, health and autonomy as basic needs as well. For in their absence, well-being is either absent, impeded or interrupted, and, where survival is not in doubt, they are needed far more than consumption, luxuries or public applause. Much the same applies also to the development of other essential capacities, such as those for meaningful work, or for understanding other people. (In a later chapter it will be suggested that social justice involves provision being made for basic needs, wherever the distribution of such provision is feasible.)

My suggestion is that the needs just mentioned are needed in every culture and every age of history. This suggestion may meet with the sceptical response that needs are culturally or historically relative. The least implausible version of this response is the claim that, while food, clothing and shelter are universal needs, some less basic needs are needed much more in one kind of society than in others (such as obedience in a monastery).

This version already concedes that there are universal needs, but adds that in different societies different skills or qualities are needed. Plausibly, though, these skills and qualities are needed for well-being or flourishing in the conditions of a given institution or society; the underlying need is universal, but there are local variations in what is required to satisfy it.

It should be added that it does not follow from a quality being regarded as a need that it really is a need. Thus too deep-seated an adoption of obedience (on the part of a monk or nun, say), even if regarded as a need, could incapacitate someone from thinking for themselves, and thus undermine the development of their autonomy, something that they might really need either in an emergency (it could be vital for someone to break the rules and call the fire brigade in the event of a fire), or if promoted to some decision-making role within their institution. (I have discussed objections to the universality of human needs in greater detail elsewhere.[3])

Thus not even the least implausible variety of objection to belief in universal human needs succeeds in undermining that belief.

2. Morality, reasons and needs

Are there reasons for being moral, and how is morality related to a worthwhile life, and to human needs? These are important issues that need to be tackled as soon as possible after human needs and worthwhile life have been considered. Although we have not yet finished investigating moral rightness and the moral virtues, the sections of Chapter 1 on Kant and on Mill (partly on rightness) and on Aristotle (partly on virtue) will allow us to consider these issues.

Hobbes, of course, had a view on all this; whatever we ought to do advances our own interests and thus satisfies our needs. But there were, as we saw in Chapter 1, good grounds to reject that view; for morality seemed not always to tally with the pursuit of personal advantage, and is oriented to satisfying the various needs of other people and creatures (both contingent needs and those constitutive of well-being), and not only those of the moral agent.

What if we build up an independent account of being moral, including all the various virtues mentioned both by Aristotle and by Mill, and then ask whether being moral in these terms is beneficial and pays off? Aristotle held (until he cast doubt on all this in *Ethics*, Book X) that having the virtues of character is a constituent of human flourishing, but Mill recognized that being virtuous does not always pay, as he recognized that virtue can take the form of self-sacrifice. Here he was surely right, for it could sometimes be virtuous to exhaust oneself or even to give up one's life for the sake of others. This might or might not occasionally be a duty, as Kant would maintain, although duties do not usually require this, if the rules that make duties obligatory are themselves based on fostering the general happiness (as Mill held) or maybe the general good. For duties that undermine the agents concerned are unlikely to promote happiness or well-being overall. All the same, being moral is not always advantageous.

This being so, people sometimes ask why we should be moral, or what reasons for being moral there might be, and why virtue (of the moral kind) is needed by anyone.[4] But these are rather peculiar questions, for several reasons. If they mean, 'Why, morally speaking, should we be moral?', then the answer is obviously that morality leaves no other option. But if the question means 'What reason of self-interest is there for being moral?', then the person asking it appears to assume that the only reasons for doing anything are self-interested ones; and this is peculiar, granted that they have enough interpersonal awareness to ask this question of someone else, and must therefore have been brought up to have some amount of consideration for others (such as the people from whom they learned language), and thus not to assume that the only reasons for doing anything are self-interested ones. Quite often, there really will be reasons of self-interest, since friendship, self-respect or reputation may require a moral course of action (or there may be rewards for doing so and disincentives for doing otherwise), but sometimes, truth to tell, there will not be.

But it by no means follows that when there are no self-interested reasons for behaving morally there is no point in doing so. For many things are worth doing that do not redound to the agent's advantage. Besides, there are reasons wherever something of value is at stake, such as someone else's enjoyment or well-being. If, as has been argued in earlier sections, the flourishing of all beings with moral standing has value, and if there is some close link between moral behaviour and the enhancement of value and/or the prevention or reduction of its opposite (disvalue), then behaving morally will always have a point and have reasons in its favour, as long as it is also recognized that there are necessarily reasons to promote what is valuable (and to prevent disvalues such as pain, disease and suffering). Morality is not some arbitrary imposition, stifling agents' enjoyment or personal development; if an action really is moral there will be reasons for it (and the reasons will often consist in furthering one or another agent's personal development or pleasure).

Where the question takes the form of someone asking whether anyone needs morality, there is a similar story. Some virtues (e.g. some amount of courage) are needed by everyone (given life's challenges and uncertainties), and Martha Nussbaum has suggested that Aristotle's virtues can be regarded as ways of tackling pervasive problems affecting humanity in general.[5] But neither being moral nor being virtuous always satisfies the agent's needs; for example, it is not impossible to combine being moral and being lonely. On the other hand, in the absence of moral behaviour and treatment, many needs would never be satisfied at all, and everyone benefits from such treatment at one time or another. So there is a strong link between morality and needs being satisfied. There is just no direct or immediate invariable link between moral behaviour and the satisfaction of the needs of the particular agent concerned.[6] (We noticed something similar about friendship, in an earlier section, when considering whether friendship is advantageous.)

Yet there is a link between one aspect of being moral and one kind of satisfaction. Moral behaviour usually involves people acting for most of the time as they believe that they ought, and recognizing this. But acting in accordance with one's own standards is necessarily satisfying as such, however unappealing it may be in other respects; indeed acting morally usually satisfies the requirements of self-respect. So most moral behaviour brings at least this kind of satisfaction in its train. Besides, since self-respect is a constituent of a worthwhile life, there is at least some link between behaving morally and leading a life of this kind.

3. Morality and leading a worthwhile life

The question of how morality is related to a worthwhile life remains to be considered. Here we need to remember that 'a worthwhile life' was not defined as a morally good one, or as a life of virtue, but as a flourishing life, or a life worth living, and that such a life, enviable as it may be, need not invariably be morally admirable or virtuous.[7] For example, academic or sporting achievements may sometimes take time and energy away from obligations such as cultivating ties to friends or family, or like campaigning for people who are disadvantaged. As Glover says: 'Music may enrich someone's life, or the death of a friend impoverish it, without him growing more or less virtuous'.[8] Besides, being moral can bring marked disadvantages or drawbacks; a focus on being fair, for example, may involve losses to one's friends or family, or to oneself.

Yet moral behaviour can contribute to a worthwhile life (even in this sense), and so can a moral character. One contribution of moral behaviour has just been mentioned, the way in which awareness of compliance with one's own moral beliefs and standards necessarily conveys self-respect, one of the constituents of a good life.[9] Moral behaviour is also frequently rewarding, as when it wins others' appreciation or gratitude, or when it builds up ties of friendship or a sense of solidarity on the part of participants sharing in a common campaign or struggle. On such occasions we speak of being enriched by such shared experiences. However, neither appreciation nor gratitude nor continuing loyalty nor solidarity can be guaranteed; life may be enriched by the pleasure and (in some cases) the understanding that they bring, but the honourable or conscientious behaviour that sometimes stimulates them has independent moral worth, and is not to be discarded when they fail or falter.

With moral character, there can be deeper links with a worthwhile life. Here much depends on what kind of person we want to be (and also to be known as). Few of us want to be the kind of person who is regarded as unreliable, self-centred or dishonest. But if we are to be reliable, generous and honest, we need to take decisions of those kinds over considerable periods of time, until they become second nature (at least if Aristotle was right about the dispositional nature of the virtues, as he surely was: see Chapter 1, Section 1). By then, behaving in these ways will usually have become a source of satisfaction, and is likely to contribute to an integrated life of settled priorities, thus playing a part in one's life being or becoming worthwhile.[10]

Yet even so, we should be aware of a paradox. Just as people who strive to be happy often fail until they forget about this aim and seek the good of others instead (the paradox of happiness), so too the attempt to become virtuous for the sake of leading an integrated and worthwhile life is likely to miscarry. (We could call this the paradox of virtue.) Having a moral character is unlikely to be achieved on the basis of reasons of self-interest, for there is a tension between virtues such as kindness and generosity and motivations such as egoism. If the real motive is personal advantage, the relevant virtues will either not be acquired at all, or will be pale substitutes for ones that are sincere and heart-felt. Thus even when having a moral character benefits the person concerned, seeking a moral character for the *sake* of such benefits is doomed to failure. Maybe, then, it is good for us all that there is a gap between having a moral character and the achievement of personal advantage.

These matters could also be related to needs. To flourish, we need to develop most of our essential capacities (or so I have argued above). Being moral contributes a great deal to attaining this, through developing powers such as understanding and deliberation, and also capacities for sympathy and participation in shared projects. It can also foster the development of other capacities (like those for perception, memory and reasoning, and for physical fitness), as we attempt to contribute to communal undertakings. Yet these other capacities could be developed for the sake of other reasons and projects; and developing exploitative skills can also serve to hone our powers of practical reasoning and even of making friends (or appearing to). So it is possible to flourish as a person while developing a moral character, or again despite not doing so. A moral character can contribute to our flourishing and thus satisfy our needs, but flourishing can take entirely different forms, and satisfy some of the same needs. While some satisfactions depend on having a good character (see above), far from all do. Thus, once again, the links between a flourishing or worthwhile or non-morally good life and a morally good or virtuous life are real but complex, and often tenuous.

Study questions

1. Is friendship a human need?
2. To what extent does moral virtue benefit its possessor?

Notes

1 G. E. M. Anscombe, 'Modern Moral Philosophy', *Philosophy*, 33, 1958, pp. 1–19, at p. 7.

2 Abraham Maslow, *Motivation and Personality*, 2nd edn, New York: Harper & Row, 1970.

3 Robin Attfield, *Value, Obligation and Meta-Ethics*, Amsterdam and Atlanta, GA: Éditions Rodopi, 1995, pp. 70–5.

4 See further William K. Frankena, *Ethics*, 2nd edn, Englewood Cliffs, NJ: Prentice-Hall, 1973, pp. 114–16.

5 Martha Nussbaum, 'Non-Relative Virtues: An Aristotelian Approach', in Martha Nussbaum and Amartya Sen (eds), *The Quality of Life*, Oxford: Clarendon Press, 1993, pp. 242–76.

6 See further Philippa Foot, 'Introduction', in Foot (ed.), *Theories of Ethics*, Oxford: Oxford University Press, 1967, pp. 1–15, at p. 7.

7 See further Frankena, op. cit., pp. 92–4.

8 Jonathan Glover, *Causing Death and Saving Lives*, Harmondsworth, UK: Penguin, 1977, p. 52.

9 See further Frederick Siegler, 'Reason, Happiness and Goodness', in James J. Walsh and Henry L. Shapiro (eds), *Aristotle's Ethics: Issues and Interpretations*, Belmont, CA: Wadsworth, 1967, pp. 30–46, at pp. 43–4.

10 For further arguments for the virtues benefiting their possessor, see Rosalind Hursthouse, *On Virtue Ethics*, Oxford: Oxford University Press, 1999, pp. 163–91.

References

Anscombe, G. E. M., 'Modern Moral Philosophy', *Philosophy*, 33, 1958, pp. 1–19.

Aristotle, *Nicomachean Ethics*, Roger Crisp (trans. and ed.), Cambridge, UK and New York: Cambridge University Press, 2000.

Attfield, Robin, *Value, Obligation and Meta-Ethics*, Amsterdam and Atlanta, GA: Éditions Rodopi, 1995.

Foot, Philippa, 'Introduction', in Foot (ed.), *Theories of Ethics*, Oxford: Oxford University Press, 1967, pp. 1–15.

Frankena, William K., *Ethics*, 2nd edn, Englewood Cliffs, NJ: Prentice-Hall, 1973.

Glover, Jonathan, *Causing Death and Saving Lives*, Harmondsworth, UK: Penguin, 1977.

Hursthouse, Rosalind, *On Virtue Ethics*, Oxford: Oxford University Press, 1999.

Maslow, Abraham, *Motivation and Personality*, 2nd edn, New York: Harper & Row, 1970.

Nussbaum, Martha, 'Non-Relative Virtues: An Aristotelian Approach', in Martha Nussbaum and Amartya Sen (eds), *The Quality of Life*, Oxford: Clarendon Press, 1993, pp. 242–76.

Siegler, Frederick, 'Reason, Happiness and Goodness', in James J. Walsh and Henry L. Shapiro (eds), *Aristotle's Ethics: Issues and Interpretations*, Belmont, CA: Wadsworth, 1967, pp. 30–46.

3
Normative Ethics

Chapter Outline

Section 1: Moral standing, value, rights and rightness

1. Moral standing and moral rights

Normative ethics is the branch of ethics concerned with theories of what is either right or obligatory, and therefore with what should be done. To study rightness, we need to build on our understanding of moral standing and of intrinsic value, studied in Chapter 2. We also need to clarify key concepts such as rightness, obligation and supererogatory actions, something attempted in the current section. We begin by reflecting on how a theory of moral standing (as developed in Chapter 2) can help with questions of right conduct, and how moral standing relates to moral rights.

To recapitulate, things with moral standing are entities which matter, morally speaking, and should be taken into account when decisions are being made. The theory presented in Chapter 2 was that moral standing attaches to all living creatures, present and future; whatever has a good of its own, it was argued, should be taken into account where it could be affected by what is done. (Here I was adopting the stance of Kenneth Goodpaster.[1])

One apparent way forward might seem to be to investigate next whether moral rights belong to the same range of entities. For if something has rights, there is such a strong case against harming it that refraining from harming it seems obligatory, and so we might seem well on the way to having a theory of rightness or even of obligation. But can we identify carriers of moral standing with the bearers of moral rights?

The answer is that we cannot. Bearers of rights are identifiable individuals (or sometimes individual corporate entities), equipped with entitlements and capable of being treated better or worse. But many carriers of moral standing are future creatures, unidentifiable in the present, and so far from being equipped with entitlements that their being brought into existence at all depends on creatures of the present (and of the near future). As such, we often cannot say whether an action of the present treats them well or badly, as the future in which they even exist may fail to come about altogether.[2] They have moral standing because we and/or other current creatures can produce the future in which they would make their appearance (or a different future in which they do not), and can affect them in that way. Yet they have no right to exist, or so too would all the other creatures that could exist instead of them, confronting us with contradictory duties to bring them all into being.

To put matters another way, the scope of morality is broader than the sphere of rights, and not all obligations correspond to rights. For example, we can have obligations to enhance the quality of life for people or other creatures in the future, whichever people and whichever other creatures may in fact come into existence then. Such obligations are not owed to future individuals, nor to anyone in particular at all, but they are still actions that it would be wrong not to perform. They are obligations with respect to future beings, without being owed to such beings. Similarly we may have obligations to relieve the poverty of current people, even when the individuals who could benefit have no rights against ourselves, and even when these individuals (and even their number) are unknown to us. As we have seen, Mill called these obligations 'duties of imperfect obligation'.[3]

I am not suggesting that rights are unimportant. For rights can be claimed, usually by their bearer; and the ability to make such claims makes awareness of rights crucial itself. Much more will be said about rights later in connection with moral rules and practices. The present point, though, is that moral standing extends far beyond the sphere of rights. For many entities matter and should be taken into consideration despite their lack of the kind of the entitlements that we call 'rights'; if these entities are ignored, our obligations will be misunderstood. If the conclusions of Chapter 2 are correct, then there is intrinsic value in the flourishing of every one of them. And if there is any link between our obligations and value, then this could still be important for our understanding of obligation, and (if so) of moral rightness as well.

2. Value, needs and obligation

It was argued in Chapter 2 that the flourishing or well-being of entities that have moral standing is intrinsically valuable; and this means that there is reason for agents to promote, protect or cherish such well-being. Could this be a foundation for a theory of obligation? This seems a promising suggestion, for the presence of value betokens the presence of reasons for action (see Chapter 2), and obligation involves the presence of overriding reasons for action, except where obligations clash.[4] And even when obligations clash, there will be strong reasons for compliance with each of the two (or more) clashing obligations (or they would not *be* obligations).[5] (Some people prefer not to speak of obligation at all, and use talk of responsibility instead. If you are one of them, please translate the language of obligation used below into the language of responsibility.)

But it would be misleading to suggest that we have obligations to (say) protect the well-being of every bearer of moral standing. For the interests of the bearers of moral standing often conflict, and in many cases the value of the well-being of one or another of them is easily outweighed by potentially conflicting values. Thus animals, including human beings, have to eat, and the eating of plants often conflicts with protecting the plants' well-being. Value, as was remarked in Chapter 2, can have different strengths or degrees, and thus greater value implies the presence of stronger reasons. Obligations, then, if they map onto value at all, will apply more readily when value is great than when it is slight.

Accordingly, as was argued in Chapter 2, we should avoid the view that all creatures should be given equal consideration, let alone the view that they should all be treated equally. Some have needs that others lack, and in each case their needs have more value and warrant higher priority than their other interests. (Needs were discussed in the final section of that chapter.) There again, some have a greater range of interests than others, and the interests of those with more sophisticated and complex capacities (such as dolphins and gorillas) should also be prioritized (over, say, those of bacteria, plants and earth-worms).[6] Otherwise we shall fail to give equal consideration to *equal* interests, the basic principle commended by Peter Singer, and one which is far superior to principles of the equal treatment either of all creatures or of all interests.[7]

Perhaps, then, human obligations relate to honouring these priorities, and satisfying those interests with greater value, as compared with the consequences of alternative actions or of inaction (let us call this a 'consequentialist' approach). The interests to be satisfied include, of course, human interests, without being confined to them, and they will often best be satisfied through compliance with moral rules or practices; otherwise the role of agents will require too much investigation and calculation, and at the same time the benefits will be lost of agents acting in a predictable and reliable manner, and in solidarity with each other. Consequentialism can be adopted in forms that uphold acting on the basis of rules or practices, where they are relevant (rather as Mill held: see Chapter 1).

However, this is not the only possible approach to obligation, even for those who recognize the intrinsic value of the flourishing of all living creatures. James Sterba, for example, suggests other inter-species principles which recognize intrinsic value, but which also authorize the self-defence of each species, on the basis that such principles are reasonable ones.[8] There is some resemblance here to the way in which Kant attempted to identify moral principles on the basis of maxims that each agent could consistently will all agents to adopt. In my view, principles of self-defence are not beyond criticism, as there is room to reason about how much self-defence is appropriate. But Sterba's approach illustrates how theories of obligation (including ones that recognize intrinsic value) could in theory avoid being grounded in the impacts of action and inaction, being grounded in (say) reasonableness instead.

In coming sections, these different approaches to obligation will be given further consideration, beginning with consequentialism (as introduced above). Rival theories, often grouped together as 'deontological' (normative theories that diverge from consequentialism) will also be considered; one example of a deontological theory is that of Kant (see Chapter 1), and another is Sterba's (see above). But before we can proceed in those directions, some conceptual issues need to be investigated, concerning acts that are either right or desirable without being obligatory, or, there again, acts belonging to obligatory kinds without always being the right thing to do.

3. Rightness and obligation

Not everything that we ought to do is an obligation or a duty. Some things ought to be done for reasons of other sorts, such as prudential, technical or aesthetic reasons, as was mentioned in Chapter 1 in the section on Hobbes. Maybe, for example, we ought to buy pears rather than apples, either because this is one viable way of feeding the family, or because they look better in a fruit bowl; the act of buying pears is hardly a duty of itself. And the reason that we ought to tighten the screws on the swivel-chair is that this is a technical necessity if it is to fulfil its function, and not (say) that either the Categorical Imperative or Millian utilitarianism demands it.

But even actions that ought to be performed for moral reasons are not all obligations or duties. Some behaviour is right because it is morally the best thing to do in the circumstances, like buying a friend a drink, perhaps, without it being obligatory, or something that it would be wrong not to do. Very large numbers of morally right actions, like smiling at acquaintances, have the same status; they are right but do not fall under moral rules, and not to behave in these ways would not be a dereliction of duty. Theories of normative ethics, therefore, should not be restricted to matters of obligation.

Certainly there is a connection between obligatory acts and right ones; for in one sense of obligation, if an act is obligatory, then it is also right. This is the sense of obligation in which actions are morally obligatory all-things-considered. In such cases, the balance of reasons makes the action obligatory. For example, perhaps you ought, all things considered, to interrupt important work to attend the funeral of a friend. When all the reasons have already been taken into account, and on balance favour this course of action, it will also be right, for there will be no considerations left with which its rightness could be questioned.

There is, however, another sense of 'obligation', in which it is obligatory to keep promises, tell the truth and avoid letting people down (obligations that are also widely known as duties). Normally it will also be right to act in these ways, but obligations can clash, and so it will not always be possible to comply with every obligation (in this sense). So these obligations cannot all be obligatory all-things-considered (although such obligations will often have this status as well, on occasions when there are no clashes). Instead they will be obligatory other-things-being-equal, and generally arise when important moral considerations are at stake.[9] When other things *are* equal, there are no clashes of obligations, and no exceptional circumstances either; but it can be important to know and recognize that a course of action is obligatory even when it cannot be adopted. For example, this knowledge may guide the person concerned to explain or apologize to the person to whom this obligation would normally be due. (Philosophers often use the Latin phrase *ceteris paribus* to mean 'other things being equal', maybe because it is shorter; it means just the same.)

It is basically types of actions that are obligatory in the other-things-being-equal sense, rather than token actions (i.e. particular actions at particular times and places). And it is because of particular circumstances that they are not always obligatory all-things-considered. A theory of normative ethics should ideally be able to explain what makes these types of actions (or action-types) obligatory and also what makes one or another override the other(s) when they clash, such that one token action is obligatory and right overall.

Not surprisingly, we use 'right' of types of actions (such as keeping promises) that are obligatory other-things-being-equal, as well as of deeds that are obligatory all-things-considered. In these cases, a right action need not be morally the best action overall (because duties can clash). When we want to use 'right' to say that a deed is morally the best action, we usually insert the word 'the' in front of 'right', as in 'the right thing to do', thus implying that this action alone is right.

But it should be added that sometimes more than one action would be right, and we can achieve what is called for in two or more different ways, which are morally on a par with each other (e.g. when it is right to go for a run, we can do so by adopting any of several different routes). So we should not assume that there is a unique solution to every moral dilemma about what to do, much less that other people are to be criticized for not adopting one particular course among the courses open to them that would have been right. A good normative theory should be capable of recognizing and accounting for there being disjunctions of right actions, that is, pairs or larger clusters of actions any one of which would be right, (say) actions X *or* Y *or* Z.

4. Supererogation

As we have seen in Chapter 1, John Stuart Mill accepts that some actions are morally desirable without being obligatory. These are praiseworthy deeds that cannot be morally required or expected of an agent, and as such are nowadays called 'supererogatory' acts. They are actions that go beyond the call of duty, but, far from being wrong, are morally admirable. Examples include the Good Samaritan in one of the New Testament parables, who tends a complete stranger, whom he finds injured by the roadside, and arranges for his sustenance and shelter for the night (Luke 10:29-37), or someone who, as was advocated by Jesus, when required to walk with an official for one mile, goes with him for two (Matthew 5:41).

At least some such actions will also be right, in the sense of being the best thing to do in the circumstances. Not all will be right in this sense (for some are extravagant or quixotic), but none will be wrong or morally forbidden, and most will be right in the sense of being one of a cluster of actions each of which would in the circumstances be morally acceptable (and not just morally indifferent). But when attention is drawn to supererogatory acts, we are reminded that moral discourse includes among acts that are right deeds that are much more significant and striking than those we most readily think of in this connection.

These further descriptions allow us to include the examples of saints and heroes, as mentioned in J. O. Urmson's celebrated article about acts of supererogation.[10] Saintly deeds are acts of conspicuous virtue in situations where most people would be disinclined so to act, such as volunteering to work in a shelter for homeless people at Christmas. Urmson's example of a heroic deed is that of a soldier who sacrifices his life to save his comrades by throwing himself on a hand-grenade that is about to explode. Another example would be that of a doctor who goes beyond her duty to tend the sick in her own town by travelling to another town where an epidemic of plague has broken out, to tend the sick there at the risk of her own life. These are conspicuous acts of virtue from which most people would be deterred by a combination of self-preservation and fear.

Urmson convincingly argues that moral theories need to provide for acts of saintliness and of heroism, as well as providing for acts that fit the recognized categories of being obligatory, or permissible, or forbidden, and to explain what makes these 'higher flights of morality' morally admirable. His own view is that the most promising theory in this connection is utilitarianism (by which he probably means a theory of a consequentialist kind), but that is a topic not for this but for another section.

Study questions

1. Are our obligations always owed to someone with rights?
2. Can actions be right without being obligatory?

Notes

1 Kenneth Goodpaster, 'On Being Morally Considerable', *Journal of Philosophy*, 75, 1978, pp. 308–25.

2 See further Derek Parfit, *Reasons and Persons*, Oxford: Clarendon Press, 1984, Part IV.

3 John Stuart Mill, 'Utilitarianism', in *Utilitarianism, On Liberty and Representative Government*, London: J.M. Dent & Sons, and New York: E.P. Dutton & Co., 1910.

4 Robin Attfield, *Value, Obligation and Meta-Ethics*, Amsterdam and Atlanta, GA: Éditions Rodopi, 1995, chapters 6 and 7.

5 Attfield, *Value, Obligation and Meta-Ethics*, pp. 242–5.

6 Ibid., chapter 6.

7 Peter Singer, *Practical Ethics*, 2nd edn, Cambridge: Cambridge University Press, 1993, pp. 16–44.

8 James Sterba, 'A Biocentrist Strikes Back', *Environmental Ethics*, 20.4, 1998, pp. 361–76.

9 Attfield, op. cit., pp. 242–5.

10 J. O. Urmson, 'Saints and Heroes', in A. I. Melden (ed.), *Essays in Moral Philosophy*, Seattle and London: University of Washington Press, 1958, pp. 198–216.

References

Attfield, Robin, *Value, Obligation and Meta-Ethics*, Amsterdam and Atlanta, GA: Éditions Rodopi, 1995.

Goodpaster, Kenneth, 'On Being Morally Considerable', *Journal of Philosophy*, 75, 1978, pp. 308–25.

Mill, John Stuart, 'Utilitarianism', in *Utilitarianism, On Liberty and Representative Government*, London: J.M. Dent & Sons, and New York: E.P. Dutton & Co., 1910.

Parfit, Derek, *Reasons and Persons*, Oxford: Clarendon Press, 1984.

Singer, Peter, *Practical Ethics*, 2nd edn, Cambridge: Cambridge University Press, 1993.

Sterba, James, 'A Biocentrist Strikes Back', *Environmental Ethics*, 20.4, 1998, pp. 361–76.

Urmson, J. O., 'Saints and Heroes', in A. I. Melden (ed.), *Essays in Moral Philosophy*, Seattle and London: University of Washington Press, 1958, pp. 198–216.

Section 2: Consequentialism and its critics

1. Intended and foreseeable consequences

We have seen that the impacts of our actions, and the difference that they make (e.g. in terms of value promoted or foregone), can be held to be relevant to their rightness. But does this apply most plausibly to all impacts, to foreseeable ones, or just to the ones that the agent intends? And does it apply too to the impacts of inaction, or of doing nothing? In this section, some answers will be presented, contrasted and discussed in the light of widespread criticisms, with a view to arriving at a defensible theory of rightness and of obligation.

To make rightness depend on all the impacts of an action (or their value) seems unreasonable. For the impacts of our actions spread out across space and time unendingly, and at least the later ones are often entirely unforeseeable. Imagine that an Ethics instructor assigns two students to the same seminar group, that they later marry, and that three hundred years later one of their descendants becomes a mass murderer. Since none of the descendants would have existed but for the action of the instructor, the theory that the rightness of actions turns on the full set of their impacts either makes that action wrong, or would do unless outweighed by other impacts (such as another descendant finding a cure for cancer). But this theory is no less unreasonable than regarding Homer's performances of the *Odyssey* in song as wrong because some people imitate the deviousness of Odysseus towards three thousand years after the event.[1]

However, if the relevance of impacts to an action's rightness is restricted to intended ones, that is just as misguided. For an agent who foresees that his or her action could trigger a world war would be able to plead that in opening hostilities he or she was only seeking to recover a few square yards or metres of territory, and that because this is an understandable and reasonable goal his/her action was right and justifiable accordingly. Similarly the driver of an automobile that swerves and causes a road crash could claim that she was only aiming to avoid a small hole in the highway (with a good prospect of success), and that her action was therefore right. But these are no justifications at all. We hold agents who could have done otherwise responsible not only for outcomes they intend but also for at least those they foresaw, and, when they fail to foresee what they could have foreseen, for those that were foreseeable.

Consequentialism can be understood as claiming that all the foreseeable impacts of actions are relevant to their rightness. (Just how they are to be seen as relevant will be discussed below, after some alternative approaches have been considered.) However, one clarification is now in place. If impacts and consequences are taken to begin only after the action is over, and if the action is described not as a basic action (e.g. 'wielding a knife') but more amply (e.g. 'killing her assailant'), then the obvious impact (the death of the person stabbed) could be omitted from consideration; for killing *simply is* causing death, rather than the death being its *consequence*. To ensure that all the foreseeable differences of an action to the world are included, we should stipulate that the impacts or consequences of an action include the foreseeable changes resulting from the act under its most basic description, such as 'wielding a deadly weapon'. In this way, murderers cannot claim that the deaths of their victims are not among the impacts of what they do, and consequentialists are free to take such deaths into account when considering the ethics of killing.

2. The principle of double effect; agents, actions and appraisal

Consider these examples, which seem to give support to a principle called 'the Principle of Double Effect'. While it is recognized to be wrong to poison someone who is trying to kill me, it is less obviously wrong to strike back at a murderous assailant, even if she or he dies in consequence. It is considered wrong for a doctor to contrive her/his patient's death, but not wrong to relieve pain, even when this can only be done by drugs that hasten the patient's demise. A bombing raid to eliminate a munitions factory may be allowable even if civilians die, whereas bombing civilians just to undermine morale may not. Thus it is sometimes held, as the Principle of Double Effect claims, that the intended consequences of actions and omissions are morally relevant, but the foreseen though unintended consequences are not relevant, except where they are extremely severe. This principle would, at least, explain these examples, and may appear to do so better than consequentialism.

But disregarding foreseen but unintended consequences has already been argued (above) to be misguided; and we may not need to resort to Double Effect to explain the examples and these widespread responses to them.[2] Thus some amount of self-defence can be justified on a consequentialist basis, whereas if premeditated killing became a common practice, trust would be undermined, and social life could well become impossible.

There again, hospitals whose staff, far from saving life, were known deliberately to shorten it would entirely forego public confidence. But towards hospitals with a policy of relieving terminal patients' pain the confidence of the public is likely to be retained and reinforced, whether or not the relief of pain is the sole intention of individual doctors and nurses, and even if the process of dying is sometimes accelerated. So the best policy is probably not so much one of observing the Double Effect Principle for itself as one of acting as if it were the invariable practice, and doing so for the sake of all the foreseeable consequences, both for patients and for non-patients.

As for bombing policies in time of war, to bomb civilians to undermine morale could be held wrong not because of the intention but because measures not directly conducive to military success, and thus disproportionate to any goods achieved or evils prevented, have long been condemned. They also tend to escalate the level of ferocity and ruthlessness among all the belligerent parties (as happened in the Second World War), to everyone's loss. Besides, this particular tactic has been widely held to be counterproductive, and to strengthen the resolve of the targeted population. So once again, the Double Effect Principle is not needed to explain our responses, because consequentialism can explain them just as well.

Yet this is not the whole story; for intentions may be recognized to have a key place in ethics. Sometimes, for example, a person's intention is relevant to the appraisal of their action, because we cannot even identify their action without knowing what they intend.[3] Thus when people stand in a queue (or in line), someone who steps into the middle of the queue might seem to be queue-jumping until they explain that they were resuming their place after briefly stepping aside; when they tell us what they see themselves as doing, by giving us the intention with which they are acting, we are enabled to tell which action they are performing, and thus to escape the temptation of misjudging it. But intentions do not always determine even the identity of actions; for many people fail to notice what they are doing, or deceive themselves about what their deeds amount to (just having a flutter, some say, when gambling away the family income). Besides, even when the identity of an action is determined by its intention, its appraisal remains an open question, except that we now know which action is to be appraised. (After all, even *un*intentional actions are often wrong.) Much less do the intended consequences of actions determine whether those actions are right or wrong, until the foreseeable consequences have been considered as well.

Here we should return to Mill's distinction (see Chapter 1) between appraisals of actions on the one hand and appraisals of motives and of character on the other. Both kinds of appraisals are important, in different contexts. When we want to know what should be done, we can often set aside the agent's motives and character, and often the consequences that they intend as well; and it is here that the consequentialist account of rightness is relevant. When, however, we are interested in people's character, or in what motivates their behaviour (as, for example, the writers of references and of obituaries often are), a different kind of appraisal is in question, which is more about goodness than rightness. For this different kind of appraisal, consequentialists can supply a relevantly different theory. For example, those traits of character and those attitudes and motives, they can say, are good ones of which the widespread manifestation among people in general would make a positive difference to the balance of value over disvalue.

Intentions are often relevant to this second kind of appraisal, because they sometimes reveal an agent's character or their motivation. They can also be relevant to issues of responsibility; for when a person does something intentionally (whether good or bad), they cannot plead that it was done inadvertently or (in most cases) reluctantly. But such issues can be deferred to the chapter on responsibility. By now enough has been said to explain our recognition that intentions have a key place in ethics, without making intended consequences the criterion of rightness.

3. The principle of acts and omissions and negative responsibility

The Principle of Acts and Omissions says that the foreseen consequences of omissions are not always morally relevant, even when identical foreseen consequences of actions are recognized to be morally relevant. It is not as bad to allow people to die of starvation in Africa as to send them poisoned food; to let elderly people die of cold as to shoot them.[4] On some views, these judgements are better explained by this principle than by the kind of consequentialism that treats the like consequences of actions and omissions as equally relevant.

But we cannot disregard the impacts of inaction, as is widely recognized in laws about negligence. Besides, imagine that on one day pressing a switch at a certain time would cause someone to be tortured, and that on another day *not* pressing a switch in the same room at that time would have the same effect, and also that there are no differentiating side-effects. Here, the relevant action and the relevant omission have to be regarded as morally alike. And if here, then why not always, when side-effects are set aside. So maybe the judgements mentioned in the previous paragraph are due to differences in side-effects.

This is a cogent explanation, at least in the case of poisoning. Poisoning is premeditated homicide, and if this were to become a widespread practice, the harms done would include a breakdown of social trust and cohesion in all the affected societies, as well as the resulting deaths. Much the same applies also in the case of shooting senior citizens; besides, shooting is potentially irreversible and cannot be countermanded by the intervention of others, whereas allowing people to die is less certain to prove fatal, in the event of intervention by others. So we can explain the judgements about these cases without resort to the Principle of Acts and Omissions. Besides, that principle appears to take too relaxed a view of the impacts of inaction; where death results from inaction, and could have been prevented through action, the agents concerned surely carry a measure of responsibility for them.

To say this is to accept *negative responsibility*, a doctrine famously criticized by Bernard Williams. Williams held that agents are morally free to pursue their own projects, even if their doing so allows great evils to take place that they could have prevented; for the evil impacts of their omissions, he held, they are not responsible.[5] But this view should be resisted, for the same reasons as those given in the two previous paragraphs. I am not suggesting that all omissions are on a par with all actions. Among the many deeds that I am omitting to do at present, many are by now beyond my powers. (Being in Britain, I would have had to travel elsewhere previously to be in a position, for example, to watch pandas in China, or to bathe in the sea at Havana.) Thus what we can compare are actions and omissions that are within our control, and which have not only similar main outcomes but similar side-effects as well. But in such cases, the foreseen (and indeed, the foreseeable) consequences of actions and omissions really should, I suggest, be appraised alike.[6]

4. Act-consequentialism and practice-consequentialism

For consequentialist theories of obligation and of rightness, the justification of acts and of moral rules and practices lies in the value (more precisely, in the balance of value over disvalue) or, in other words, in the non-moral good which they would bring about in one way or another,[7] where non-moral good consists in states such as pleasure, happiness and flourishing. This, for example, is what makes right actions right. For deontological theories, on the other hand, the justification lies either not in the consequences at all, or at most only partly.

However, each type of theory exists in at least two forms, distinguished by whether single acts and/or their consequences are in question, or rules or practices and/or their consequences too. But this at once raises a problem for theories with no place for moral rules, and which make rightness turn either on the consequences of single acts (act-consequentialism) or on our judgements about such acts, with or without regard to their consequences (act-deontology). This is because most people hold that if an action involves breaking a promise, there is some sort of obligation not to do it, however good the consequences, just because it falls under a moral rule. Even if this were an exceptional case in which the rule should be broken, the fact that it would amount to breaking a promise is agreed to count against it,[8] contrary to what act-consequentialism and act-deontology both imply. But this counts strongly against both these theories.

This leaves us with theories that take moral rules seriously. Some of these claim that there is nothing to justify the rules, but that we simply recognize their correctness by intuition. But stances of this kind are unable to explain why the currently recognized rules are the correct ones (and no others), how the list might ever be revised and what makes these rules *moral* ones. Stances that have answers to these questions seem more promising, since finding such answers seems far from impossible. It is clearly not impossible to reason about rules.[9]

Among the more promising stances are consequentialist ones, although, as we shall see in the coming section, there are others, based on hypothetical contracts or on what agents would agree to (in certain imaginary circumstances). Thus rule-consequentialists hold that those actions are right which fall under rules overall compliance with which produces or would produce the best overall consequences, or better overall consequences than alternative rules or an absence of rules; and that is what makes these rules moral ones. However, when there is no rule of an overall beneficial (or optimific) kind in place or in prospect, then those actions will be right that have the best overall consequences themselves.

So as to stress that the main difference here from act-consequentialism arises from people acting together in mutual solidarity, which changes the entire social context of action, it is best to call this stance 'practice-consequentialism', for it is not abstract rules that are beneficial, but practices in which people stand together cooperatively and in this way make a difference to society, through, for example, keeping their promises or through mutual consideration. Besides, since some advocates of rule-consequentialism limit its scope to existing rules, and omit optimific ones that are not currently in place, but that would bring overall benefits if introduced, the stance introduced here (including possible optimific practices as it does) is better and more accurately depicted as 'practice-consequentialism'.[10]

This means that acts can be justified through contributing to optimific practices, and that practices can be justified, compared and criticized by reference to the desirability or undesirability of their overall impacts. What is more, acts will be obligatory where the foreseeable consequences of relevant practices make a serious difference, or, where no practice is relevant, when this holds good of the foreseeable consequences of the act itself. In this way, one of the requirements of a satisfactory theory presented in the previous section is satisfied, for it supplies a cogent criterion of acts being obligatory.

Further, consequentialism can readily explain why sometimes more than one act (from a cluster of acts) is right, and it is right to perform any one of the cluster. For the foreseeable outcomes will sometimes leave it indifferent which of several actions should be performed, and so whichever of them is selected will be right. Thus another of the requirements presented in the previous section (the capacity to explain there sometimes being more than one right action) is also satisfied (even if other normative theories could satisfy this requirement too).

Practice-consequentialism is broadly in line with the stance of Mill, a rule-utilitarian who was prepared to envisage alternative optimific practices, but who tended to omit non-human interests from consideration, despite recognizing them in theory, and who characterized the good of individual humans as 'happiness', arguably omitting the development of essential human capacities. As Mill held, a strength of stances of this kind is that they need not be silent about situations where two rules clash, because an appeal can be made to the general good (see the section on Mill).

But Mill is less than clear about what form such an appeal would take. Here is what a practice-consequentialist can say. Imagine a clash between telling the truth and keeping a promise (and that there is enough time to deliberate). We should first consider the difference made by each of these practices, and then, bearing this in mind, consider how much difference on this occasion compliance with one and infringement of the other would make to their overall value or importance (including people's trust in their intactness), and decide accordingly. This would include taking into account impacts on the persons to whom the promise had been made, and on those relying on the truth being told, who would be the people most closely and most certainly affected. This would obviously not be easy, but the rare situations where rules conflict cannot be expected to be easy in any case. So the theory predicts just what we would expect.

Here consequentialism appears to fare at least as well as rival theories, which (in situations such as this one) either appeal (dubiously) to intuitions, or ask still less tractable questions such as which priorities between rules we would agree to if society were being founded all over again. Many further problems for consequentialism remain to be addressed. But so far it emerges as a seriously defensible normative theory.

Study questions

1. Are unforeseeable consequences a problem for consequentialists?
2. Ought we to maximize what is of value?

Notes

1 For the problem, see James Lenman, 'Consequentialism and Cluelessness', *Philosophy and Public Affairs*, 29.4, 2000, pp. 342–70; for a reply, see Elinor Mason, 'Consequentialism and the Principle of Indifference', *Utilitas*, 16.3, 2004, pp. 316–21.

2 Robin Attfield, *Value, Obligation and Meta-Ethics*, Amsterdam and Atlanta, GA: Éditions Rodopi, 1995, pp. 128–31.

3 See Michael Ridge, 'Mill's Intentions and Motives', *Utilitas*, 14, 2002, pp. 54–70.

4 Jonathan Glover, *Causing Death and Saving Lives*, Harmondsworth, UK: Penguin, 1977, pp. 92–103.

5 Bernard Williams, 'A Critique of Utilitarianism', in J. J. C. Smart and Bernard Williams, *Utilitarianism: For and Against*, Cambridge, UK: Cambridge University Press, 1973, pp. 75–150, at pp. 95, 116–17.

6 Robin Attfield, *Value, Obligation and Meta-Ethics*, pp. 122–5; see also Attfield, 'Supererogation and Double Standards', *Mind*, 88, 1979, pp. 481–99.

7 Thomas Hurka, *Perfectionism*, New York and Oxford: Oxford University Press, 1993, p. 20.

8 William K. Frankena, *Ethics*, 2nd edn, Englewood Cliffs, NJ: Prentice-Hall, 1973, pp. 36–7.

9 See Brad Hooker, 'Ross-style Pluralism versus Rule-Consequentialism', *Mind*, 105, 1996, pp. 531–52.

10 See Attfield, *Value, Obligation and Meta-Ethics*, pp. 108–11, 176–9.

References

Attfield, Robin, 'Supererogation and Double Standards', *Mind*, 88, 1979, pp. 481–99.

—, *Value, Obligation and Meta-Ethics*, Amsterdam and Atlanta, GA: Éditions Rodopi, 1995.

Frankena, William K., *Ethics*, 2nd edn, Englewood Cliffs, NJ: Prentice-Hall, 1973.

Glover, Jonathan, *Causing Death and Saving Lives*, Harmondsworth, UK: Penguin, 1977.

Hooker, Brad, 'Ross-style Pluralism versus Rule-Consequentialism', *Mind*, 105, 1996, pp. 531–52.

Hurka, Thomas, *Perfectionism*, New York and Oxford: Oxford University Press, 1993.

Lenman, James, 'Consequentialism and Cluelessness', *Philosophy and Public Affairs*, 29.4, 2000, pp. 342–70.

Mason, Elinor, 'Consequentialism and the Principle of Indifference', *Utilitas*, 16.3, 2004, pp. 316–21.

Ridge, Michael, 'Mill's Intentions and Motives', *Utilitas*, 14, 2002, pp. 54–70.

Williams, Bernard, 'A Critique of Utilitarianism', in J. J. C. Smart and Bernard Williams, *Utilitarianism: For and Against*, Cambridge, UK: Cambridge University Press, 1973, pp. 75–150.

Section 3: Deontology, contractarianism and consequentialism

1. Rights, rules and practices

Several areas of ethics have sometimes been considered not to be adequately accommodated by consequentialism. For example, Kant (as we saw in Chapter 1) thought our obligation to tell the truth could not rest on anything as contingent as consequences; but he was almost certainly relying on the consequences of practices such as truth-telling to uphold his Categorical Imperative, without realizing it. In the twentieth century, Sir David Ross took the view that (alongside the duty to be beneficent) several moral principles, including truth-telling and promise-keeping, have to be accepted as binding in the absence of any consequentialist justification.[1] But, as we have seen in the last section, this view leaves unanswered such questions as how these principles (and no others) are to be recognized, what makes them moral ones, how we could ever revise the list and what to do when these principles clash.[2] This section considers further areas that appear to cry out for a deontological theory (i.e. a normative theory that rejects consequentialism), and investigates whether such a theory is needed or not. It further considers the view that rightness relates rather to what would be agreed in a society-forming contract (contractarianism).

A promising area for deontological theories is that of rights. For rights such as the right of a person to life or their right not to be tortured seem too unquestionable and too unqualified for them to be contingent on consequences or on the general good. To make them contingent in this way seems to make their validity fluctuate from case to case, or, in other words, seems to undermine them, and act-consequentialism really seems to be open to this charge. Hence several writers argue that recognition of such rights is a principle not grounded in consequences, or in other words a deontological principle.[3]

This approach, however, risks depriving rights of grounds or justification. (It is sometimes suggested that human rights are grounded in the presuppositions we have to make when recognizing someone as an agent; but this would at best restrict rights to children and adults, as opposed to infants; and even some children and adults would be excluded too, contrary to most views of the wide scope of human rights.) So it is worth asking whether consequentialism can, after all, underpin rights and the importance of observing them.

Respect for rights involves respecting rules which prohibit certain forms of treatment; the human beings (or the animals) to whose treatment these rules apply are then the bearers of the relevant rights. As soon as the question is raised of whether there could be grounds resting on the general good for respecting such rules, the answer becomes clear.[4] For without rules of this kind, no society would be secure, and no one could feel free from arbitrary mistreatment. Accordingly, practice-consequentialism is well capable of underpinning and justifying as wide a range of rights as those that are standardly recognized. To elaborate precisely which ones would take us too far afield, although it is worth saying that this approach can also supply grounds for not recognizing supposed rights that might newly be proposed, for example the right to burn books on feast days in public places. In any case it has already become manifest that rights (including most of those mentioned in the United Nations Universal Declaration of Human Rights of 1948) can be given due recognition without adopting a deontological theory.

2. Integrity, overdemandingness and alienation

As we saw in the previous section, Bernard Williams rejects belief in negative responsibility, holding that people are not responsible for the bad impacts of their omissions, however serious. Consequentialism, by contrast, he holds to be too demanding, in expecting agents to interrupt their projects to prevent such evils. He also supposes it to alienate people from cultivating their relationships when the greater good could otherwise be furthered, and to alienate them from their own moral beliefs when pursuing the best consequences clashes with those beliefs.[5] Having already responded to his criticism of negative responsibility, I will consider here his remaining criticisms of consequentialism, which amount (once again) to advocacy of a deontological normative theory.

One form that his claim that consequentialism is overdemanding could take would be the suggestion that it cannot cope with supererogatory actions (morally desirable actions that exceed the call of duty: see the opening section of this chapter), through making such actions obligatory. But consequentialists need not make promoting the good obligatory in all circumstances. They can explain that what makes supererogatory acts morally desirable is their optimific character (their tendency to promote the best available balance of good over bad outcomes), without making this the criterion of obligation (or of what it is wrong not to do). Thus the criterion of obligation might be an action's either complying with an optimific practice or making a serious difference to the balance of outcomes; it would be this serious difference that makes such an action obligatory rather than optional.[6] Accordingly consequentialism need not suggest that agents may never relax from the quest of promoting good consequences, much less that they must be constantly ready, for the sake of making the slightest difference to that quest, to disrupt their family life or the cultivation of their friendships.

Yet consequentialism might still alienate people either from their integrity (and their moral beliefs) or from their relationships, even if it can accommodate supererogatory actions in the way just presented. It might do this simply by advocating different moral beliefs from those that a person happens to hold. But if so, this is no less a problem for any normative theory whatever that could encourage a change of direction; Kantianism could be subject to the same criticism, and so could virtue ethics (see the coming section). Besides, this will not be a problem for those who either accept consequentialism or reject it outright, but rather for those who are self-divided between these different stances. But that is not a distinctive problem for consequentialism either, for the same criticisms could be made of any other proposed normative theory, deontological ones included.[7] The only way to avoid such problems is to give up theories altogether, and thus the valuable guidance that they sometimes offer at the same time.

However, the objection could instead be that consequentialism supposedly makes loyalty to friends and relations or caring for the one's nearest and dearest contingent on all this serving the greater good. Peter Railton has replied to this objection that it may be a problem for what he calls 'subjective consequentialism', which bids us constantly refer to the greater good in making decisions, but not to 'objective consequentialism', which instead advocates compliance with practices, relationships and dispositions that are beneficial (or optimific) overall, but which does not require us constantly to review whether (say) personal loyalty continues to be justified. On occasion, we may add, agents may need a consequentialist decision-procedure (e.g. when considering whether to support new legislation). But Railton is right to hold that consequentialism does not require people continually to calculate whether to adhere to relationships, or care for those dear to them.[8] Thus, contrary to Williams' claims, it need not be a source of personal alienation, let alone undermine their integrity.

Railton's defence of consequentialism also means that there is no need to modify it to avoid it requiring excessive sacrifices. Samuel Scheffler has proposed that, to avoid consequentialism making excessive demands that conflict with the interests of agents and their families and friends, it should be adjusted through recognition of an 'agent-centred prerogative'.[9] This modification was intended to make sacrificial behaviour supererogatory rather than obligatory; at the same time it comprised a significant departure from consequentialism in the direction of a deontological position. But Railton's defence shows how objective consequentialism (in the sense of the previous paragraph) has no need for any such modification; for it is already consistent with fostering one's relationships, caring for one's nearest and dearest and adhering to dispositions needed for an agent's self-preservation (including willingness to draw the line and sometimes reject opportunities to enhance the world), rather than with duties to pursue optimific courses of action until the agent suffers emotional burn-out, and becomes alienated and unfit to continue making a positive difference.

3. The problem of justice

Another reason for adopting a deontological understanding of normative ethics is that consequentialism seems unable to account for distributive justice. It seems indifferent between different ways of distributing goods such as happiness (even when the total of happiness rises), some of which are much more unequal than others. We have seen in Chapter 1 how Mill attempted to reconcile justice with utilitarianism. His underlying claim is that the rules of justice (including distributive justice) make so much difference to the general good that they take priority over other rules, and that, far from being neutral in their regard, utilitarianism requires that they be prioritized. A version of this defence will be presented shortly for practice-consequentialism. But where the good is held to consist simply in happiness (or in the balance of happiness over unhappiness), this defence seems vulnerable to the charge that distributions involving evils other than unhappiness are tolerated, even when these evils are avoidable, contrary to widespread beliefs about justice.

Here is another way of expressing how justice is a problem for consequentialists. Consequentialists explain what is right in terms of what is good (good outcomes, that is, or the balance of good ones over bad ones). But justice (or what is just) seems independent of what is good, and what is right is frequently determined by what is just. If so, then consequentialism seems unable to cope with justice, and therefore with rightness, and a theory that is at least partly deontological is needed. Both William Frankena and John Rawls reject consequentialism on this basis.[10]

However, a version of Mill's response can be presented, which recognizes goods other than happiness and evils other than unhappiness. If the account of value of Chapter 2 is accepted, great value attaches to the satisfaction of needs, and particularly to that of basic needs, and plausibly it is provision for such basic needs that just states of society uphold. If it is also granted that rightness and obligation are related to maximizing value (or rather the balance of value over disvalue), then actions that are just and for that reason right will precisely be ones that promote or preserve such just states of society. Practices of satisfying basic needs will make such a large difference to value as almost invariably to outweigh other considerations, and so a consequentialism geared to such practices turns out to be able to accommodate distributive justice after all, and explain why promoting it should have a high priority. Just states of society will be valuable not in themselves but because of their benefits to the individuals affected; but their high value will still make just and therefore right the actions that promote or preserve them.[11]

But another field of justice, corrective justice, is sometimes held to require a deontological rather than a consequentialist theory, since punishment is only just if it is backward-looking and matches offenders' deserts. This is a genuine problem for act-consequentialists. But practice-consequentialists can support backward-looking practices, such as judicial punishment for infringements of the law, on consequentialist grounds such as their overall benefits to society. The relation of rule-consequentialism to this kind of justice was well explained in John Rawls' paper 'Two Concepts of Rules', where readers will find a fuller and clearer account than there is room for here.[12] As Rawls explains, such consequentialists are committed not to punishing the innocent or inflicting draconian penalties (as some critics claim), but to due process and to penalties proportioned to the deterrence and prevention of offences. At the same time, consequentialism has the advantage of being able to present a social justification for systems of punishment (to the extent that they can be justified at all), an advantage unavailable to deontological theories that regard punishment as retribution carried out for its own sake, rather than for any good that it might do.

4. Contractarian theories of rightness

So far, it seems better to find the justification of rules or practices in the difference that they make, rather than in themselves and in our ability to discern or intuit their obligatory nature (as Ross and others have maintained). However, another approach justifies them as what would be agreed to in a fair bargaining situation. Prominent among such thinkers is John Rawls, when (some years after the paper just mentioned) he wrote *A Theory of Justice*.[13] Since this approach represents ethical principles as what people would be willing to buy into by way of a contract, let us call this stance 'contractarianism'. Many variants of such a stance have been proposed, both previously (including that presented by Thomas Hobbes: see Chapter 1) and subsequently, but contractarianism is illustrated here by the theory of Rawls.

Rawls asks us to imagine some rational and self-interested people who know they will have to live together as a society, somehow understand a good deal about human sociology and psychology, but have no idea what their own prospects are, or even what their own identity will be. From this 'initial position', he infers that they will agree to certain principles for their society, and that this makes these principles just and right. (The principles include ones ensuring that whoever is worst off in society is better off than they would be in any alternative social system. But we need not pursue further the principles that would be selected.) A key assumption here is that whatever would be agreed in such a situation is just and right, or rather that there is nothing else to rightness than this. Ultimately, every contractarian theory makes a parallel assumption, relating justice and/or rightness to its hypothetical contract.

Granted this assumption, and granted a sound derivation of social rules or practices from the situation in which the contract is made, these rules or practices would be defensible, and thus justifiable, on that basis. But there are good reasons to question this assumption. One reason concerns its failure to guarantee that the interests of future generations will be provided for. (This issue is further discussed in the section 'The Emergence of Applied Ethics'.) Another concerns its failure to make any provision for the interests of non-human creatures, argued above (in Chapter 2) to have moral standing, and thus to have to be taken into account in any adequate theory of normative ethics. A third concerns its failure to guarantee that the interests of those humans who are unable to enter into contracts will be heeded. Thus we cannot assume that what would be agreed is either just or right. The model of the contract could still be a valuable device for appraising proposed rules for society, but it cannot be assigned any definitive status for shaping ethical theory.

Rawls' model has also been well criticized by feminist writers for undue abstraction. His contracting parties are deprived of any sense of belonging in a network of relationships, or even of identity, and so the society and the social rules they construct can be seen as so much the product of this abstraction as to be themselves unreliable.[14] This criticism may apply more particularly to Rawls' variety of contractarianism than to others involving less abstraction, but so much abstraction will be needed to generate any contractarian theory that it raises doubts, to say the least, about all such theories. As Seyla Benhabib argues, we need a less 'disembedded and disembodied' model of human life to theorize adequately about ethics.

This suggests the need to return to reflection on the good of individuals and of society (as Benhabib also suggests) when reasoning about what is right. Contractarian theories are too unreliable, valuable as the use of contractarian models can sometimes be. Consequentialist approaches, however, such as the practice-consequentialism presented and defended in the previous and the present section, still seem to supply the best theories of normative ethics. The next section, however, will consider whether theories of normative ethics should instead be abandoned.

Study questions

1. What are moral rights, and can they be reconciled with consequentialism?
2. Does consequentialism belittle integrity?
3. Can consequentialism be reconciled with the obligation to be just?

Notes

1 W. D. Ross, *The Right and the Good*, Oxford: Clarendon Press, 1930.

2 Robin Attfield, *Value, Obligation and Meta-Ethics*, Amsterdam and Atlanta, GA: Éditions Rodopi, 1995, pp. 106–7; Brad Hooker, 'Ross-style Pluralism versus Rule-Consequentialism', *Mind*, 105, 1996, pp. 531–52.

3 A. I. Melden, *Rights and Right Conduct*, Oxford: Blackwell, 1959; Alan Gewirth, *Human Rights: Essays on Justification and Applications*, Chicago: University of Chicago Press, 1982.

4 See, for example, R. M. Hare, *Moral Thinking: Its Levels, Method and Point*, Oxford: Clarendon Press, 1981, pp. 147–68.

5 Bernard Williams, 'A Critique of Utilitarianism', in J. J. C. Smart and Bernard Williams, *Utilitarianism: For and Against*, Cambridge, UK: Cambridge University Press, 1973, pp. 75–150.

6 Robin Attfield, *Value, Obligation and Meta-Ethics*, pp. 115–19.

7 Ibid., pp. 120–1.

8 Peter Railton, 'Alienation, Consequentialism and the Demands of Morality', *Philosophy and Public Affairs*, 13, 1984, pp. 134–71; Robin Attfield, *Value, Obligation and Meta-Ethics*, pp. 176–83.

9 Samuel Scheffler, *The Rejection of Consequentialism*, Oxford: Clarendon Press, 1982.

10 William Frankena, *Ethics*, 2nd edn, Englewood Cliffs, NJ: Prentice-Hall, 1973, pp. 41–5; John Rawls, *A Theory of Justice*, London, Oxford, New York: Oxford University Press, 1972, pp. 446–52.

11 See further Robin Attfield, *Value, Obligation and Meta-Ethics*, pp. 133–41.

12 John Rawls, 'Two Concepts of Rules', in Philippa Foot (ed.), *Theories of Ethics*, Oxford: Oxford University Press, 1967, pp. 144–70; see particularly pp. 144–53. See also Robin Attfield, *Value, Obligation and Meta-Ethics*, pp. 145–6.

13 John Rawls, *A Theory of Justice* (see note 10 above).

14 Seyla Benhabib, *Situating the Self: Gender, Community and Postmodernism in Contemporary Ethics*, New York: Routledge, 1992.

References

Attfield, Robin, *Value, Obligation and Meta-Ethics*, Amsterdam and Atlanta, GA: Éditions Rodopi, 1995.

Benhabib, Seyla, *Situating the Self: Gender, Community and Postmodernism in Contemporary Ethics*, New York: Routledge, 1992.

Frankena, William, *Ethics*, 2nd edn, Englewood Cliffs, NJ: Prentice-Hall, 1973.

Gewirth, Alan, *Human Rights: Essays on Justification and Applications*, Chicago: University of Chicago Press, 1982.

Hare, R. M., *Moral Thinking: Its Levels, Method and Point*, Oxford: Clarendon Press, 1981.

Hooker, Brad, 'Ross-style Pluralism versus Rule-Consequentialism', *Mind*, 105, 1996, pp. 531–52.

Melden, A. I., *Rights and Right Conduct*, Oxford: Blackwell, 1959.

Railton, Peter, 'Alienation, Consequentialism and the Demands of Morality', *Philosophy and Public Affairs*, 13, 1984, pp. 134–71.

Rawls, John, 'Two Concepts of Rules', in Philippa Foot (ed.), *Theories of Ethics*, Oxford: Oxford University Press, 1967, pp. 144–70.

—, *A Theory of Justice*, London, Oxford, New York: Oxford University Press, 1972.

Ross, W. D., *The Right and the Good*, Oxford: Clarendon Press, 1930.

Scheffler, Samuel, *The Rejection of Consequentialism*, Oxford: Clarendon Press, 1982.

Williams, Bernard, 'A Critique of Utilitarianism', in J. J. C. Smart and Bernard Williams, *Utilitarianism: For and Against*, Cambridge, UK: Cambridge University Press, 1973, pp. 75–150.

Section 4: Virtue ethics

1. Introduction

There are other answers to the question what makes right actions right besides consequentialist, contractarian and deontological ones. Many of them appeal, directly or indirectly, to Aristotle. Some suggest that there is no need for a theory of rightness at all; anyone who has practical wisdom (as depicted by Aristotle) can discern what to do in particular circumstances, and needs no further principles. (But this appears to leave practical wisdom itself with no criteria, and few prospects of being taught to new generations.) Others appeal to the centrality of the virtues, understood as dispositions to choose reasonably in a wide range of situations, and sometimes suggest that whatever the virtuous person would do is right of itself. Those of them who do not go as far as this still claim that fostering the virtues is central in moral education (which at least begins to answer the above question about how to educate people in practical wisdom), sometimes adding that in matters of moral education nothing more can usefully be said. Those who appeal to the centrality of the virtues in any of these ways are adherents of 'virtue ethics'.

In this section, stances that reject normative theory are discussed, both those that resist principles altogether and, more particularly, those that appeal to virtue ethics, with its partial rejection of theory and its endorsement of virtuous dispositions as crucial even if little or nothing else of normative theory remains credible and acceptable.

2. The rejection of theory

One influential advocate of discarding traditional theories of normative ethics has been Jean-Paul Sartre. Objecting to any values imposed on the individual by others, Sartre makes values depend on the individual's choice and commitment; such is his 'existentialism'.[1] He thus rejects principles like those deriving from Kant's categorical imperative, and valorizes judgements made by the individual in response to particular circumstances, regarding them as also precedents, as far as that individual was concerned, for the whole of humanity. Failure to recognize one's responsibility to make choices he regarded as 'bad faith'. Sartre's appeal to commitment has a little in common with Richard Hare's appeal to the prescriptions of moral agents as the basis of moral discourse (see Chapter 5); but, unlike Hare, Sartre had no place for the principles which, according to Hare, our particular judgements commit us to. (Sartre's stance on freedom is further discussed in the section 'The Future is Open', the final section of Chapter 6.)

Sartre's emphasis on commitment and authenticity can readily be appreciated, but it is implausible that an entire value-theory can be derived from it alone, let alone an ethic. The value of an individual's autonomy seems to be presupposed, but that of the flourishing of people or of other creatures seems not to be recognized, except in cases where an individual chooses commitment to it. Here an objector can rightly claim that some things are valuable whether individuals commit to them or not; otherwise our value-theory will be severely impoverished, and our actions may well be either whimsical or anarchic or egoistic. In later life, Sartre adopted Marxism, but his doing so appears to require ampler claims about human nature and about values than his existentialism allows of.

An earlier proponent of rejecting traditional ethical theory was Friedrich Nietzsche. Nietzsche regarded received morality as a slave-morality, which needed to be superseded in a 'transvaluation of values',[2] issuing in the emergence of values of nobility and of egoism suited to a Superman (Übermensch), expressing his Will to Power. Interpreters diverge over whether Nietzsche was an ethicist proposing a new ethic, or a critic of ethics in general. While he was in part seeking a return to the values of the heroic age of ancient Greece, what he was proposing can be seen as highly ambiguous (allowing it later to be used in support of Nazi ideology, almost certainly in ways that Nietzsche would have contemptuously rejected).

Since Nietzsche was appealing to a conception of what is good for human life, it is possible to understand him as a moralist, albeit one who rejects most of what is recognized as morality.[3] At the same time, there are few grounds if any for endorsing either his indifference to the badness of suffering, or his rejection of non-competitive qualities such as kindness. While his critiques of both Kantianism and of utilitarianism are sometimes on target, his implicit case against moral principles in general is unpersuasive.

A much more impressive case against there being defensible moral principles has been put forward recently by defenders of moral particularism like Jonathan Dancy. If there is a role for principles, they claim, it is at best as rules of thumb which save the need to reflect anew in every situation. For principles as such have no privileged place in moral reasoning, neither as absolute and unqualified principles, which never prove equal to the full range of situations, nor as 'contributory' principles, supposed to supply reasons (even if not conclusive reasons) wherever they apply. This is because different features prove relevant and supply reasons in different situations, and none are relevant in all.[4]

However, the fact that a course of action would amount to breaking a promise is usually agreed to count against it, even if not always to settle the question of its wrongness; thus the wrongness of promise-breaking is usually held to be a principle of the kind that Dancy labels 'contributory' (see Section 2 of this chapter, on Consequentialism and Its Critics). The debate about principles is further pursued in some detail in the section about Medical Ethics in the chapter on Applied Ethics; there it is granted that our judgements about cases are sometimes more secure than our confidence in principles, but denied that this supplies any reason to abandon principles or moral reasoning involving them. If so, then even if not all moral reasoning involves reasoning from principles, the whole weight of moral discernment and decision-making cannot be imposed on our judgement of individual cases, with little or no help from principles, in the manner credited by particularists.

Accordingly we should not discard those forms of normative theory that involve reasoning with the aid of principles. But it could still be that our focus in normative matters should be on the virtues, rather than other tracts of theory, or even that what the virtuous person would do is the criterion of rightness. So we need to return to the range of positions introduced at the beginning of this section, and thus to virtue ethics.

3. What virtue ethicists affirm

Some of the considerations motivating a rejection of ethical theory have at times motivated virtue ethics, which has sometimes denied either the need for or the possibility of ethical codes or principles.[5] For principles can be held futile in the absence of the virtues, and of the practical wisdom that goes with them, and when virtues and practical wisdom are present, the need for principles can seem open to question. (The concept of practical wisdom originated with Aristotle: see Chapter 1.) However, the need for virtuous dispositions and for practical wisdom does not of itself mean that there is no place for principles, for practical wisdom is sometimes the capacity to interpret principles in complex situations, or to interpret such situations so as to discern the relevance of one or another reason for action or moral principle. Similarly the presence of virtues need not mean that an agent's actions will be as reflective and as self-critical as they would be if the agent had a grasp either of principles or of underlying reasons for action. Hence the importance of the virtues should not be treated as a reason for discarding principles, rules, reasons or generally normative theory.

However, virtue ethicists need not reject rules or principles. As Rosalind Hursthouse remarks, many rules can readily be derived from virtues and vices, rules such as 'Do what is honest/charitable; do not do what is dishonest/uncharitable'.[6] Avoiding recognized vices, such as being arrogant, inconsiderate, presumptuous or self-indulgent, readily supplies a lengthy list of such rules. So virtue ethics has a great deal of guidance to offer, and at the same time may serve to explain how some deeds are duties, when omitting them would involve one or more of the vices. This does not remove all the problems virtue ethics faces, such as what makes apparent virtues and vices genuine ones, whether the virtuous person's actions are always right, what to do when the behests of different virtues clash or what to do when avoiding the vices apparently rules out every course of action (including that of doing nothing). On the answers to questions such as these turns the answer to the question of whether virtue ethics discards too much that other normative theories uphold.

Besides making virtues and vices central in the moral life, virtue ethics usually claims that a truly virtuous person will have practical wisdom, the kind of knowledge or understanding that 'enables its possessor' to 'do the right thing'.[7] While this is not infallible knowledge, as the virtuous person will sometimes be unavoidably ignorant of circumstances, this person will otherwise have the moral understanding, judgement and sensitivity to act rightly. Hursthouse grants that the virtues (in the ordinary senses of virtue-terms) are compatible with faulty judgement, but herself uses 'virtue' in a sense that involves rational choice and practical wisdom as such; this kind of virtue is held to distinguish virtuous adults from 'nice adolescents' who frequently lack such judgement. She adds that even virtue ethicists such as Michael Slote who make no mention of practical wisdom uphold a similar link between virtue and rightness through claiming that having virtuous motives involves having a 'balanced' character, and is a sufficient condition for acting rightly.[8] Sceptics could here contest Hursthouse's claim that anyone is persistently virtuous in her demanding sense, and Slote's corresponding claims about virtuous motivation and its sufficiency.

In addition, virtue ethicists standardly claim that having the moral virtues is, as Aristotle held, an aspect of well-being or *eudaemonia*. As Hursthouse puts it, virtue is necessary for *eudaemonia*; far from being a state independent of virtue, virtue is 'partially constitutive' of a flourishing life. (This helps explain her claims for practical wisdom, for the virtuous person understands *eudaemonia* and thereby what is important in life, and is thus likely to judge correctly about which course of action to pursue.) In the final section of Chapter 2, I have argued, to contrary effect, that flourishing is possible without a virtuous character. Being virtuous, it could be replied, comprises an achievement and is intrinsically valuable, and thus can figure among the goods that contribute to a flourishing life. However, as Brad Hooker, who makes this point, goes on to argue, we would not pity someone for failing to be virtuous if their life goes well in other respects; so, while virtue can contribute to a flourishing life, it seems not to be a necessary condition of such a life.[9]

Virtue ethicists often supply one or another account of what makes virtues virtuous, and thus how virtues can be identified. Some combination is usually included of contributing to the good of the person concerned, and to the good of other people. Such an account can generate problems, if the link between virtue and rightness is to be maintained. For critics can now suggest either that it is not the virtues that make actions right, as it is what makes the virtues virtuous (the justifications of virtue) that has this role, or that the actions of virtuous people can fail to be right when the justifications support alternative courses of action. This criticism also implies that virtue ethics fails to recognize the centrality of these justifications, and in this way discards something important that other theories (or some of them) recognize.

4. Virtues and rightness

According to virtue ethics, virtues are standardly beneficial to their possessor, at least in favourable circumstances, and this relation is one of the factors that confers on traits the status of virtues. If the claim were that virtues are always beneficial to the person concerned, there would be room to doubt that (in this sense) kindness and compassion are virtues at all. But the qualifications ('standardly' and 'in favourable circumstances') overcome this doubt, for in a virtuous society these traits would probably be favourably regarded and thus beneficial. (At the same time, the need for these qualifications reinforces the above reasons to doubt that all the virtues are always necessary for one's own flourishing.)

Besides this criterion of standardly benefiting the agent, Hursthouse supplies some other-regarding criteria for qualities being virtuous. Thus dispositions of character will be virtuous only if they promote the survival of the human species and also the good functioning of their possessor's social group.[10] But when challenged by Hooker about the criteria being restricted to human interests as opposed to those of other species, Hursthouse supplies a revised account in which compassion extends to the suffering of animals and courage to protecting those for whom one is responsible, domestic animals included.[11] It would also be open to her (at least in theory) to interpret the virtues as involving concern for future generations and their quality of life, and even as compatible with recognition of impersonal obligations to whoever will live in future centuries (see the section of Chapter 4 on the Re-emergence of Applied Ethics).

So a good deal turns on whether these extensions modify her account of what makes virtues to be virtues. If the rationale of virtues remains unchanged (as conducive to human survival and the good of human society, rather than that of non-human creatures and future generations as well), then it seems an unduly narrow and unreliable account of which the virtues are and what they involve; and this affects the credibility of the theory that right action is simply what the person with these virtues would do. If, however, the rationale is modified, then we are offered a much more cogent account of what the virtues consist in and involve, and how the virtuous person (newly understood) would behave becomes a better indicator of rightness. However, the reason for this now appears not to consist in the judgement or the practical wisdom of the virtuous person, but in the application of an improved theory of moral standing and of intrinsic value, or, in other words, an improved understanding of the reasons that make actions morally right.

Here it is appropriate to return to a distinction made in Chapter 1, in the section on Aristotle. As was said there, virtue ethics can be followed either in a weaker or in a stronger form. In its weaker (or less demanding) form, it affirms the centrality of the virtues in the moral life and in moral education. This version of virtue ethics does not face the problems mentioned above, and is compatible with both deontological, contractarian and consequentialist theories of obligation and of rightness. For all these theories can readily agree to the importance of agents internalizing the principles or rules that they favour and forming dispositions not only to behave but also to feel, react and reflect accordingly; and such multi-track dispositions are precisely what virtue ethicists advocate. Since, however, this approach to the virtues does not belong distinctively to virtue ethics, it and its relations to one or another account of the virtues is usually called 'virtue theory' instead. Hence one form of virtue theory relates virtues such as compassion and courage to sympathy for and protection of the wider range of holders of moral standing recognized in books such as this one, supplying a biocentric rather than an anthropocentric variety of virtue theory, and recognizing links between intrinsic value and right action in the manner of consequentialism.

By contrast, virtue ethics in its stronger form asserts (as that section goes on to relate) either that right action simply consists in doing what the virtuous person would do, or that there is no criterion of rightness beyond that of doing just this. But there are good reasons to doubt whether this is all that there is to rightness, as if a person who has attained the virtues and the practical wisdom they require is likely to act rightly, when not unavoidably ignorant of circumstances, in all the complex situations of the modern technological world, and as if our understanding of rightness cannot be enhanced by reflection on the moral standing of (for example) non-human creatures and future beings (human and non-human), or on the possibilities for intrinsic value in their lives. Similarly there are good reasons to doubt whether the practical wisdom and judgement and moral imagination associated with mature virtues are likely to come up with right decisions all the time as such, and were not likely to be enhanced by reflection on the foreseeable impacts of action and of practices on affected parties, whether human or non-human.

It seems wiser to hold that rightness can be understood independently of virtue, and that virtuous dispositions will be dispositions to reflect, react, feel and behave accordingly, with due sensitivity for the moral standing of all affected parties and for the value of their flourishing, and to participate in practices that make all this possible (with dispositions to choose and to act rightly included among them). For this approach, the virtues remain central to the moral life, but rightness is a more basic concept than virtue, rather than virtue defining rightness.

In the coming section, more will be said about the relations of the virtues to a range of ethical theories, and thus to duties and to rightness, and at the same time to moral goodness, an area where virtue ethics has further contributions to make.

Study questions

1. Consider the case for and against moral particularism.
2. To what extent does virtue ethics form a coherent and convincing ethical theory?

Notes

1 Jean-Paul Sartre, *Existentialism and Humanism*, trans. Philip Mairet, London: Methuen, 1948.

2 Friedrich Nietzsche, *On the Genealogy of Morality*, ed. Keith Ansell Pearson, trans. Carol Diethe, Cambridge and New York: Cambridge University Press, 2007.

3 G. J. Warnock, *The Object of Morality*, London: Methuen, 1971, pp. 160–1.

4 Jonathan Dancy, *Ethics Without Principles*, Oxford: Clarendon Press, 2004; 'Moral Particularism', *Stanford Encyclopedia of Philosophy*, http://plato.stanford.edu/entries/moral-particularism/ (revised 2009).

5 John McDowell, 'Virtue and Reason', *Monist*, 62, 1979, pp. 331–50.

6 Rosalind Hursthouse, 'Virtue Ethics', *Stanford Encyclopedia of Philosophy*, http://plato.stanford.edu/entries/virtue-ethics (revised 2007), p. 8.

7 Hursthouse, ibid., p. 6.

8 Michael Slote, *Morals from Motives*, Oxford: Oxford University Press, 2001.

9 Brad Hooker, 'The Collapse of Virtue Ethics', *Utilitas*, 14.1, 2002, pp. 22–40, at p. 25.

10 Hursthouse, *On Virtue Ethics*, Oxford: Oxford University Press, 1999, pp. 198–210.

11 Hursthouse, 'Virtue Ethics vs. Rule-Consequentialism: A Reply to Brad Hooker', *Utilitas*, 14.1, 2002, pp. 41–53.

References

Dancy, Jonathan, *Ethics Without Principles*, Oxford: Clarendon Press, 2004.

—, 'Moral Particularism', *Stanford Encyclopedia of Philosophy*, http://plato.stanford.edu/entries/moral-particularism/ (revised 2009).

Hooker, Brad, 'The Collapse of Virtue Ethics', *Utilitas*, 14.1, 2002, pp. 22–40.

Hursthouse, Rosalind, *On Virtue Ethics*, Oxford: Oxford University Press, 1999.

—, 'Virtue Ethics vs. Rule-Consequentialism: A Reply to Brad Hooker', *Utilitas*, 14.1, 2002, pp. 41–53.

—, 'Virtue Ethics', *Stanford Encyclopedia of Philosophy*, http://plato.stanford.edu/entries/virtue-ethics (revised 2007).

McDowell, John, 'Virtue and Reason', *Monist*, 62, 1979, pp. 331–50.

Nietzsche, Friedrich, *On the Genealogy of Morality*, ed. Keith Ansell Pearson, trans. Carol Diethe, Cambridge and New York: Cambridge University Press, 2007.

Sartre, Jean-Paul, *Existentialism and Humanism*, trans. Philip Mairet, London: Methuen, 1948.

Slote, Michael, *Morals from Motives*, Oxford: Oxford University Press, 2001.

Warnock, G. J., *The Object of Morality*, London: Methuen, 1971.

Section 5: Practice-consequentialism and virtue-consequentialism

1. Blending virtue theory with traditional approaches

This section considers whether normative ethics theories other than virtue ethics can find room for the virtues, and what form a consequentialist version of virtue theory would best take. We begin with traditional ethical theories such as Kantianism and contractarianism.

It is sometimes supposed that Kant's ethical theory is so strongly focused on duty and his Categorical Imperative criterion for identifying it as to have nothing to say about virtue or the virtues. In fact, however, he composed a work entitled 'Doctrine of Virtue' (part of the *Metaphysics of Morals* (1797)), in which he supplied an account of virtue in terms of a disposition to do one's duty.[1] Indeed Kantians and other deontologists can readily accommodate the virtues in this kind of way, which suggests that the notion of virtue is derivative from and dependent upon the notion of duty. However, we do not hold that all deviations from virtue are failures to do one's duty, nor that all virtuous deeds are instances of dutifulness. While some virtuous deeds are also duties, many are not, being supererogatory instead (see Section 1 of this chapter); and while many deviations from virtue are derelictions of duty, some of them are not (but just cases of someone holding back from an act of supererogation). The Good Samaritan, while showing compassion, was not discharging his duty, but exceeding it; and the priest and the Levite, who passed by on the other side, were short on compassion, but not on compliance with obligations (Luke 10:29-37). This being so, there are grounds to doubt the close ties of dependence between virtue and duty suggested by Kant.

Nevertheless, Kant's project of extending deontology to cover virtue was not misguided in itself, even if he gives duties too great a prominence in his detailed doctrine. Indeed, as Brad Hooker says, it is not only Kantianism that can, in principle, accommodate the virtues; for any kind of normative ethics that recognizes rules and is concerned that agents internalize them until they become second nature can do so too. For to internalize relevant rules and develop dispositions to behave, think and react accordingly is just what acquiring and possessing the virtues involves.[2] Among the kinds of normative ethics that treat rules in this way, contractarianism and rule-consequentialism are included (and thus practice-consequentialism is to be included too). Maybe there is a little more to the virtues than this, in the form of the dimensions of practical wisdom that allow agents to bring moral imagination to bear on new situations; but if so, these dimensions can readily be added to Hooker's account.

So it is unsurprising that John Rawls holds that once we have the principles of right and of justice (understood, of course, as contractarians understand them), we are in a position to define the virtues. For the virtues are 'families of dispositions and propensities regulated by a higher-order desire, in this case a desire to act from the corresponding moral principles'.[3] True to his view of society, Rawls later spells this out as follows: '. . . it seems clear that the fundamental virtues are among the broadly based properties that it is rational for members of a well-ordered society to want in one another'.[4] Whether or not we have doubts about Rawls' contract theory (see the section on 'The Re-emergence of Applied Ethics' for some reservations on this topic), these statements bear out Hooker's view that normative theories which endorse moral rules can readily be expanded so as to incorporate theories of the virtues as well. Hobbesian contractualists too can endorse most of the virtues, insofar as their egoistic assumptions permit.

This kind of expansion is available to rule-consequentialism as well. David Hume was in this regard a predecessor of rule-consequentialism, and held that the virtues are characteristics that are either useful or agreeable either to their possessor or to others.[5] Thus reflective tendencies to act on beneficial rules will be among the virtues (although we may hesitate to include among the virtues tendencies mainly beneficial to the agent, rather than to others, and also tendencies that do not arise, as Aristotle requires, from past choices). Whatever reservations we may have about the detail of Hume's theory, it well indicates how rule-consequentialists can readily accommodate the virtues.

However, a distinction made by John Stuart Mill serves to warn consequentialists not to assume too readily that virtuous deeds and right actions are identical. As was mentioned in Chapter 1, Mill distinguishes between the rightness of actions, to which their impacts on happiness are directly relevant, and the worth of agents and their characters (and thus of traits of character), where the links with enhancement of happiness are much more indirect.[6] This allows him to hold that actions that are virtuously motivated can fail to be right, and that not all right actions need have virtuous motives either. It follows that right actions will not always be ones that the virtuous person (let alone the well-brought-up person) would perform, although if the virtuous person's virtues are informed by sound principles, then they will often be. Nonetheless, a consequentialist account can still be supplied of what makes virtuous traits virtuous (such as the overall tendency of such traits, or the difference that their presence makes). But such an account needs to be independent in some degree of a consequentialist's account of what makes right actions right.

Thus virtue ethics should not be construed as the only theory capable of understanding virtue and the virtues; several other theories have this ability as well. Also it should not be assumed that whatever deeds are virtuous are right; the virtuous person has no privileged access to moral rectitude, and may need to struggle with moral dilemmas, just as the less-than-virtuous person must.

2. Objective consequentialism and dispositions

As was mentioned in Section 3 (above), Peter Railton presents two contrasting forms of consequentialism, 'subjective consequentialism', which bids us constantly refer to the greater good in making decisions, and 'objective consequentialism', which instead advocates compliance with practices, relationships and dispositions that are beneficial (or optimific) overall, but which does not require us constantly to review whether (say) personal loyalty continues to be justified. The generally optimific character of these practices, relationships and dispositions makes compliance with them right, and means that we have no need continually to reflect on whether (for example) loyalty to our relationships is justified; rather, we are enabled to act from regard or love for the friend or loved-one, and not abstractly for the sake of the greater good. Adherence to such objective consequentialism allows Railton to counter Bernard Williams' objections to the supposed alienating tendencies of consequentialism.[7]

Besides practices like promise-keeping and truth-telling, and relationships like friendship and marriage, Railton assigns a parallel role to optimific dispositions, and there is every reason to include the virtues among them. Virtues such as courage, sensitivity and mercy can readily be seen to be generally optimific, and, as was argued in the same section, this can cogently be claimed about justice as well. These are, of course, dispositions acquired through an accumulation of past choices (as Aristotle maintains), and, as Hursthouse argues, propensities not only to behave in certain ways, but also to think, feel and react in corresponding ways. Thus supporters of Railton can claim that living in accordance with virtues such as these can be upheld by objective consequentialists, and that compliance with virtues such as these is normally right. If so, the resulting position enlarges forms of objective consequentialism such as practice-consequentialism into what might be called 'virtue-consequentialism'.

Such a stance has clear merits, not least because adherence to these virtues liberates the agents concerned from having to resort continually to attempts to scrutinize their behaviour or their plans by reference to the general good. Besides, better outcomes are likely to result from widespread adherence to virtue-based principles such as 'Be compassionate' and 'Avoid irresponsibility' than from the same people calculating how to promote the best outcomes. Yet the problem remains that far from all virtuous behaviour is likely to be right. When virtues clash (just as when rules clash), there is a need to appeal beyond them. Adherence to virtues also has the same problem as adherence to rules; in exceptional circumstances, it will be better to diverge from the path of virtue, just as it can be better to infringe the rule. To suggest that true virtue involves having an inerrant form of inbuilt practical wisdom which will solve these problems of itself is too close to seeking to resolve the difficulty by stipulation or sleight of hand.

However, virtue-consequentialism has its replies. In all but exceptional circumstances, the best outcomes are likely to be generated by adherence to the recognized virtues (as well as by adherence to moral practices and by loyalty to people's relationships). Where circumstances are exceptional, consequentialism (unlike deontology) can appeal to the criterion of the balance of foreseeable good outcomes over foreseeable bad ones. In theory, this leaves the problem of deciding whether or not circumstances are exceptional, because in theory that is a possibility all the time. But in practice, exceptional circumstances are likely to be identifiable with not much greater difficulty than exceptional weather; the signs and forecasts will not always succeed, but will often prove reliable. So far, then, virtue-consequentialism seems a defensible extension of practice-consequentialism, with some distinct advantages over rival theories ranging from deontology to virtue ethics.

3. Consequentialism, green virtues and practical wisdom

A number of consequentialists have upheld versions of virtue-consequentialism, including Julia Driver and Roger Crisp.[8] As with Railton, consequentialism is held in an objective form, as the ultimate justification of rules and virtues alike, but utilitarian calculation is rejected as a decision-theory suited to the generality of cases. Rather we should adopt and live by the virtues. As Crisp expresses matters: 'An agent ought to live virtuously, consulting the BU criterion [which requires agents to maximize utility] only on certain special occasions'. These special occasions would almost certainly include exceptional circumstances.

Dale Jamieson defends a nuanced form of this view. In our actual circumstances in the actual world, with its anthropogenic species-extinctions and climate change, the best outcomes will come about from a focus on character rather than on individual acts, even though in imaginable circumstances the reverse would be the case. Our situation requires agents to minimize their contributions to global environmental change, whatever they believe about the behaviour of others or the prospects of others acting likewise; and this requires, in turn, a focus on non-calculative generators of character, such as appropriate virtues. Subsequently Jamieson attempts to identify some relevant examples of such virtues, in the form of humility, temperance and mindfulness.[9]

One objection considered by Jamieson has been raised by John Doris and others: empirical studies suggest that contextual factors (like being in a hurry) are stronger predictors of human behaviour than facts about individual character.[10] The apparent impotence of character is potentially a problem for virtue ethicists as well as for virtue-consequentialists. But both can reply that virtues are multi-track dispositions, involving a diversity of sensitive responses to different kinds of contexts, and capable of explaining not only behaviour but also inclinations and attitudes;[11] thus the differences made by contexts revealed in these studies fail to show that advocacy of dispositions such as virtues is futile or condemned to being ineffectual, and cannot enhance the world accordingly.

Jamieson, however, believes that any consequentialist theory should emphasize this kind of responsiveness to changing circumstances, to the extent of advocating the promotion of the good through new responses to new situations (what he calls 'non-complacency'); otherwise something less than the good will be promoted. But this in his view raises problems for any indirect form of consequentialism, such as virtue-consequentialism, and might seem to indicate the need in many circumstances for utilitarian calculation all over again.[12] To this it could be replied that in no world at all similar to our own is frequent use of such calculation likely to be the best guarantor of the balance of good over bad being maximized. What Jamieson himself argues about the characteristic failure of calculation in face of problems such as environmental change applies more widely to most real-world situations, and suggests that being virtuous is usually best, and that 'non-complacency' is not, after all, a radical problem for virtue-consequentialism.

Yet the difficulty that we encounter in supplementing Jamieson's list of 'green virtues' beyond humility, temperance and mindfulness illustrates how virtue-consequentialism is best regarded as an extension of practice-consequentialism and not as a complete, self-standing theory. For example, being cautious about projects that might adversely affect the environment is probably a desirable disposition. But if this description is all that we can appeal to, the outcome is likely to be undue caution about projects capable of reducing ecological problems, while at the same time having undesirable side-effects, such as estuarial barrages constructed for the sustainable generation of electricity, which also disrupt some of the wildlife of adjacent wetlands. Generally the outcome could involve a failure to do anything adventurous even when inaction means leaving a bad situation intact. What is needed is not so much a disposition as a principle such as the Precautionary Principle: where there is reason to believe that there is a risk of serious irreversible harm, scientific uncertainty should not be treated as of itself a reason against intervention to avert that risk. While this principle itself stands in need of interpretation, preferring it to a commendable but inevitably vague virtue of caution is likely to have much better outcomes. Accordingly this principle should be embedded in our practices, something that practice-consequentialism (unlike virtue-consequentialism considered in isolation) is well able to support and justify.

A related issue for virtue-consequentialism is whether adherence to generally optimific virtues makes actions right. While right actions will often flow from such virtues, sometimes they will not, as when two generally optimific virtues clash. For just as there can be clashes between optimific practices such as truth-telling and promise-keeping, so there can be conflicts between the corresponding virtues of veracity and fidelity (even though both of them are generally optimific). The resources of consequentialism for addressing such conflicts were discussed in the above section on Consequentialism; and it is important that, unlike both deontology and virtue ethics, consequentialism has such resources. But it should be added that, while it is often right to adhere to one or other of the virtues, such adherence does not make actions (or inaction) right in exceptional circumstances such as when virtues or practices clash; in such cases further reflection will be needed to discover which course of action is optimific (in terms of foreseeable outcomes) and thus right.

Matters would be otherwise if it could be held that true virtues are always associated with the kind of practical wisdom, moral imagination and judgement which allows agents to attain a balanced and thus correct conclusion to their deliberation. But the possessors of actual virtues usually lack such insight, and there is no clear-cut way of distinguishing whether in particular cases such insight is present, weakly present, defective or absent. On the other hand, agents can build up habits of reflection on the circumstances of action and thus on its impacts (long-term impacts included), and this seems to be what Jamieson has in mind in commending 'mindfulness'. Here is Jamieson's example: 'A virtuous green would see herself as taking on the moral weight of production and disposal when she purchases an item of clothing (for example). She makes herself responsible for the cultivation of the cotton, the impacts of the dyeing process, the energy costs of the transport, and so on'.[13] There is some exaggeration here, for the purchaser cannot be responsible for activities such as cotton-growing that have taken place already without her consent. Yet she can take into account the impact on such processes of supporting them by her purchase and thus with her custom.

Jamieson represents mindfulness as a virtue involving the creation of new values, since this kind of awareness is rare in our society. Yet it is also an example of practical wisdom, as commended by Aristotle, involving as it does an intelligent appreciation of what one would be doing through adopting one or another of the practical options available. Until recently, discerning the global impacts of action and inaction was seldom possible, and deliberation was confined to more local and short-term implications. Recently, however, awareness of distant but foreseeable impacts has become possible (many of them indirect), and consequentialism can accordingly support and encourage the kind of virtue that fosters such awareness.[14] To represent acting accordingly as obligatory would be unduly demanding, in view of the far-reaching range and extent of even the foreseeable impacts of action and inaction. But to represent the corresponding disposition as a virtue, vital if our actions are to be as informed and as beneficial as possible, is no more than a third-millennium rediscovery of the philosophical wisdom of the period before those millennia began.

Study questions

1. Need virtuous people be motivated, as Rawls suggests, by a desire to act from the corresponding moral principles?
2. How strong is the case for consequentialists to adhere to 'green' virtues?
3. Has the virtue of practical wisdom become more relevant in the face of ecological and technological problems?

Notes

1 Immanuel Kant, *The Doctrine of Virtue: Part 2 of 'The Metaphysics of Morals'*, trans. Mary J. Gregor, New York: Harper & Row, 1964.

2 Brad Hooker, 'The Collapse of Virtue Ethics', *Utilitas*, 14.1, 2002, pp. 22–40, n. 14 (p. 28).

3 John Rawls, *A Theory of Justice*, Cambridge, MA: Harvard University Press, 1971, p. 192.

4 Rawls, ibid., p. 436.

5 David Hume, *An Inquiry Concerning the Principles of Morals*, Sections V to VIII; available in David Hume, *Enquiries Concerning Human Understanding and Concerning the Principles of Morals*, ed. P. H. Nidditch, 3rd edn, Oxford: Clarendon Press, 1975.

6 John Stuart Mill, 'Utilitarianism', in J. S. Mill, *Utilitarianism, On Liberty and Representative Government*, London: J.M. Dent & Sons, and New York: E.P. Dutton & Co., 1910, p. 17.

7 Peter Railton, 'Alienation, Consequentialism and the Demands of Morality', *Philosophy and Public Affairs*, 13, 1984, pp. 134–71.

8 Julia Driver, *Uneasy Virtue*, Cambridge and New York: Cambridge University Press, 2001; Roger Crisp, 'Utilitarianism and the Life of Virtue', *Philosophical Quarterly*, 42, 1992, pp. 139–60.

9 Dale Jamieson, 'When Utilitarians Should Be Virtue Theorists', *Utilitas*, 19.2, 2007, pp. 160–83.

10 John Doris, *Lack of Character: Personality and Moral Behavior*, New York, 2002.

11 Jonathan Webber, 'Virtue, Character and Situation', *Journal of Moral Philosophy*, 3, 2006, pp. 193–213; see also Nancy E. Snow, *Virtue as Social Intelligence*, New York and London: Routledge, 2010.

12 Jamieson, op. cit., pp. 172–6.

13 Jamieson, op. cit., p. 182.

14 See Robin Attfield, 'Mediated Responsibilities, Global Warming and the Scope of Ethics', *Journal of Social Philosophy*, 40.2, 2009, pp. 225–36; also in Ruth Irwin (ed.), *Climate Change and Philosophy*, London: Continuum, 2010, pp. 183–96.

References

Attfield, Robin, 'Mediated Responsibilities, Global Warming and the Scope of Ethics', *Journal of Social Philosophy*, 40.2, 2009, pp. 225–36; also in Ruth Irwin (ed.), *Climate Change and Philosophy*, London: Continuum, 2010, pp. 183–96.

Crisp, Roger, 'Utilitarianism and the Life of Virtue', *Philosophical Quarterly*, 42, 1992, pp. 139–60.

Doris, John, *Lack of Character: Personality and Moral Behavior*, New York, 2002.

Driver, Julia, *Uneasy Virtue*, Cambridge and New York: Cambridge University Press, 2001.

Hooker, Brad, 'The Collapse of Virtue Ethics', *Utilitas*, 14.1, 2002, pp. 22–40.

Hume, David, *An Inquiry Concerning the Principles of Morals*; available in David Hume, *Enquiries Concerning Human Understanding and Concerning the Principles of Morals*, ed. P. H. Nidditch, 3rd edn, Oxford: Clarendon Press, 1975.

Jamieson, Dale, 'When Utilitarians Should Be Virtue Theorists', *Utilitas*, 19.2, 2007, pp. 160–83.

Kant, Immanuel, *The Doctrine of Virtue: Part 2 of 'The Metaphysics of Morals'*, trans. Mary J. Gregor, New York: Harper & Row, 1964.

Mill, John Stuart, 'Utilitarianism', in J. S. Mill, *Utilitarianism, On Liberty and Representative Government*, London: J.M. Dent & Sons, and New York: E.P. Dutton & Co., 1910.

Railton, Peter, 'Alienation, Consequentialism and the Demands of Morality', *Philosophy and Public Affairs*, 13, 1984, pp. 134–71.

Rawls, John, *A Theory of Justice*, Cambridge, MA: Harvard University Press, 1971.

Snow, Nancy E., *Virtue as Social Intelligence*, New York and London: Routledge, 2010.

Webber, Jonathan, 'Virtue, Character and Situation', *Journal of Moral Philosophy*, 3, 2006, pp. 193–213.

4

Applied Ethics

Chapter Outline

Section 1: The re-emergence of applied ethics

1. The disappearance of applied ethics

In recent decades, many ethicists have studied the practical implications of ethics in a wide range of fields, from the ethics of war to the ethics of sex, and from medical ethics to the ethics of the environment. These are examples of applied ethics, in which philosophical reasoning is applied to practical issues in an attempt to clarify them and sometimes to defend or justify stances such as vegetarianism or pacifism, or policies such as overseas aid or sustainable development. But as recently as the 1960s, these issues played little or no part in the philosophy curriculum of the universities of Anglo-Saxon countries, and philosophy was regarded as excluding them. Studies such as these had been in abeyance since the beginning of the twentieth century.

They had not always been in abeyance. In earlier centuries, there had been no reluctance to apply philosophical theories to practical questions affecting the social order, either among the philosophers of the ancient world or of the early modern period, or those from the intervening period. (Think of Plato, Aristotle, Aquinas and Locke: Plato and Aristotle applied philosophy to politics, Aquinas to war, Locke to education and religious toleration.) Nor was there any awareness of a distinction between first-order discourse, the realm of observable reality and practical life, and second-order discourse, the realm of philosophical analysis. This distinction was very much a twentieth-century invention.

But early in the twentieth century, the kind of practical reasoning characteristic of applied ethics disappeared from the philosophical scene. Part of the explanation may lie in the increased focus among philosophers on ordinary language, the distinctions that it embodies and what its speakers use it to do. Another part undoubtedly lies in the impact of G. E. Moore's influential claim, made in *Principia Ethica* (1903), that to move from facts to claims about what is good involves the 'naturalistic fallacy', in which 'good' (which he considered indefinable) is tacitly defined.[1] Yet even if Moore were right about this, nothing follows about the impossibility of reasoning about values, as emerges from the fact that Moore himself proceeded to publish a reasoned contribution to normative ethics in his book *Ethics* (1912). But the inference was widely drawn that reasoning about the good and the right had no basis, since it lay outside the realm of facts.

Some of those who thought along these lines took the view that ethical language consists not in statements or truth-claims, but in expressions of the speaker's or writer's feelings. But if so, then there is little or no basis for reasoning in ethics. This kind of position is called 'emotivism' (see the section on Non-cognitivism), and was conveyed in extreme form when A. J. Ayer defended (in *Language, Truth and Logic* (1936)) the view that ethical claims do not express propositions, capable of truth and falsity, but merely pseudo-propositions, and are literally meaningless.[2] The central target of Ayer's charges of meaninglessness was metaphysics, but the extremity of his account of ethics has usually been held to indicate a major weakness in his general 'verificationist' theory of meaning. Yet a whole generation accepted either his kind of emotivism or the comparable stance of C. L. Stevenson, and the consequent irrationalist view of ethical language effectively precluded any reasoned study of applied ethics. Even normative ethics went into abeyance too for a while. (The influential view of Ludwig Wittgenstein that attempts to write ethics run up against the boundaries of language, on the ground

Table 4.1

SOME PRACTITIONERS OF META-ETHICS
George Edward Moore, 1873–1958
Charles Leslie Stevenson, 1908–79
Alfred Jules Ayer, 1910–89
Richard Mervyn Hare, 1919–2002

that values supposedly form no part of the world, probably contributed to the same effect.)

Within the field of meta-ethics (the study of the status of ethical discourse), emotivism was eventually superseded (during the 1950s) by the prescriptivism of Richard Hare. Hare's view of ethical language was just as non-cognitivist as that of the emotivists; for him, such language consisted not in statements but in prescriptions, made either to others or to oneself. But because it implicitly turned on universal prescriptions, and these prescriptions were open to rational review, prescriptivism provided room for ethical reasoning, at least with regard to the consistency of those who used such language. Initially, however, this provision seemed not to increase the scope for inter-personal reflection or for public debate; for prescriptivism seemed to be saying that almost any prescriptions could defensibly be adopted as long as the holders adhered to them consistently. Ethical language was always 'evaluative' and separated from factual language by an uncrossable gulf, the fact/value divide, and this of itself seemed to undermine the prospects of reasoning for or against any ethical stance on any agreed basis.[3] Later, Hare himself became one of those who contributed to the re-emergence of applied ethics, but well into the 1960s the ascendancy of prescriptivism seemed to make any such resurgence improbable in the extreme, at least in Anglo-Saxon philosophy circles. Ethics, as a branch of philosophy, continued to see itself as a second-order investigation of language, having no involvement with the first-order commitments of ethical language as actually used in ordinary discourse.

2. Philosophical roots of the re-emergence of applied ethics

Some of the philosophical doctrines that re-inforced the restriction of ethics to a second-order study had already come increasingly under scrutiny. These included Moore's claim that definitions of 'good' involve a 'naturalistic fallacy', and also acceptance on the part of non-cognitivists of the fact/value distinction itself.

Moore's assertion of the 'naturalistic fallacy' was challenged by the American philosopher William Frankena, who suggested, in effect, that Moore had assumed his own conclusion. Let 'X' be a proposed definition of 'good'. Moore claimed that questions concerning whether things that are X are really good are always *open* questions, with 'no' as a possible answer, and used this claim to show that 'good' is indefinable. Frankena replies that Moore *assumes* here that 'X' is never equivalent to 'good', which is what he is attempting to prove. Until he or his followers can produce an independent argument to this effect, there is no reason to believe that a successful definition of 'good' (or 'naturalism', in Moore's terminology) is impossible.[4] But if so, the route from 'is' to 'good' (and possibly to 'ought' as well) may be an open one, at least where Moore's argument is concerned.

There might still be some other reason why reasoning from facts to 'evaluations' (or 'ought'-conclusions) is invalid, as the non-cognitivists held. But John R. Searle and Philippa Foot now challenged this view. Searle's challenge consisted in presenting a valid argument from one man saying to another 'I promise to pay you five dollars' (without acting or jesting, and when both understood ordinary English) to the conclusion that the speaker is under an obligation to pay five dollars to the other, and therefore ought, as far as his obligation goes, to pay this sum. The validity of this reasoning depends, as Searle acknowledged, on the institution of promising; but this very institution makes it a necessary truth that people who utter words such as these in circumstances of these kinds make promises and, as such, enter into an obligation. So Searle managed to show that the fact that certain words were uttered in specific circumstances entailed the undertaking of an obligation, and thus (other things being equal) of an 'ought' and therewith an 'evaluative' conclusion. Thus, moves from facts to such conclusions could not always be invalid.[5]

Philippa Foot used a different route to show that such logical moves (or inferences) are sometimes valid. For human good and harm cannot be held to be morally irrelevant, and so there will sometimes be valid inferences from cases where causing injury (a factual matter) is in question to what morally ought to be done in such cases. (More is said about such reasoning in the section on Naturalism.) Besides showing that not just any moral judgement is compatible with recognized facts, this approach also indicated which kinds of facts and which kinds of moral judgements go together. Thus reasoning from facts to values was vindicated, and the non-cognitivism of the emotivists and the prescriptivists was thrown into question. For the possibility had emerged that some moral 'oughts' can after all be known.[6]

3. Key non-philosophical factors

While Foot's revival of naturalism re-opened the possibility of applied ethics, the stimuli that led more directly to its re-emergence were political and social developments. One of these was undoubtedly the Vietnam War, or rather American participation in this war in the 1960s and early 1970s. Whole generations of American students due to be drafted to serve in Vietnam demanded that first-order issues such as the ethics of war be studied in ethics courses (and not only second-order theories), plus issues relating to the civil rights movement and to the environment. Given the urgency of modern dilemmas, philosophy (which was known to have addressed, for example, the ethics of war, if only in the distant past) could no longer be confined to abstract theories.

Another influential factor was the publication in 1963 of Rachel Carson's book *Silent Spring*, which exposed the impacts of pesticides on wildlife and on human health, together with the attitudes of human domination and of unreflective preference for short-term technological solutions that underpinned their use. Issues such as these further contributed to the demand that philosophy be applied to significant practical matters. So did the Civil Rights Movement and the Women's Movement of the 1960s and 1970s. The new trends soon received recognition with the launch in 1971 of the journal *Philosophy and Public Affairs*.

4. Some philosophical influences

The first volume of *Philosophy and Public Affairs* included Peter Singer's celebrated article 'Famine, Affluence and Morality', which took a radical line on people's responsibilities to avert famine. Singer argued that agents who could alleviate famine (e.g. through financial contributions) without sacrificing anything of comparable importance should do so. This claim continues to be debated.[7]

That year also saw the publication of an even more influential philosophical work which revived the contractarian approach to ethics and political philosophy. This was John Rawls' *A Theory of Justice.* The underlying idea was that whatever rules or arrangements would be freely agreed by people bargaining about the shape of the society in which they are all going to have to live will be just and fair ones, provided that they are bargaining on a basis of equality, which Rawls ensures by requiring that they have no knowledge of their future identity and prospects (the veil of ignorance).[8] While this underlying idea is itself open to challenge, Rawls' model of a fair bargaining situation allowed others (Charles Beitz and Brian Barry in particular) to use it to study international equity and to criticize the current state of international relations (in ways that took his contractarianism far beyond his own ambitions for it), and others still to apply it to relations between generations, and thus to environmental issues. Rawls' approach, in other words, not only revived political and social philosophy but also nourished applied ethics in several of its branches.

Another contributor to applied ethics was Richard Hare, who now claimed that his universal prescriptivism supported utilitarianism. This was not the classical form of utilitarianism, which advocates aiming for the greatest happiness of the greatest number, but a modern variant which aims at the fulfilment of interests through maximizing the satisfaction of preferences. Rational agents, Hare claimed, would recognize that they are effectively prescribing for situations in which what happens to others might just as easily happen to themselves; and so what they would not prescribe for themselves they will be unwilling to prescribe for others. They will accordingly consider the interests of all the parties affected by action when they judge actions to be right. (See Hare's book *Moral Thinking* (1981), and the section of this book on Non-cognitivism.) So everyone should be guided by a normative ethic of preference-satisfaction, and can tackle practical issues (from environmental planning, *via* whether to eat meat, to the issue of what is wrong with slavery) on that basis.[9] Many philosophers expressed reservations about this approach, some objecting to utilitarianism on general grounds, or to Hare's new claims for its objectivity, and others objecting to the restriction of interests to the holders of preferences, excluding from consideration, as it does, those animals and other creatures lacking preferences but having a good of their own (see Attfield, *Value, Obligation and Meta-Ethics* (1995)).[10] Nevertheless, this approach enabled Hare (despite his remaining a non-cognitivist) and many of his followers not only to participate in applied ethics, but also to claim that certain solutions (or prescriptions, as he called them) were rationally far preferable to all other options.

5. The multiple spheres of applied ethics

Some of the fields to which ethics was now applied were ones with a long history of ethical reflection. Of these, the ethics of war was one, and medical ethics (including issues surrounding abortion) another. The ethics of war had been discussed by theologians in the Middle Ages, and medical ethics had been the subject of the Hippocratic Oath in the ancient world, and more recently of codes of ethics for the medical profession. The ethics of the treatment of animals had also been discussed in ancient times, but now attracted new attention because of the practices of factory farming and animal experimentation. Further fields became subject to philosophical reflection for the first time. One of these was environmental ethics, fostered by a wave of environmental concern generated by problems such as the use of pesticides (see above), the defoliation of forests (in the Vietnam War), the growth of deserts, the loss of arable land and the extinction of species and of habitats. Another was development ethics, a field in which concern to alleviate famine (see above) was broadened to include the underlying causes of famine (malnutrition and poverty), and pathways for moving away from them towards what came to be known as 'development'.

All these five fields are considered in separate sections below, although a further recently revived field, business ethics, cannot be discussed in this book. Here, two further areas will be considered, the related fields of obligations to future generations and of population ethics. These fields are of course inter-connected with (for example) development ethics and environmental ethics, since one of our prime responsibilities to future generations may well be to prepare the way for sustainable development and for a sustainable world population. Yet, as we shall see, they also raise distinctive issues which need to be reflectively considered.

6. Future generations and population ethics

While future generations have never been forgotten (see Exodus 3:15 and Deuteronomy 7:9 in the Bible), it was only during the Enlightenment of the eighteenth century that people realized that the current generation can make changes that will affect them for better or for worse, and that we of the present stand to be judged by 'posterity' (or our successors). More recently John Rawls attempted to cover obligations to posterity through defending a 'Just Savings Principle', whereby each generation makes savings to benefit its successor such as it would have expected to receive from the previous generation.

While there is much to be said for this principle, it did not fit well with the contract-making situation of Rawls' basic theory (see above), in which all the parties know that they are going to be contemporaries, and not strung out over successive generations. To provide for future generations, Rawls had to modify his basic model, and require that each of the parties, while otherwise remaining self-interested, is concerned about his or her descendants (Rawls, section 22). But this modification (or afterthought) appears even more arbitrary than his original depiction of these isolated decision-makers; for they are still not allowed to have ties to family or friends, yet are presumed to care about the next generation just the same. Followers of Rawls have tried to solve this problem by changing the basic model such that the decision-makers, instead of being contemporaries, represent all the generations that there will be. Yet this proposal too is fundamentally flawed. For the principles selected by these decision-makers make a difference to how long humanity survives, and thus to how many generations there will be. Therefore it cannot be assumed that the answer to this latter question is known before the decision-makers begin their work, as it would have to be if all the generations are somehow to be represented.

Brian Barry, a philosopher sympathetic to Rawls' general approach, suggests that equity between generations would be attained if similar resources are made available to future generations as to the present generation, this being the responsibility of those current societies that consume and deplete existing resources.[11] This Equal Resources Principle sounds like what would be agreed if any three or four successive generations could discuss the relations between them, and is thus a Rawlsian solution. The main problem is that the current generation could seldom if ever bring this about, in view of the uncertainty of future needs and problems. Perhaps we should instead say that those current societies able to do so should make provision for the basic needs of future generations (and not only human generations at that) insofar as these can be foreseen, and also facilitate the development of characteristic human capacities (and thus of human culture) insofar as current agents can foresee what this requires; this view would also be in line with the ethical theory upheld in this book. Central to delivering these obligations in the present would be efforts to preserve a habitable environment by drastically reducing carbon emissions and other forms of pollution (see the section on Environmental Ethics).

Thomas Schwartz has presented a problem for all such views. The identity of future people is not yet determined, depending as it does on the timing of their conception; different people would result if different sperms and eggs happen to coalesce. Thus, apart from people already conceived, there are no future people in existence to whom obligations could be owed. Hence we can have no obligations to future generations at all.

This is called the Non-Identity problem. However, Derek Parfit has responded to this problem as follows. Granted that different sets of future people may be brought into being dependent on what current people (and their successors) do, we can still make a difference to the quality of life of whoever will actually live, and could well have related responsibilities. So it does not follow from there being no one to whom such responsibilities are owed that we have no responsibilities to contribute to the quality of life of whoever there will be. Thus our future-related responsibilities are to be construed as obligations with regard to whoever there will be, and not as *owed* to identifiable future individuals. Hence we should reject the Person-Affecting View, which represents all obligations as owed to identifiable recipients, and adopt instead some version of the Total View, which relates our obligations to making the maximum foreseeable difference to the quality of life of all the possible recipients that could be affected.[12] (Fortunately this coheres with the ethical theory commended in this book.)

The Person-Affecting View was itself introduced to solve a problem apparently raised by utilitarianism, with its advocacy of maximizing happiness. For if happiness could be maximized by enlarging the human population, utilitarianism seems to advocate doing so continuously until the stage where happiness ceases to increase (a nightmare scenario if all this happens on one small planet). The suggested cure was to restrict obligations to identifiable people (and thus largely to existing people), and to disregard the happiness of people not yet in existence. But this solution would discriminate against future generations, whose quality of life could be adversely affected by the policies that it would enjoin (see Parfit, *Reasons and Persons*, section 123). Besides, consequentialist theories (particularly ones for which well-being is the goal, rather than happiness) need not advocate population increases, at least if only one planet is available. For they can take into account the impacts on other species and their habitats, together with the impacts on human beings of congestion and loss of privacy; as Richard Hare argued, small increases to population density can cause quality of life to plummet.[13] Thus the Total View turns out not to advocate increasing the human population but stabilizing it, in the overall interests of all creatures present and future, human and non-human alike. Even if population levels are likely to increase in any case for some decades, policies of moving in this direction should be favoured.

Coercive population policies are sometimes advocated. However, population policies need not be coercive, and should not in any case be considered in isolation from other social policies, in the fields of education, health and land tenure, for example. When families have land security or equivalent, and are confident that their children will grow to adulthood, population growth rates are found to fall away without coercion, in (what is known as) a 'demographic transition' (see Ryberg).[14] This is best secured where people (and particularly women) perceive themselves as participating in social decisions, for which the prerequisites include education and literacy. It is measures such as these, I suggest, that contribute to desirable population policies. (We return to such issues in the section on Development.)

Study questions

1. How would you explain the re-emergence of applied ethics in the later decades of the twentieth century?
2. What are the basis and extent of our obligations towards future people?

Notes

1 See G. E. Moore, *Principia Ethica* (1903), Cambridge: Cambridge University Press, 1968.

2 See A. J. Ayer, *Language, Truth and Logic* (1936), London: Gollancz, 1967.

3 R. M. Hare, *Freedom and Reason*, Oxford: Clarendon Press, 1963.

4 See William K. Frankena, 'The Naturalistic Fallacy', *Mind*, 48, 1939, pp. 464–77.

5 See John R. Searle, 'How to Derive "Ought" from "Is"?', *Philosophical Review*, 73, 1964, pp. 43–58.

6 See Philippa Foot, 'Moral Beliefs', *Proceedings of the Aristotelian Society*, 59, 1958–9, pp. 83–104; 'Moral Arguments', *Mind*, 67, 1958, pp. 502–13.

7 Peter Singer, 'Famine, Affluence and Morality', *Philosophy and Public Affairs*, 1, 1971–2, pp. 229–43.

8 John Rawls, *A Theory of Justice*, Cambridge, MA: Harvard University Press, 1971.

9 R. M. Hare, *Moral Thinking: Its Levels, Method and Point*, Oxford: Clarendon Press, 1981.

10 Robin Attfield, *Value, Obligation and Meta-Ethics*, Amsterdam and Atlanta, GA: Éditions Rodopi, 1995.

11 Brian Barry, 'The Ethics of Resource Depletion', in Barry, *Liberty and Justice: Essays in Political Theory 2*, Oxford: Clarendon Press, 1991, pp. 259–73.

12 Derek Parfit, *Reasons and Persons*, Oxford: Clarendon Press, 1984.

13 R. M. Hare, 'Possible People', in Hare, *Essays in Bioethics*, Oxford: Clarendon Press, 1993, pp. 67–83.

14 Jesper Ryberg, 'Population and Third World Assistance: A Comment on Hardin's Lifeboat Ethics', *Journal of Applied Philosophy*, 14.3, 1997, pp. 207–19.

References

Attfield, Robin, *Value, Obligation and Meta-Ethics*, Amsterdam and Atlanta, GA: Éditions Rodopi, 1995

Ayer, A. J., *Language, Truth and Logic* (1936), London: Gollancz, 1967.

Barry, Brian, 'The Ethics of Resource Depletion', in Barry, *Liberty and Justice: Essays in Political Theory 2*, Oxford: Clarendon Press, 1991, pp. 259–73.

Carson, Rachel, *Silent Spring*, London: Hamish Hamilton, 1963.

Foot, Philippa, 'Moral Arguments', *Mind*, 67, 1958, pp. 502–13.

—, 'Moral Beliefs', *Proceedings of the Aristotelian Society*, 59, 1958–9, pp. 83–104.

Frankena, William K., 'The Naturalistic Fallacy', *Mind*, 48, 1939, pp. 464–77.

Hare, R. M., *The Language of Morals*, Oxford: Clarendon Press, 1952.

—, *Freedom and Reason*, Oxford: Clarendon Press, 1963.

—, *Moral Thinking: Its Levels, Method and Point*, Oxford: Clarendon Press, 1981.

—, 'Possible People', in Hare, *Essays in Bioethics*, Oxford: Clarendon Press, 1993, pp. 67–83.

Moore, G. E., *Ethics* (1912), London and New York: Oxford University Press, 1966.

—, *Principia Ethica* (1903), Cambridge: Cambridge University Press, 1968.

Parfit, Derek, *Reasons and Persons*, Oxford: Clarendon Press, 1984.

Rawls, John, *A Theory of Justice*, Cambridge, MA: Harvard University Press, 1971.

Ryberg, Jesper, 'Population and Third World Assistance: A Comment on Hardin's Lifeboat Ethics', *Journal of Applied Philosophy*, 14.3, 1997, pp. 207–19.

Schwartz, Thomas, 'Obligations to Posterity', in R. I. Sikora and Brian Barry, *Obligations to Future Generations*, Philadelphia: Temple University Press, 1978, pp. 3–13.

Searle, John R., 'How to Derive "Ought" from "Is"?', *Philosophical Review*, 73, 1964, pp. 43–58.

Singer, Peter, 'Famine, Affluence and Morality', *Philosophy and Public Affairs*, 1, 1971–2, pp. 229–43.

Stevenson, C. L., *Ethics and Language*, New Haven, CT: Yale University Press, 1945.

Section 2: Medical ethics

1. Introduction: medical ethics before bioethics

While the discipline of bioethics may be said to have originated in the 1970s, medical ethics is very much older. There has been a profession of medicine in the West since the fifth century BCE (and probably much earlier), and the Greeks even had a god of healing, Asclepius, whose daughter, Hygieia, was worshipped as the goddess of health. Both of these deities were mentioned in

Table 4.2

THE HIPPOCRATIC OATH
1. I swear by Apollo Physician and Asclepius and Hygieia and Panacea and all the gods and goddesses, making them my witnesses, that I will fulfil according to my ability and judgment this oath and this covenant.
3. I will apply dietetic [that is, dietary and lifestyle-related] measures for the benefit of the sick according to my ability and judgment; I will keep them from harm and injustice.
4. I will neither give a deadly drug to anybody if asked for it, nor will I make a suggestion to this effect. Similarly I will not give to a woman an abortive remedy. In purity and holiness I will guard my life and my art.
6. Whatever houses I may visit, I will come for the benefit of the sick, remaining free of all intentional injustice, of all mischief and in particular of sexual relations with both female and male persons, be they free or slaves.
7. Whatever I hear in the course of my treatment or even outside of the treatment in regard to the life of men, which on no account one must spread abroad, I will keep to myself holding such things to be shameful to be spoken about.
8. If I fulfil this oath and do not violate it, may it be granted to me to enjoy life and art, being honoured with fame among all men for all time to come; if I transgress it and swear falsely, may the opposite of all this be my lot.[1]

the Hippocratic Oath, named after the famous physician Hippocrates of Cos (469–399 BCE). It runs (in part) as in Table 4.2:

We may notice here the commitment to benefiting the sick (the underlying point of medicine), to the avoidance of harm, to confidentiality and to avoiding injustice and exploitation; all these themes recur in modern bioethics. We may also remark the specific commitment neither to administer poison nor to perform abortions. (These commitments help explain the honour received by Hippocrates in the Christian church during the Middle Ages, although at the time abortion was only forbidden after 'quickening', when the foetus could be felt to move within the womb. This criterion was not formally discarded until 1869.[2]) As well as the Oath, some other Hippocratic texts have survived; jointly they bear out the desirability of doctors' self-imposed constraints at a time when there was otherwise little or no state regulation of their activities. As far as we are aware, there was no contribution to this code of conduct from contemporary philosophers, although Plato held strong views on related issues (e.g. in the 'Laws'), and Aristotle was himself the son of a prominent doctor.

This holds good also of the re-appearance of codes of professional ethics in the nineteenth and early twentieth centuries, both in America and in Britain. Medical practitioners were concerned to unify, strengthen and protect their profession against rival claimants to the healing of the sick (such as homeopaths, bone-setters and chiropractors), by recognizing professional standards and expelling from the profession those who failed to comply. The American Medical Association was first in the field with its 'Code of Medical Ethics' of 1848,[3] followed by the British Medical Association which established its Central Ethical Committee in 1902, to maintain an accepted standard of professional conduct and present cases for expulsion from the Association for conduct 'detrimental to the honour and interests of the medical profession'.[4] In more recent decades, comparable codes of professional conduct have been adopted for many non-medical professions such as accountants, architects and engineers.

The medical experiments carried out by Nazis on unwilling subjects in concentration camps during the Second World War led to a code being drawn up in advance of the Nuremberg War-Crimes Trials held at the end of that War. This Nuremberg Code expressed standards of conduct intended to apply to all future research on human subjects, and considered to be ones that should have been in place for the experiments of the recent past, even though it was drawn up afterwards. The very first Article of the Code stresses the requirement of informed consent on the part of experimental subjects: see Table 4.3.

Table 4.3

THE NUREMBERG CODE, ARTICLE ONE

The voluntary consent of the human subject is absolutely essential. This means that the person involved should have legal capacity to give consent, should be so situated as to be able to exercise free power of choice, without the intervention of any element of force, fraud, deceit, duress, over-reaching, or other ulterior form of constraint or coercion, and should have sufficient knowledge and comprehension of the elements of the subject matter involved as to enable him to make an understanding and enlightened decision. This latter element requires that before the acceptance of an affirmative decision by the experimental subject there should be made known to him the nature, duration, and purpose of the experiment, the method and means by which it is to be conducted, all inconveniences and hazards reasonable to be expected, and the effects upon his health or person which may possibly come from his participation in the experiment.

The duty and responsibility for ascertaining the quality of the consent rests upon each individual who initiates, directs or engages in the experiment. It is a personal duty and responsibility which may not be delegated to another with impunity.[5]

The new stress on the informed consent of experimental subjects was incorporated into codes of medical ethics in general. Further, what held good for experimental subjects was soon recognized to apply to medical patients as well, and the traditional themes of medical ethics were now supplemented with the requirement to respect patients as persons and ensure that their fully informed consent be given to treatments that doctors deemed it necessary for them to undergo. Later this theme was to re-appear among the principles of biomedical ethics as the principle of autonomy. The importance of patient participation was emphasized as Western populations became more educated, and movements of the 1960s (such as the women's movement) increasingly questioned the authoritarianism of doctors, which earlier generations had accepted, and demanded that the rights of patients be recognized.

Post-war trends also brought a new importance to the traditional theme of justice. The unaffordability of medical treatment for many citizens led first countries such as New Zealand (in the 1930s), then Britain and other developed Commonwealth countries (in the 1940s and 1960s) and eventually other countries of Western Europe such as Sweden, France and Germany (in the 1950s, 1960s and 1970s) to abolish fees for most such treatment, and to bring medical services under state control. This was seen as a move in the direction of social justice, making medicine 'free at the point of need', and funded not from fees but from taxation. In Britain, doctors were allowed some degree of independence, and despite initial reluctance broadly accepted the new system, which has widespread and strong popular support. In the USA such an approach has until recently been resisted on grounds of the freedom of taxpayers. However, issues of distributive justice, such as the availability of treatments and of who should have access to them, have everywhere become more prominent in an age in which scientific advances have made many forms of therapy too expensive for most people without some form of either medical insurance or state provision. Issues of the allocation of scarce medical resources have thus assumed a high profile, and are likely to retain it for the foreseeable future.

2. The emergence of bioethics

As we have seen in Section 1 of this chapter, philosophers newly turned their attention in the 1970s to issues of medical ethics and a number of related issues. Already one philosopher, Abraham Kaplan, had contributed in 1966 to a conference held at Portland, Oregon on 'The Sanctity of Life'; Kaplan stressed the role of philosophers in clarifying principles and concepts such as the sanctity of life, and also in studying diverse traditions (including the Kantian tradition) capable of informing judgements in practical situations.[6]

However, John Rawls' book *A Theory of Justice* (1971) was the work that seemed to show how philosophical reflection could more reliably generate practical guidance. If people in a fair bargaining situation would agree to certain principles for their community, those principles will apparently be fair ones. Furthermore, this approach could be applied to issues of medical services and their distribution, and also, as we have seen in Section 1, to issues of what earlier generations owe to later ones. (As we shall see, Rawls also put forward a further method, felt by some to have yet greater value, that of Wide Reflective Equilibrium.)

Among other leading philosophers who now contributed to biomedical issues, there were Hans Jonas, who was able to draw on continental traditions, and discussed experimenting with human subjects,[7] and Richard Hare, whose version of utilitarianism required the preferences and thus the interests of all affected parties (abnormal infants included) to be taken into consideration.[8] Two research centres for the philosophical study of biomedical issues were now set up, the Hastings Centre (in 1970) and the Kennedy Centre (in 1971).[9] Meanwhile Hare was among those who applied normative theory to the topic of abortion, one of the earliest biomedical issues to take centre stage (see below).

3. Abortion

In matters of abortion, two views were held among American doctors in the early twentieth century: the strict view, which forbade abortions altogether, except in the direst of circumstances, because of the value of the life of the foetus, and the broad or liberal view that the foetus had a limited right to life, but one which counted for less than the mother's.[10] Philosophers in this period had other preoccupations and abstained from comment, but liberal theologians such as Joseph Fletcher, who objected to a top-down view of morality, advocated instead an ethic more sensitive to situations, interpreted in the light of the New Testament concept of love (agape), and were able to defend abortion in some cases.[11] While mainstream Catholic teaching was (and remains) uncompromisingly opposed to abortion (now that the criterion of quickening had been finally discarded), certain theologians objected to this principle-driven approach, preferring the longstanding approach of casuistry, which seeks agreement about particular cases, and reasons from these to other cases by analogy. Some who took this approach and occasionally condoned abortions eventually felt obliged to leave the Catholic church.[12]

Writing in *Philosophy and Public Affairs*, the philosopher Judith Jarvis Thomson now brought a new approach to this topic. The conservative argument can be presented as follows: Every person (including the foetus) has a right to life. While a mother has a right to make decisions about her own body, a person's right to life is stronger than this right, and outweighs it. So abortions may not be performed. Instead of denying the much-disputed opening premise, Thomson contests the second one. If a person wakes to find themselves in a hospital ward, back to back with a famous violinist who needs the service of the person's kidneys for nine months if he is to survive (and to learn that they have been kidnapped by a society of the violinist's fans for this purpose), the violinist has no right to the use of the person's body. While it would be generous to grant it all the same, there would be no obligation to do so. Thomson compares this case to pregnancies incurred either through rape or despite the use of contraceptives, and concludes that in such cases abortion is far from wrong.[13]

Thomson's method involves an appeal to a parallel and would-be clearer case (in the manner of casuistry), and also illustrates how philosophical techniques can be brought to bear on biomedical topics. However, maybe the issue cannot be settled by appeal to rights, for it may not always be right actually to do whatever one has a right to do (think of Shakespeare's Shylock). Hence philosophers who appeal beyond rights to the consequences of actions (or types of actions) have been prone to question Thomson's reasoning (even when, like Peter Singer, they largely agreed with her conclusion).[14] A consequentialist appraisal of abortion was supplied by Richard Hare three years later in the same journal; Hare argued that, since we are glad to be alive, and would be glad, if we imagine ourselves as a foetus, not to be aborted, there is always something to be said against abortion, even though in many cases the interests of the mother outweigh those of the foetus and make abortion right.[15] Hare's reasoning has proved as controversial as Thomson's, but serves to illustrate how his method of imaginative substitution (imagining oneself at the receiving end of an action that is contemplated) can be salutary.

4. The principles of biomedical ethics

In *Principles of Biomedical Ethics*, Beauchamp and Childress (of the Kennedy Centre) presented four principles which they took to supply the guidance necessary for ethical decision-making in medicine.[16] Three of these principles have ancient origins: the principle of beneficence (which conveys that interventions should always be for the benefit of the patient), that of non-maleficence (which forbids causing harm), and the principle of justice (which requires fairness and forbids exploitation). The remaining principle, that of autonomy, could be held to arise from the requirements of the Nuremberg Code, is supported by the ethics of Kant and of Mill alike and had recently been expressed in *The Belmont Report* of 1978 as the requirement of respect for persons.[17] The approach of *Principles* was to be pre-eminent in bioethics for decades to come; its sixth edition was published in 2009.[18]

Principles were required to be coherent, comprehensive, simple and broadly in accordance with ordinary judgements, while being capable, where judgements conflict, to adjudicate between them. Judgements and actions, they held, are justified by rules (such as a rule against killing innocent human beings), which are justified by principles (such as, in this case, non-maleficence), which are justified by an ethical theory (such as consequentialism or alternatively a deontological basis such as Kant's Categorical Imperative). However, the formulation of principles involves an interplay between accepted judgements and apparently persuasive principles and theories; rules and principles are proposed by systematizing judgements, and then tested by considering whether they generate acceptable judgements. If they generate unacceptable judgements, then the rules, principles and (if necessary) the underlying theory have to be revised accordingly. This is a method put forward by Rawls and known as 'Wide Reflective Equilibrium'. How this might be applied to the four proposed principles will be considered shortly.

The four principles are discussed in greater detail in *Principles*, and readers should look at these discussions. The principle of non-maleficence is distinguished from that of beneficence largely because duties to avoid or avert harm are widely held more stringent than duties to do good. Yet duties of beneficence are also recognized in *Principles*; indeed the entire practice of medicine has all along been held to turn on the goal of benefiting patients. Many have doubted whether non-maleficence and beneficence are really separate principles; thus failures to help often constitute harm, and so the two principles may be regarded (at least in practice) as one. The principle of justice is clearly important, and needs separate expression (to make it clear that unfairness and exploitation must be avoided), whether or not it can be derived from (say) consequentialism; but in face of competing theories of justice, this principle is not given a precise and detailed formulation. The principle of autonomy inherited many of the requirements of the Nuremberg Code, adjusted to the context of therapy, including that of informed consent (expounded in some detail in *Principles*).

Let us consider an example (presented by Earl R. Winkler), with a bearing on how to interpret the principle of autonomy. A man suffering from multiple sclerosis who has contracted a treatable bacterial infection enters hospital and requests not to be treated. The principle of beneficence suggests that he should be treated, but the principle of autonomy suggests otherwise. Should doctors simply allow one principle to override another? (There must be cases where pairs of principles conflict, and resolving such cases is in any case a problem for Beauchamp and Childress.) However, investigation discloses that the patient has been suffering from depression, and so doubt is cast on whether his request was really autonomous. After treatment with antibiotics and some family counselling, his attitude changes and his health improves. Such cases suggest that the principle of autonomy needs to be interpreted in a manner that questions the autonomy of the patient's original request, requiring that expressions of wishes (as well as being informed and voluntary) come from people competent to make decisions;[19] thus a better and more sophisticated 'reflective equilibrium' is reached between judgements about cases and the formulation of principles.

But Winkler has a further example, intended to show that the interpretation of cases matters more than an understanding of principles. A motorcyclist, now paraplegic as a result of an accident, is so pervasively angry and resentful that (after years of refusing help and counselling) he refuses to eat. The patient is competent, and yet his decision is inauthentic (conflicting with his own earlier values). But to force-feed him would be brutal, and would also have to be continued indefinitely. In the absence of other solutions, we should accordingly allow him to die. We should also modify further any interpretation of the principle of autonomy that disregards inauthentic decisions. This supposedly emerges only through reflection on cases rather than on principles.[20] However, even if we accept Winkler's judgement about the case described, this does no more than suggest that the inauthenticity of decisions does not invariably invalidate them, particularly where failure to respect them would cause prolonged harm. The traditional reluctance of ethicists such as Mill to endorse paternalism is thus upheld, and how to interpret the principle of autonomy is further clarified. The principle (together with that of non-maleficence) can still be held to supply the reason for the judgement mentioned, and thus its justification.

There was a tendency in the 1990s to resist the view, often attributed to the first edition of *Principles*, that principles represent secure knowledge and that judgements about cases can, after due reflection, be deduced from them (the 'deductivist' model). Instead, writers such as Winkler advocated a 'situationist' view (rather like that of Fletcher), on which it is judgements about cases which are more secure, and to which principles have to be adapted. It cannot be denied that sometimes such judgements are more secure than the principles that we take to underpin them. An example can be found in Renford Bambrough's (much earlier) work *Moral Scepticism and Moral Knowledge* (1979). As he says, 'We know that this child, who is about to undergo what would otherwise be painful surgery, should be given an anaesthetic before the operation'.[21] (Or at least, we know this if there are safe anaesthetics available and local medical staff are trustworthy.) And as he adds, no reason that could be given to doubt this would be more secure than our judgement itself. Yet this judgement can still be deduced from the principles of beneficence and non-maleficence, plus the facts just supplied about the circumstances, and these principles continue to supply reasons for, and thus justify, our judgement. So there is no need to discard the 'deductive' component of deductivism. All that needs to be conceded to situationism is that the detailed formulation of principles needs constantly to be revised in the light of clear-cut cases (which is sometimes called a 'dialectical' approach).

Other ethicists suggest that instead of principles, what conduces to ethical conduct is a virtuous character (and in particular an attitude of care: see the section on Virtue Ethics). It cannot be denied that a good character is likelier to generate good clinical practice than good principles plus good reasoning are. But principles should not reasonably be jettisoned (for this reason or for any other). As was argued in the section on Aristotle, there is no guarantee that the person of good character will always do what is right; and guidance about what is right is at least as likely to be derivable from sound principles as if it is from reflection about what the caring person would do. Nor is it likely that an attitude of caring will ensure behaviour that is fair. Thus appeal to principles plausibly remains crucial.

This helps explain why Beauchamp and Childress continue to make bioethics focus on the four principles in their sixth edition of 2009. But this latest edition, without endorsing situationism, may be held to embody a move away from full reliance on the deductivist model in the direction of a greater reliance on the approach of reflective equilibrium, as illustrated above.[22]

5. Some recent implications of the principle of justice

As we have seen, issues of the allocation of medical resources have widely become prominent. This is true not only at national level, but internationally too. One such issue concerns the comparative neglect on the part of medical research to invest resources in tropical medicine, in view of the comparative poverty of most of the affected populations, and the better prospects for profit of investment in maladies affecting the populations of temperate climates. Medical researchers, Western governments and pharmaceutical companies can be held to have a responsibility to invest much more heavily in measures (both preventative and therapeutic) to contain and counteract tropical diseases.[23] Such a responsibility is indicated whether we ground ethics on a Kantian basis, a consequentialist basis, a rights basis or a Rawlsian basis.[24]

The phenomenon of global warming makes this responsibility both more pressing and more urgent. The vectors of tropical illnesses (such as the Anopheles mosquito) are moving into higher altitudes and higher latitudes, putting more people at risk of diseases like malaria. Simultaneously, millions of people are being forced to leave their homes and migrate because of droughts, typhoons or floods, generated by climate change, and thereby become more vulnerable than previously to such illnesses. Third World countries often cannot cope with the resulting medical problems without assistance from Western countries, whose consumption has in any case brought climate change about. So the ancient principle that the allocation of medical resources must be fair and equitable turns out to have international implications of vast dimensions, unforeseen until recently, but ones which can no longer be neglected by the practitioners of medical ethics.

Study questions

1. What principles should be employed to arrive at decisions in matters of abortion?
2. What should medical staff do when following the principle of beneficence clashes with respecting a patient's autonomy?
3. Should medical staff adopt either the Principle of Double Effect, or the policy of behaving as if it were correct (see Chapter 3, Section 2, Sub-section 2)?

Notes

1 Paul Carrick, *Medical Ethics in Antiquity: Philosophical Perspectives on Abortion and Euthanasia*, Dordrecht and Boston, MA: D. Reidel, 1985, pp. 69–70.

2 Albert R. Jonsen, *The Birth of Bioethics*, New York and Oxford: Oxford University Press, 1998, p. 289.

3 American Medical Association, *Original Code of Medical Ethics*; see http://www.ama-assn.org.

4 Andrew A. G. Morrice, 'Honour and Interests: Medical Ethics and the British Medical Association', in Andreas-Holger Maehle and Johanna Geyer-Kordesch (eds), *Historical and Philosophical Perspectives on Biomedical Ethics*, Aldershot and Burlington, VT: Ashgate, 2002, pp. 11–35, at p. 20.

5 'Nuremberg Code' in *Trials of War Criminals before the Nuremberg Military Tribunals under Control Council Law No. 10,* vol. 2, pp. 181–2; available at http://ohsr.od.nih.gov/guidelines/nuremberg.html.

6 Abraham Kaplan, 'A Social Ethics and the Sanctity of Life. A Summary', in Daniel H. Labby et al., *Life or Death: Ethics and Options*, Seattle: University of Washington Press, 1968, pp. 152–67; Jonsen, *The Birth of Bioethics*, p. 18.

7 Jonsen, *The Birth of Bioethics*, p. 150.

8 R. M. Hare, 'The Survival of the Weakest', in Samuel Gorovitz et al. (eds), *Moral Problems in Medicine*, Englewood Cliffs: Prentice-Hall, 1976, pp. 364–9.

9 Jonsen, *The Birth of Bioethics*, pp. 20–3.

10 Kristin Luker, *Abortion and the Politics of Motherhood*, Berkeley, CA and London: University of California Press, 1984, p. 39.

11 Joseph Fletcher, *Morals and Medicine*, Princeton, NJ: Princeton University Press, 1954, and *Situation Ethics*, London: SCM Press, 1966.

12 Jonsen, *The Birth of Bioethics*, p. 301.

13 Judith Jarvis Thomson, 'A Defense of Abortion', *Philosophy & Public Affairs*, 1, 1970–1, pp. 47–66.

14 Peter Singer, *Practical Ethics,* 2nd edn, Cambridge: Cambridge University Press, 1993, pp. 146–8.

15 R. M. Hare, 'Abortion and the Golden Rule', *Philosophy & Public Affairs*, 4, 1974–5, pp. 201–22.

16 T. L. Beauchamp and J. F. Childress, *Principles of Biomedical Ethics,* 1st edn, Oxford: Oxford University Press, 1979.

17 National Commission for the Protection of Human Subjects of Biomedical and Behavioural Research, *The Belmont Report*, Washington, DC: U.S. Government Printing Office, 1978; see Jonsen, *The Birth of Bioethics*, pp. 20–1.

18 Beauchamp and Childress, *Principles of Biomedical Ethics,* 6th edn, Oxford: Oxford University Press, 2009.

19 Earl R. Winkler, 'From Kantianism to Contextualism: The Rise and Fall of the Paradigm Theory in Bioethics', in E. R. Winkler and J. R. Coombs (eds), *Applied Ethics: A Reader*, Oxford: Blackwell, 1993, pp. 343–65, at pp. 377–8.

20 Winkler, pp. 358–60.

21 Renford Bambrough, *Moral Scepticism and Moral Knowledge*, London and Henley: Routledge & Kegan Paul, 1979, p. 15.

22 Beauchamp and Childress, *Principles*, 6th edn, p. 375.

23 For a study of ethical issues relating to the pharmaceutical industry, see Dianna Melrose, *Bitter Pills: Medicines and the Third World Poor*, Oxford: Oxfam, 1982.

24 See Robin Attfield, 'The Global Distribution of Health Care Resources', *Journal of Medical Ethics*, 16.2, 1990, pp. 153–6.

References

American Medical Association, *Original Code of Medical Ethics*; see http://www.ama-assn.org.

Attfield, Robin, 'The Global Distribution of Health Care Resources', *Journal of Medical Ethics*, 16.2, 1990, pp. 153–6.

Bambrough, Renford, *Moral Scepticism and Moral Knowledge*, London and Henley: Routledge & Kegan Paul, 1979.

Beauchamp, T. L. and J. F. Childress, *Principles of Biomedical Ethics*, 1st edn, Oxford: Oxford University Press, 1979.

—, *Principles of Biomedical Ethics*, 6th edn, Oxford: Oxford University Press, 2009.

Carrick, Paul, *Medical Ethics in Antiquity: Philosophical Perspectives on Abortion and Euthanasia*, Dordrecht and Boston, MA: D. Reidel, 1985.

Fletcher, Joseph, *Morals and Medicine*, Princeton, NJ: Princeton University Press, 1954.

—, *Situation Ethics*, London: SCM Press, 1966.

Hare, R. M., 'Abortion and the Golden Rule', *Philosophy & Public Affairs*, 4, 1974–5, pp. 201–22.

—, 'The Survival of the Weakest', in Samuel Gorovitz et al. (eds), *Moral Problems in Medicine*, Englewood Cliffs: Prentice-Hall, 1976, pp. 364–9.

Jonsen, Albert R., *The Birth of Bioethics*, New York and Oxford: Oxford University Press, 1998.

Kaplan, Abraham, 'A Social Ethics and the Sanctity of Life. A Summary', in Daniel H. Labby et al. (eds), *Life or Death: Ethics and Options*, Seattle: University of Washington Press, 1968, pp. 152–67.

Luker, Kristin, *Abortion and the Politics of Motherhood*, Berkeley, CA and London: University of California Press, 1984.

Melrose, Dianna, *Bitter Pills: Medicines and the Third World Poor*, Oxford: Oxfam, 1982.

Morrice, Andrew A. G., 'Honour and Interests: Medical Ethics and the British Medical Association', in Andreas-Holger Maehle and Johanna Geyer-Kordesch (eds), *Historical and Philosophical Perspectives on Biomedical Ethics*, Aldershot and Burlington, VT: Ashgate, 2002, pp. 11–35.

National Commission for the Protection of Human Subjects of Biomedical and Behavioural Research, *The Belmont Report*, Washington, DC: U.S. Government Printing Office, 1978.

Nuremberg War Crimes Tribunal, *Trials of War Criminals before the Nuremberg Military Tribunals under Control Council Law No. 10*, vol. 2; available at http://ohsr.od.nih.gov/guidelines/nuremberg.html.

Singer, Peter, *Practical Ethics*, 2nd edn, Cambridge: Cambridge University Press, 1993.

Thomson, Judith Jarvis, 'A Defense of Abortion', *Philosophy & Public Affairs*, 1, 1970–1, pp. 47–66.

Winkler, Earl R., 'From Kantianism to Contextualism: The Rise and Fall of the Paradigm Theory in Bioethics', in E. R. Winkler and J. R. Coombs (eds), *Applied Ethics: A Reader*, Oxford: Blackwell, 1993, pp. 343–65.

Section 3: Animal ethics

1. Introduction

Concern among philosophers about the proper treatment of animals was present in the ancient world, among philosophers of the early centuries of the common era such as Plutarch and the neo-Platonists, Plotinus and Porphyry, and re-appeared during the early modern period among thinkers such as Locke, Leibniz, Pope and Voltaire, and among their humanitarian successors who initiated legislation in Britain against cruelty to animals. But, unlike medical ethics, the study of this branch of applied ethics was not continuously pursued until a new wave of concern arose during the 1970s, in response to developments in agricultural technology such as factory farming and in research such as animal experimentation, together with increases in the practice of farming animals for their fur. The new trail was blazed by Stanley and Roslind Godlovitch and John Harris when they published in 1972 their collection *Animals, Men and Morals: An Enquiry into the Maltreatment of Non-humans.*[1] This was also the stage of a related wave of environmental concern, which overlapped with concerns about animal welfare over issues such as whaling and seal-culling.

The case for including non-human animals among the bearers of moral standing has already been presented in the section on 'Moral Standing, Value and Intrinsic Value', and was brought to renewed prominence in this period. On the one hand, Peter Singer (an Australian ethicist) argued that in view of the ethical centrality of pleasure and pain, all sentient creatures must be regarded as having moral standing, whose interests were to be taken into consideration alongside those of human beings.[2] Singer's case is a consequentialist one, of the utilitarian kind, adjusted to take into account the preferences of self-conscious creatures (including most human beings but also some non-humans such as dolphins and chimpanzees). On the other hand, Tom Regan, an American critic of utilitarianism who argues from a rights perspective, claims that those animals that are 'subjects of a life' (a majority, perhaps) have a right not to be killed or subjected to gratuitous suffering. While rights can be overridden in exceptional circumstances, nothing justifies current practices of food rearing.[3] Both these animal-welfarist thinkers deploy their arguments in favour of vegetarianism.

In this section, these arguments will be discussed, together with related ones, and related to factory farming (a practice well reported in Singer's book), animal research, transgenic engineering and commercial fishing. The environmental impacts of some of these practices will also be considered, together with continuities and discontinuities between animal welfarism and environmentalism.

2. Animal rights and the equal consideration principle

Regan argues cogently that if humans have a right not to be made to suffer gratuitously, then so do non-human animals. And since most farming, and almost all factory-farming, involves avoidable suffering, this already supplies a strong case against consuming its products, and thus for vegetarianism, even before the supposed right to life of food-animals is as much as considered.

But are such rights exceptionless and ethically fundamental? Regan does not (unlike some theorists of rights) consider them entirely exceptionless, but expects the cases where very significant good could be done by infringing a right to be very rare. In his view, rights are more far-reaching than the entitlements upheld by utilitarian rules could be, and defeat utilitarian (and generally consequentialist) considerations; rights, that is, are to be observed (except in rare cases) even when greater good could have been done by infringing them.

However, this stance is liable to generate contradictions, if it is granted that most parties with interests have rights (something Regan would be likely to grant). For it will not be possible to respect rights and forego the greater good which often could have been brought about instead, without at the same time failing to respect the rights of the parties to which this greater good could instead have been done. In other words, if rights are as strong and as widely distributed as Regan thinks, then they are bound quite frequently to clash; but such clashes are unacceptable if rights can never rightly be infringed except in rare cases. If acting rightly involves respecting rights, then it will frequently be impossible to do so, or thus to act rightly at all.

As I have argued in the section on 'Deontology, Contractarianism and Consequentialism', we should adopt instead a rule-consequentialist understanding of rights. Given this approach, respect for rights involves honouring rules which prohibit certain forms of treatment; these are rules in the absence of which significant harms or injuries would be liable to take place. The human beings or animals to whose treatment these rules apply are thus the bearers of the relevant rights. This view is consistent with Singer's approach, to which we now turn.

Singer defends the Principle of the Equal Consideration of Equal Interests. This means that two creatures with the same interests at stake should be considered equally, whereas greater interests (such as an interest in not suffering greater pain) should receive greater consideration, irrespective of the species to which the creature belongs. (This Principle coheres well with the kind of consequentialism supported in this book.) Thus the suffering inflicted in the course of factory-farming, being much greater than the interest of human diners in the pleasures of taste, means that the products of factory-farms should be avoided and boycotted.

However, self-conscious creatures with a concept of themselves as ongoing individuals with a future have an interest in shaping their own future, an interest lacked by creatures that are sentient and conscious but lack *self*-consciousness. These interests take priority where they are at stake, and explain what is wrong with killing such creatures, which include most human beings and also (as mentioned above) some intelligent creatures of other species.

From the outset Singer included pigs among self-conscious creatures, and therefore objected to their being farmed and killed for food, quite apart from the suffering that these processes involve. With other food-animals, his objection was not to killing (as these animals are in principle replaceable), but to the suffering that they undergo. Singer added that, to ensure that they are not upholding and supporting the practice of factory-farming, people should avoid meat-eating altogether, and become vegetarians.

Regan at one point commented that this is only a conditional basis for vegetarianism, and thus an insecure one, and that his own rights approach was much more secure. Indeed Singer could not criticize someone who consumed (say) a sheep that had died in a road accident after living a happy life.[4] Singer replied that boycotting factory-farms was in his view a strategy rather than a principle, and agreed about the sheep; his vegetarianism was indeed conditional, and none the worse for that. The issue of principle was not vegetarianism but equal consideration of equal interests.[5]

3. A critique of vegetarian ethics

Vegetarianism can in fact be supported on a number of bases, as is conveyed by the spirit of a passage of Stephen Clark, a sturdy philosophical defender of vegetarianism. Listing metaphysical and religious influences supportive of his overall stance, Clark writes, '. . . I am an Aristotelian on Mondays and Wednesdays, a Pyrrhonian Sceptic on Tuesdays and Fridays, a neo-Platonist on Thursdays and Saturdays and worship in the local Episcopalian church on Sundays'.[6] Yet other philosophers have adduced further bases; for example, Mark Rowlands has proposed an extended version of Rawls' contractarianism.[7] However, for present purposes a critique of vegetarian ethics from a consequentialist perspective will be considered, as it allows the kind of conclusions adopted elsewhere in this book to be applied critically to an issue that is at the same time controversial and offers ethical options to readers.

In his book *Rights, Killing and Suffering: Moral Vegetarianism and Applied Ethics*, R. G. Frey, another American philosopher, considers in turn the three kinds of moral grounds supplied by Regan and Singer (and considered above) for vegetarianism, arguments from rights, killing and suffering.[8]

His appraisal of arguments from rights is that such arguments achieve nothing that cannot be achieved without them. What underpins such arguments is interests, and it is simpler and clearer to argue from interests direct. Such an appraisal can take the breath away from people who regard rights as ethical bedrock, beyond which there is no appeal. For consequentialists, however, rights are (so to speak) conclusions, or the content of derivative principles, based on the good or harm of the people or creatures in question. This does not detract from the importance of rights and of appealing to them, but it does mean that appeal can be made to these more basic considerations, and that at the same time we can avoid the often exaggerated rhetoric of rights.

Where arguments from the wrongness of killing are concerned, Frey objects that it is not invariably wrong to kill, and that talk of a right to life is misleading, granted that some killing is justified. In this way, Regan's case against killing animals needs more qualification. However, the reasons given by Singer for the wrongness of killing self-conscious creatures that want to remain alive (see above) could well be held to remain unaffected.

Where the argument from suffering is concerned, Frey agrees that we should actively seek to prevent suffering, but claims that this does not require vegetarianism; there is no formal contradiction in eating food against the rearing of which you are campaigning. Many people, however, find a pragmatic contradiction between campaigning against factory farming and willingness to consume its products; charges of hypocrisy against such campaigners are likely to stick. Hence, while Frey is right in holding that opposition to factory farming does not require vegetarianism, there is a strong case for the view that it does require abstaining from the products of factory farms, and perhaps consuming instead the produce of free-range farming.

4. Animal research and genetic engineering

Similar principles apply to the testing of products on non-human animals. Since unnecessary suffering is to be avoided, the argument from suffering counts strongly against the testing on animals of unnecessary products such as cosmetics. This does not make all animal testing wrong, let alone all animal research. For some research saves the lives of self-conscious beings, and the testing of some life-saving or life-prolonging pharmaceutical products has a similar justification. Nevertheless the suffering that such testing often causes means that alternatives should be sought and employed where possible, and that the scale and the repetition of testing should be minimized.

There was a time when animals were regarded as mechanisms without feeling, and when vivisection (that is, surgical procedures conducted on living animals) was regarded as unobjectionable. Besides the obvious inhumanity of this practice, it is open to the objection that if animals are so unlike human beings, little or nothing of relevance about human beings was likely to be discovered. If, on the other hand, animals resemble humans in having feelings (sensations and emotions) and being liable to pain, then the claim that we cannot be sure that they suffer needs to be abandoned, together with unspeakable practices like vivisection performed without anaesthetics.

Newer kinds of research include genetic engineering, in which animals with genetic material from more than one species (transgenic animals such as Dolly the sheep) are produced. Such genetic engineering is sometimes considered to raise ethical issues. If the resulting creatures suffer (perhaps from genetically implanted diseases), that clearly requires a strong justification. But the objection that genetic engineering of itself involves violence to natural kinds through failing to respect naturally evolved species and should therefore be discontinued is not in itself convincing.

However, that does not make it right to generate dysfunctional creatures, such as the pigs engineered to have short legs and thus a higher proportion than usual of meat to bone, which turned out to suffer from conditions of the joints like arthritis. Generally, those responsible for producing a new strain or species need to reflect beforehand on whether such a creature will be able to function healthily as naturally evolved species do, and not to be a burden to itself; they cannot plead that because the new creatures will belong to no natural kind, nothing will count as harming them.[9] Ethics does not turn exclusively on considerations of harm, and can instead turn on avoiding the quality of life of new creatures being avoidably low or wretched. Nor is it acceptable to avoid this by rendering new animal species insensible or insentient (as is suggested by Frey), and thus to replace vigorous creatures with stupefied ones; while this might prevent suffering, it also prevents intrinsically valuable animal lives being lived.[10] (Once again, it turns out that our value-theory should not be restricted to hedonism, which lacks grounds on which to resist this suggestion.)

Further, those responsible for releasing new strains or species into the environment need to reflect beforehand on the possible impacts of doing this on the natural ecosystems in question. There have been many cases of exotic species whose introduction has caused havoc (from rabbits in Australia to eucalyptus in Africa). Thus genetic engineering can cause harm not through the nature conferred on the new species but through its unintended impacts on other species. For unintended impacts are just as relevant in the field of animal ethics as we have seen them to be in that of inter-human ethics.

5. Environmental impacts of agriculture and fisheries

This mention of unintended consequences prompts us to consider the ethics of animal rearing and of fishing with respect to their side-effects on local and global ecosystems. Not all unintended impacts are regrettable ones. For example, it is sheep rearing that makes possible the continued existence of certain rare species such as some kinds of the fritillary butterfly. But some of the relevant impacts have a bearing on the ethics of the practices in question.

Grazing animals can be a sustainable practice across the generations, but pressures of population and limits of space sometimes give poor people incentives to over-graze the available pasturage, which then degenerates and undergoes erosion. This happened, for example, in South Africa in the apartheid period (prior to 1994), when blacks were confined by law to limited landholdings; in many places the land remains degraded. The ethical issue concerned not the actions of pastoralists, who had little choice about where to graze their animals, but the oppressive system that caused these problems.

Animal rearing by and for wealthier people can also generate environmental problems. Currently large areas of the Amazonian rainforest are being cut down for the sake of cattle rearing, to supply burgers for wealthy Westerners. Numerous rare forest species are thus being lost, and irrecoverable forest destroyed. Besides, the processes involved in supplying meat (largely for rich consumers) altogether emit 18 per cent of global carbon emissions.[11] Even if the cattle are well-treated, consuming the products of such farming is ethically problematic in view of its unintended ecological impacts.

Fishing too can be conducted sustainably, but in recent decades has been so intensively pursued that many species, such as the once plentiful cod, have become endangered, fishing grounds such as the Grand Banks (off Newfoundland) are so depleted that fishing has had to be abandoned, and the entire ecological balance of the oceans has been placed at risk. An example has been the deaths of many dolphins in the course of fishing for tuna. Once again, consumers need to reflect on the ethical issues raised by the practices involved in food production.

6. Animal ethics versus environmental ethics

The examples just given show that animal ethics needs to expand to consider the far-reaching environmental implications of food rearing. However, some philosophers have seriously argued that animal welfarism and environmental ethics are fundamentally in conflict.[12]

Areas of apparent contrast include the following. Animal ethics is concerned about the welfare of individual creatures, whereas environmental ethics (as the section on Environmental Ethics attests) is often concerned with the survival of species, habitats and ecosystems. Animal ethics has among its objects the prevention of pain and suffering, whereas environmental ethics aims at a much broader range of goods and evils, and often regards pain as a side-effect of predation, one of the drivers of evolution. Further, animal ethics is usually focused on the ethics of individual consumption, while environmental ethics takes seriously the systems and structures on which life depends, and the importance of not subverting them.

With contrasts such as these in mind, J. Baird Callicott has suggested that these two branches of ethics (animals welfarism and environmental ethics) form two apices (or apexes) of an equilateral triangle, of which the third is traditional humanism, the kind of ethics that pays little or no heed to anything but the interests of human beings.[13] Later, however, he revised this view, in a paper entitled 'Animal Liberation and Environmental Ethics: Back Together Again'.[14] Without following the twists and turns of Callicott's thinking, we can recognize grounds on which conflict between these approaches can be avoided.

Thus environmental ethics need not and should not be entirely preoccupied with collectives such as species, habitats and ecosystems (ethical holism), since its adherents and participants need to reflect on how to interact with individuals as well, both human and non-human, and need a consistent and comprehensive ethic to enable them to do so. At the same time, animal ethics can include systems within its purview, wherever they are relevant. Since wild creatures depend on untrammeled wild ecosystems, animal ethicists are not committed to policing them to reduce suffering or premature death (as Mark Sagoff suggests[15]). Animal ethics is right to emphasize the importance of the avoidance of suffering (and if environmental ethicists sometimes disregard this, they do so at their peril), but it need not simultaneously disregard other dimensions of well-being.

Most importantly, neither of these branches of ethics should be seen as committed beforehand to a fragmentary ethic or value-theory. Environmental ethics need not be committed to ethical holism (as if there were no intrinsic value in the lives of individuals), while animal ethics need not be blind to the importance of the systems and structures within which individual consumption and the treatment of individual creatures take place. Animal ethics and environmental ethics are primarily concerned with different sectors of ethics, but they need not (for that reason or any other) be committed to different values. (The section on Environmental Ethics takes these matters further.)

Study questions

1. Is vegetarianism defensible on consequentialist grounds, on animal rights grounds, on other grounds, or not at all?
2. Does giving priority to human beings over other animals amount to speciesism?

Notes

1 Stanley Godlovitch, Roslind Godlovitch and John Harris (eds), *Animals, Men and Morals: An Enquiry into the Maltreatment of Non-humans*, New York: Taplinger, 1972.

2 Peter Singer, *Animal Liberation: A New Ethic for Our Treatment of Animals*, London: Jonathan Cape, 1976.

3 Tom Regan, *The Case for Animal Rights*, London: Routledge, 1983.

4 Tom Regan, 'Utilitarianism, Vegetarianism and Animal Rights', *Philosophy and Public Affairs*, 9, 1979–80, pp. 305–24.

5 Peter Singer, 'Utilitarianism and Vegetarianism', *Philosophy and Public Affairs*, 9, 1979–80, pp. 325–37.

6 Stephen R. L. Clark, *The Moral Status of Animals*, Oxford: Oxford University Press, 1977, pp. 4–5.

7 Mark Rowlands, *Animal Rights: A Philosophical Defence*, London: Macmillan, 1998.

8 R. G. Frey, *Rights, Killing and Suffering: Moral Vegetarianism and Applied Ethics*, Oxford: Blackwell, 1983.

9 Robin Attfield, 'Genetic Engineering: Can Unnatural Kinds Be Wronged?', in P. R. Wheale and R. M. McNally (eds), *Animal Genetic Engineering: Of Pigs, Oncomice and Men*, London: Pluto Press, 1995, pp. 201–8.

10 Frey, op. cit., pp. 179–80. Robin Attfield, 'Intrinsic Value and Transgenic Animals', in Andrew Johnson and Alan Holland (eds), *Animal Biotechnology and Ethics*, London: Chapman and Hall, 1998, pp. 172–89.

11 United Nations Food and Agriculture Organization, *Livestock's Long Shadow: Environmental Issues and Options*, Rome: FAO, 2006.

12 J. Baird Callicott, 'Animal Liberation: A Triangular Affair', *Environmental Ethics*, 2, 1980, pp. 311–28; reprinted in Callicott, *In Defense of the Land Ethic, Essays in Environmental Philosophy*, Albany; NY: State University of New York Press, 1989, pp. 15–38; Mark Sagoff, 'Animal Liberation and Environmental Ethics: Bad Marriage, Quick Divorce', *Osgoode Hall Law Journal*, 22, 1984, pp. 297–307; reprinted in David Schmidtz and Elizabeth Willott (eds), *Environmental Ethics: What Really Matters, What Really Works*, New York and Oxford: Oxford University Press, 2002, pp. 38–44.

13 Callicott, op. cit.

14 J. Baird Callicott, 'Animal Liberation and Environmental Ethics: Back Together Again', in Callicott, *In Defense of the Land Ethic*, pp. 49–59.

15 Sagoff, ibid., p. 42 (in Schmidtz and Willott).

References

Attfield, Robin, 'Genetic Engineering: Can Unnatural Kinds Be Wronged?', in P. R. Wheale and R. M. McNally (eds), *Animal Genetic Engineering: Of Pigs, Oncomice and Men*, London: Pluto Press, 1995, pp. 201–8.

—, 'Intrinsic Value and Transgenic Animals', in Andrew Johnson and Alan Holland (eds), *Animal Biotechnology and Ethics*, London: Chapman and Hall, 1998, pp. 172–89.

Callicott, J. Baird, 'Animal Liberation: A Triangular Affair', *Environmental Ethics*, 2, 1980, pp. 311–28.

—, 'Animal Liberation: A Triangular Affair', in Callicott, *In Defense of the Land Ethic, Essays in Environmental Philosophy*, Albany, NY: State University of New York Press, 1989, pp. 15–38.

—, 'Animal Liberation and Environmental Ethics: Back Together Again', in Callicott, *In Defense of the Land Ethic*, pp. 49–59.

Clark, Stephen R. L., *The Moral Status of Animals*, Oxford: Oxford University Press, 1977.

Frey, R. G., *Rights, Killing and Suffering: Moral Vegetarianism and Applied Ethics*, Oxford: Blackwell, 1983.

Godlovitch, Stanley, Roslind Godlovitch and John Harris (eds), *Animals, Men and Morals: An Enquiry into the Maltreatment of Non-humans*, New York: Taplinger, 1972.

Regan, Tom, 'Utilitarianism, Vegetarianism and Animal Rights', *Philosophy and Public Affairs*, 9, 1979–80, pp. 305–24.

—, *The Case for Animal Rights*, London: Routledge, 1983.

Rowlands, Mark, *Animal Rights: A Philosophical Defence*, London: Macmillan, 1998.

Sagoff, Mark, 'Animal Liberation and Environmental Ethics: Bad Marriage, Quick Divorce', *Osgoode Hall Law Journal*, 22, 1984, pp. 297–307.

—, 'Animal Liberation and Environmental Ethics: Bad Marriage, Quick Divorce', in David Schmidtz and Elizabeth Willott (eds), *Environmental Ethics: What Really Matters, What Really Works*, New York and Oxford: Oxford University Press, 2002, pp. 38–44.

Singer, Peter, *Animal Liberation: A New Ethic for Our Treatment of Animals*, London: Jonathan Cape, 1976.
—, 'Utilitarianism and Vegetarianism', *Philosophy and Public Affairs*, 9, 1979–80, pp. 325–37.
United Nations Food and Agriculture Organization, *Livestock's Long Shadow: Environmental Issues and Options*, Rome: FAO, 2006.

Section 4: Development ethics

1. The concept of development and related problems

In this section, the concept of development and the field of development ethics are introduced, together with related disagreements. We then turn to related ethical principles and debates, to the concept of sustainable development and related issues, and to issues surrounding the Millennium Development Goals.

'Development' here refers to social and economic development, as opposed to development of the biological or psychological kinds. Thus it is societies and countries that can develop (or fail to develop) in the relevant sense. Such development is best understood through the contrasting notion of 'under-development', which refers to a state of affairs in which most of the following evils reinforce one another: poverty, malnutrition, high rates of infant mortality, low life expectancy, high rates of morbidity, low rates of health care, widespread illiteracy and low average productivity. By contrast, development is both the process of moving away from these evils to more satisfactory levels of life expectancy, health, literacy and/or productivity, and the condition of a society which has largely attained more satisfactory levels, provided that development also involves some degree of autonomy and self-help on the part of the society in question, and some enhancement of social justice.

Since development involves moving or having moved away from evils, some writers take the view that it is itself necessarily good, and as such automatically favoured by all users of the term, and that the term 'development' is thus itself 'evaluative'.[1] But as we shall shortly see, some other people, far from regarding development as progressive, actually reject development as a goal and as a programme altogether. For there are many routes away from the evils mentioned above, of which most introduce new problems. Hence not all processes of development warrant our approval or deserve to be favoured as such. In every case somebody somewhere regards them as progressive, but in using the word 'development' we are not committed to agreeing with them.

Indeed a variety of values are embodied in development discourse. Accordingly, as Denis Goulet, one of the pioneers of development ethics, explained in 1977, development ethics deals with 'the ethical and value questions posed by development theory, planning and practice'.[2] The study of these debates and their implications became institutionalized with the establishment in 1984 of the International Development Ethics Association. So development ethics is a more recent branch of ethics than animal ethics or environmental ethics. However, some of the issues that it addresses had been current since the late 1940s.

The term 'under-development' was coined in 1949 by US President Harry Truman. 'We must embark', he declared, 'on a bold new program for making the benefits of our scientific advances and industrial progress available for the improvement and growth of under-developed areas', adding that this is 'a program of development' with no place for 'the old imperialism' or 'exploitation for foreign profit'.[3] But a condescending and exploitative approach is just what this programme has been accused of by the Latin American writer Gustavo Esteva, who remarks that two-thirds of the peoples of the world were now stigmatized as 'under-developed' and in need of American-led 'development', and that the underlying motive was to secure them from the threat of communism.[4]

While Esteva may have been right about Truman's motivation, Truman was surely right about the problems, for poverty, malnutrition, illiteracy and early deaths were widespread and self-reinforcing problems across the entire former colonial world, affecting billions of people. Truman's model of development is also open to criticism, with its implicit suggestion that economic growth and technological investment will eventually trickle down through society and enhance the lives of the poor; this is the model that development ethicists would later castigate as unrealistic, indulgent towards large corporations and objectionably indifferent towards oppressed people. Nevertheless Truman's core concept of development as the process of movement away from these evils and the state of society where they are overcome, far from being perverse, was to prove indispensable, and to be welcomed at the United Nations and across the world, even by people inclined to reject his model and his programme.

Accordingly we need to distinguish the concept of development from conceptions of it, whether capitalist, communist, nationalist, religious or eclectic. In 1986, the United Nations proclaimed that everyone has a right to development, and in its Declaration on the Right to Development defined 'development' as follows:

> Development is a comprehensive economic, social, cultural and political process, which aims at the constant improvement of the well-being of the entire population and of all its inhabitants on the basis of their active, free and meaningful participation in development and in the fair distribution of the resulting benefits therefrom.[5]

A strong merit of this definition is its emphasis on (and requirement of) the engagement and participation of the entire population in development. A weakness is its inclusion in the definition of the term to be defined (in the phrase 'participation in development'), for definitions that do this are circular, failing to explain the term to be defined; but this fault could easily be cured by replacing this phrase with 'participation in this process'. A more serious weakness is the absence of any mention of the priority within development of poverty reduction. However, the Declaration is overwhelmingly important because of its global recognition of the moral entitlement of all peoples to freedom from under-development and its evils, and to participation in the development process. (Use another term such as 'poverty' if you object to the term 'under-development'.) Without endorsing Truman's model or programme, the United Nations thus endorsed his core concept and also its moral urgency.

2. Hunger, poverty, need and ethics

Much earlier, in the inaugural number of *Philosophy and Public Affairs*, Peter Singer presented his Famine Relief Argument, defending a principle which was later much discussed by development ethicists. According to this principle, 'if we can prevent something bad happening without sacrificing anything of comparable moral importance, we ought to do so'. In conjunction with the facts of widespread famine and of the disposable income available to affluent people, this implies that affluent people should use this income to send aid and reduce starvation elsewhere in the world.[6] Singer's principle, while compatible with consequentialism, could also be endorsed by some deontologists. But in making famine relief an obligation, it was widely held to be unduly demanding, and to be representing supererogatory acts as obligatory.

Yet if the issues had been as Singer presented them, there would have been a strong case for his view of obligations. But, as David Crocker has argued, the issues need to be reinterpreted, not least because famine arises from long-term malnutrition, and this is the underlying problem in need of a remedy.[7] Besides, as Jean Drèze and Amartya Sen cogently claim, the remedies for persistent malnutrition differ from those for hunger, and involve institutional change rather than emergency relief.[8] There again, both famine and chronic hunger turn out not only to be remediable but also to be preventable;[9] if so, our obligations may relate to prevention as much as to cure. In any case, reflection on hunger needs to recognize that hunger is often due not to lack of food but to inability to acquire it; people are often hungry when food is plentiful, because they cannot secure it. So its prevention involves redistribution of resources, and not invariably moving food and people into close proximity.[10]

Thus, where the goal is the well-being of a country's entire population, the ethical debate needed to shift from focusing on famine relief and the ethics of aid to the ethics of development, including not only international aid but also the development goals pursued by developing countries themselves. This stress on active participation is reflected in Crocker's revised account of development (based on the thought of Sen) as 'a process of change that protects, restores, strengthens and expands people's valued and valuable capabilities'.[11] Perceptive readers will notice here a resemblance to the account of the good life in terms of the development of essential capacities, presented in the section on 'Worthwhile Life and Meaningful Work'.

Not all development ethicists make capabilities central. Some, for example, prioritize basic needs,[12] while others such as Jim Nickel stress human rights,[13] While these concepts have their place (particularly when accounts of justice are required), the language of capabilities has the advantage of foregrounding the activities which both constitute well-being and are essential for participatory development. The capabilities approach of Amartya Sen has itself been developed by Martha Nussbaum and David Crocker as fundamental within development ethics.[14]

There is some common ground between this line and the Kantian approach to development issues presented by Onora O'Neill in *Faces of Hunger*,[15] which underlines how extreme poverty undermines the exercise of rational agency, and thus the proper functioning of human beings. O'Neill argues cogently in support of voluntary population policies (discussed in the section on Re-emergence), but mistakenly assumes that famines cannot be prevented.

We should also remember the persistent problems for Kantianism, depicted in the section on 'Some Kantian Themes'.

Others have drawn on the contractarian approach in support of international development. John Rawls did not derive international obligations from the original position and the rules that would there be chosen, regarding it (in *A Theory of Justice* and elsewhere) as a model for participants in one and the same land or society, rather than for global society (see the section on The Re-emergence of Applied Ethics). But (as that section goes on to relate), his model of a fair bargaining situation has allowed others to use it to study international equity and to criticize the current state of international relations;[16] for if we could choose the rules of international relations and international trade and finance, we would be unlikely to endorse current practices, which have often had the effect of diverting resources from developing to developed countries, and thus of entrenching poverty.

However, Rawls' list of 'basic goods' (such as liberty and self-respect) needs to be supplemented as an account of human good by the capacities of the capabilities approach. Besides, the limitations of contractarianism (relating to its treatment of future generations and of non-human creatures) indicate that a theory with a broader understanding of moral standing, as well as a broader value-theory, is needed, such as the biocentric consequentialism defended in other chapters of this book. The centrality of provision for future generations to the development of all human societies is also central to the topic of sustainable development, to which we now turn.

3. Sustainable development

In 1987, the Brundtland Report (the report of the World Commission on Environment and Development) was published under the title *Our Common Future*, blending developmental and environmental issues in a global programme of sustainable development. 'Sustainable development' was defined as development that 'meets the needs of the present without compromising the ability of future generations to meet their own needs'.[17] Successive chapters applied this concept to sectors such as population, food, conservation of species and energy generation.

The above definition turns out to underdefine 'sustainable development'. Such development, as the Report goes on to make clear, does not merely refrain from placing obstacles in the way of future generations, but actively promotes sustainable practices (of sustainable farming, renewable energy generation, etc.) the benefits of which are intended to endure through successive generations. Further, sustainable development, as it also makes clear, involves development that is sustainable not only economically but also socially and environmentally, as the chapter on species and ecosystems proceeds to emphasize. In places, the Report (despite the frequent assertions of commentators to the contrary) even rejects anthropocentrism and endorses the intrinsic value of non-human creatures.[18] Those focusing on the central definition have been prone to neglect these themes, although the definition of another report partially makes good the omissions by defining 'sustainable development' as 'improving the quality of life while living within the carrying capacity of supporting ecosystems'.[19]

Altogether the Brundtland Report conveyed a message of hope that environmental problems and the problems of under-development could be tackled and surmounted both simultaneously and recurrently. Yet we should not assume that any process that is sustainable is thereby morally desirable or just. Sustainable processes can be inegalitarian or otherwise defective (think of slavery), rather as processes of development can be.[20]

Five years later, a World Summit was held at Rio de Janeiro, at which over 180 nations endorsed sustainable development and agreed to implement it in their own national policies. The Rio Declaration (1992), however, was explicitly anthropocentric; there again, different countries were soon stressing different aspects (some development and some sustainability). Further, the global endorsement given to sustainable development had the result that the governments and corporations of wealthy states attempted to reinterpret 'sustainable development' in ways that suited their own interests. It was, for example, frequently treated as equivalent to 'sustainable growth', despite the chasm of divergence between economic growth and development (as defined above). This tendency led in turn to the criticism that 'sustainable development' meant 'business as usual', and to Esteva's view that it amounted to a mere repackaging of the ideology of Harry Truman.[21]

But adherents of sustainable development (often now referred to as 'sustainability') are free to remind the revisionists and the sceptics that they can consistently take into account the interests of future generations (without discounting them as conventional economics does) and the good of non-human creatures (just as the Brundtland Report itself does), and at the same time plan sustainably to mitigate problems such as poverty, deforestation and climate change.[22] The Rio Conference inaugurated sequences of conferences on both of these latter themes, and the one on climate change later issued in the

Kyoto accord of 1997 (see the section on Environmental Ethics). Sustainable development enjoys the unusual status of a radical concept to which most governments in the world at least nominally subscribe. Its supporters are thus well placed to insist on its practical realization.

4. The Millennium Development Goals

At the turn of the millennium, the United Nations further agreed to eight Millennium Development Goals (MDGs), to be attained by 2015.[23] The goals range from halving extreme poverty to halting the spread of HIV/AIDS, ensuring environmental sustainability and providing universal primary education. Just one of these goals, to halve the incidence of global poverty, is likely to be attained in part, mainly because of the economic rise of India and China, but the others are almost certain to be unfulfilled.

Major structural changes at international level will be required to fulfil these goals, and to transcend them by discharging the obligation (which would still exist even if they were to succeed) to prevent avoidable poverty, a goal far beyond the reach of the MDGs. Integrated policies of development, including policies for stabilizing and sustaining population levels (see the later part of the first section of this chapter), are likely to be needed. One proposal is for the recognition of 'Greenhouse Development Rights' for every living human being, and a related plan to tax everyone with income above a certain level, and require governments to pay this amount to a global authority authorized to supervise and fund both development, climate change mitigation and adaptation to such climate change as cannot be prevented.[24]

Whether this ambitious plan for new global institutions is the best strategy is open to debate. It may prove better to have separate authorities charged to supervise development on the one hand and climate change mitigation and adaptation on the other. But the proposal serves at least to stress the importance of supporting some form of institutional change to satisfy the obligations of all agents in a position to make a difference, both in matters of climate change and in matters of development.

We also have responsibilities to consider personal and domestic lifestyle changes in both these causes, and to generate a cultural climate in which large national and international changes are more likely to be supported and thus implemented. Ultimately, though, what will be required is agreement about these matters at government level, and the establishment of new global institutions with the funds and powers necessary for the scale of these unfinished tasks.

Study questions

1. Should human capabilities be central to our understanding of development?
2. How is the idea of sustainable development best interpreted?

Notes

1 Nigel Dower, 'Development Ethics', in Ruth Chadwick (ed.), *Encyclopedia of Applied Ethics*, San Diego: Academic Press (4 vols), vol. 1, pp. 755–66.

2 Denis Goulet, *The Uncertain Promise*, New York: Apex Press, 1977; this passage is quoted by Dower, ibid., at p. 756.

3 Harry Truman, speech of 20 January 1949, quoted in Gustavo Esteva, 'Development', in Wolfgang Sachs (ed.), *The Development Dictionary: A Guide to Knowledge as Power*, London: Zed Books, 1992, pp. 6–25.

4 Esteva, ibid.

5 United Nations, Preamble to 'Declaration on the Right to Development', quoted in Nigel Dower, *World Ethics: The New Agenda*, Edinburgh: Edinburgh University Press, 1998, pp. 152–3.

6 Peter Singer, 'Famine, Affluence and Morality', *Philosophy & Public Affairs*, 1, 1972, pp. 229–43.

7 David Crocker, 'Hunger, Capability and Development', in W. Aiken and H. LaFollette (eds), *World Hunger and Morality*, 2nd edn, 1996, pp. 211–30; reprinted in Des Gasper and Asuncion Lera St. Clair (eds), *Development Ethics*, Farnham, UK and Burlington, VT: Ashgate, 2010, pp. 383–402.

8 Jean Drèze and Amartya Sen, *Hunger and Public Action*, Oxford: Clarendon Press, 1989, pp. 7–8.

9 Crocker, op. cit., p. 388 (Gasper and St. Clair).

10 Crocker, ibid., pp. 389–91.

11 Crocker, ibid., p. 410.

12 Paul Streeten, with S. J. Berki, M. Haq, N. Hicks and F. Stewart, *First Things First: Meeting Basic Needs in Developing Countries*, Oxford: Oxford University Press, 1981.

13 James W. Nickel, 'Rights and Development', in Kenneth Aman (ed.), *Ethical Principles for Development: Needs, Capacities or Rights?*, Montclair, NJ: Institute for Critical Thinking, 1991, pp. 200–12.

14 David Crocker, 'Functioning and Capability: The Foundations of Sen's and Nussbaum's Development Ethic', *Political Theory*, 20, 1992, pp. 584–612.

15 Onora O'Neill, *Faces of Hunger: An Essay on Poverty, Hunger and Development*, London: Allen & Unwin, 1986.

16 Brian Barry, *The Liberal Theory of Justice: A Critical Examination of the Principal Doctrines in A Theory of Justice by John Rawls*, Oxford: Clarendon Press, 1973; Charles Beitz, *Political Theory and International Relations*, Princeton, NJ: Princeton University Press, 1979.

17 World Commission on Environment and Development (WCED), *Our Common Future*, Oxford and New York: Oxford University Press, 1987, p. 43.

18 WCED., ibid., pp. 13, 57, 147, 148, 155.

19 International Union for the Conservation of Nature, *Caring for the Earth: A Strategy for Sustainable Living*, Gland, Switzerland: IUCN/UNEP/WWF, 1991. For discussion of problems raised by this definition, see Robin Attfield, *Environmental Ethics: An Overview for the Twenty-First Century*, Cambridge: Polity and Malden, MA: Blackwell, 2003, pp. 135–6.

20 See Robin Attfield and Barry Wilkins, 'Sustainability', *Environmental Values*, 3, 1994, pp. 155–8.

21 Esteva, op. cit., p. 16.

22 Adherents include Paul Ekins, a lone voice among the contributors to Wolfgang Sachs (ed.), *Global Ecology*, whose view is that sustainable development remains a possibility, but involves restructuring the world. See Paul Ekins, 'Making Development Sustainable', in Wolfgang Sachs (ed.), *Global Ecology*, London and Atlantic Highlands, NJ: Zed Books, 1993, pp. 91–103.

23 United Nations, 'United Nations Millennium Declaration', 2000: www.un.org/millenniumgoals/.

24 Paul Baer, Tom Athanasiou and Sivan Kartha, *The Right to Development in a Climate Constrained World: The Greenhouse Development Rights Framework*, EcoEquity, 2007: www.ecoequity.org/docs/TheGDRsFramework.pdf.

References

Attfield, Robin, *Environmental Ethics: An Overview for the Twenty-First Century*, Cambridge: Polity and Malden, MA: Blackwell, 2003.

Attfield, Robin and Barry Wilkins, 'Sustainability', *Environmental Values*, 3, 1994, pp. 155–8.

Baer, Paul, Tom Athanasiou and Sivan Kartha, *The Right to Development in a Climate Constrained World: The Greenhouse Development Rights Framework*, EcoEquity, 2007: www.ecoequity.org/docs/TheGDRsFramework.pdf.

Barry, Brian, *The Liberal Theory of Justice: A Critical Examination of the Principal Doctrines in A Theory of Justice by John Rawls*, Oxford: Clarendon Press, 1973.

Beitz, Charles, *Political Theory and International Relations*, Princeton, NJ: Princeton University Press, 1979.

Crocker, David, 'Functioning and Capability: The Foundations of Sen's and Nussbaum's Development Ethic', *Political Theory*, 20, 1992, pp. 584–612.

—, 'Hunger, Capability and Development', in W. Aiken and H. LaFollette (eds), *World Hunger and Morality*, 2nd edn, 1996, pp. 211–30.

—, 'Hunger, Capability and Development', in Des Gasper and Asuncion Lera St. Clair (eds), *Development Ethics*, Farnham, UK and Burlington, VT: Ashgate, 2010, pp. 383–402.

Dower, Nigel, 'Development Ethics', in Ruth Chadwick (ed.), *Encyclopedia of Applied Ethics*, San Diego: Academic Press (4 vols), 1998, vol. 1, pp. 755–66.

—, *World Ethics: The New Agenda*, Edinburgh: Edinburgh University Press, 1998.

Drèze, Jean and Amartya Sen, *Hunger and Public Action*, Oxford: Clarendon Press, 1989.

Ekins, Paul, 'Making Development Sustainable', in Wolfgang Sachs (ed.), *Global Ecology*, London and Atlantic Highlands, NJ: Zed Books, 1993, pp. 91–103.

Esteva, Gustavo, 'Development', in Wolfgang Sachs (ed.), *The Development Dictionary: A Guide to Knowledge as Power*, London: Zed Books, 1992, pp. 6–25.

Goulet, Denis, *The Uncertain Promise*, New York: Apex Press, 1977.
International Union for the Conservation of Nature, *Caring for the Earth: A Strategy for Sustainable Living*, Gland, Switzerland: IUCN/UNEP/WWF, 1991.
Nickel, James W., 'Rights and Development', in Kenneth Aman (ed.), *Ethical Principles for Development: Needs, Capacities or Rights?*, Montclair, NJ: Institute for Critical Thinking, 1991, pp. 200–12.
O'Neill, Onora, *Faces of Hunger: An Essay on Poverty, Hunger and Development*, London: Allen & Unwin, 1986.
Singer, Peter, 'Famine, Affluence and Morality', *Philosophy & Public Affairs*, 1, 1972, pp. 229–43.
Streeten, Paul, with S. J. Berki, M. Haq, N. Hicks and F. Stewart, *First Things First: Meeting Basic Needs in Developing Countries*, Oxford: Oxford University Press, 1981.
United Nations, *Declaration on the Right to Development*, New York: United Nations, 1986.
—, 'United Nations Millennium Declaration', 2000: www.un.org/millenniumgoals/.
World Commission on Environment and Development (WCED), *Our Common Future*, Oxford and New York: Oxford University Press, 1987.

Section 5: Environmental ethics

1. Ecological problems and the origins of environmental ethics

This section, after introducing ecological problems, covers the rise of environmental ethics in the 1970s, and then moves in turn to related theories of value and to normative theories. After a brief discussion of the causes of the problems, it turns to some relevant environmental policies, which prove to include climate change adaptation and mitigation.

Ecological problems are problems arising from humanity's dealings with natural systems.[1] Accordingly, without pausing at present to reflect on what makes them problems, we can plausibly cite as ecological problems pollution, deforestation, the depletion of natural resources, losses of wildlife and natural habitats, the degradation of cultivable land and the growth of deserts. Climate change, in the forms of ozone depletion, acid rain and greenhouse gas emissions[2] can cogently be added to this list. Population increases are sometimes regarded in the same light, but, despite their connection with modern technology, can better be understood as an aspect of the problem of under-development (see the later part of the first section of this chapter).

Most if not all of these problems derive in part from the technology of the late twentieth century (that of the period after 1945) and its commercial exploitation. So it is not surprising that environmentalism (campaigns to preserve tracts of the natural environment and of its wildlife) originated in this period, in works like Aldo Leopold's *A Sand County Almanac* (critical of the degradation of 'the land' and its community) and Rachel Carson's *Silent Spring* (critical of herbicides and pesticides).[3]

Philosophers and social theorists had, it is true, been protesting at deforestation long before: among them Plato in the *Critias* in the fourth century BCE, against that of Attica (in Greece), and John Evelyn, in *Silva, or a Discourse on Forest Trees*, in the seventeenth century against that of England.[4] But it was in the early 1970s that environmental philosophy (with its concern for issues of value and ethics and underlying issues about reality) was born.

Thus the Australian philosopher Richard Routley presented his paper 'Is There a Need for a New, an Environmental Ethic?' at the World Congress of Philosophy at Varna, Bulgaria in 1973, later revised jointly by Val Routley and himself as 'Human Chauvinism and Environmental Ethics'.[5] The pioneering monograph of their celebrated compatriot John Passmore, *Man's Responsibility for Nature*, appeared in 1974 (for some years the only monograph on environmental philosophy).[6] In America, Holmes Rolston III, destined to become 'the father of environmental ethics', published in *Ethics* in 1975 'Is There an Ecological Ethic?'.[7] Meanwhile Arne Naess, a veteran philosopher from Norway, had produced in *Inquiry* in 1973 'The Shallow and the Deep, Long-Range Ecology Movement: A Summary'.[8] (Later, in 1990, Rolston was to found the International Society for Environmental Ethics.)

A common strand of the work of the Routleys, Rolston and Naess (though not of Passmore) is that moral standing should be recognized to apply to non-human creatures, and intrinsic value should be located in their well-being as well as that of human beings (rejection, that is, of anthropocentrism in favour of a non-anthropocentric value-theory and ethic: see the section on Moral Standing, Value and Intrinsic Value). This was the core of Routley's proposed new environmental ethic and of Rolston's defence of values in nature, and part of the Deep Ecology platform championed by Naess. Naess also advocated taking into account the environmental problems of poor (as well as of rich) countries, and the needs of future generations as well as of the present. (These themes too have been endorsed above: see the first and the previous sections of this chapter.) While not every aspect of the Deep Ecology platform is equally defensible (such as its advocacy of considerably reducing the human population), these proved to be themes crucial to a defensible comprehensive ethic, applicable both to inter-species issues and to inter-human issues as well.

2. Ecocentrism, anthropocentrism and biocentrism

Several of these founders of environmental ethics recognized the moral standing not only of individual non-human creatures but also of ecosystems (such as mountains and rivers) and of species. In other words, they favoured replacing anthropocentrism with 'ecocentrism', the normative stance that holds that species and ecosystems have a good independent of that of their component members, and as such carry moral standing, and that their attaining this good has intrinsic value.[9]

Some of the supporters of this holistic approach (i.e. an approach focused on wholes rather than on individuals) were influenced by Aldo Leopold's Land Ethic. Leopold regarded the land as an interactive community, including both living and non-living components, a community which warranted respect as a whole. Passmore responded that members of communities must be capable of awareness of mutual obligations, and that our attitudes to human communities cannot be carried over to ecological 'communities', where the term 'community', if applicable at all, does not imply mutual recognition among the members.[10]

Leopold also claimed that the core of ethics is to be found in the integrity, stability and beauty of the biotic community; actions are right when they tend to preserve such integrity, stability and beauty, and wrong when they tend otherwise.[11] But, while this is a salutary reminder to take into consideration the impacts of our actions on natural systems, it cannot be regarded as a cogent criterion of rightness. Thus the breaking of promises makes little or no difference to the integrity (etc.) of the biosphere, but cannot therefore be regarded as morally neutral, any more than homicide can.

Yet in the hands of the philosopher J. Baird Callicott, the Land Ethic was worked up into an ethical system, with concentric circles of obligation on the part of human beings towards others (whether human or non-human), some of them being more central and others less so.[12] Not surprisingly, this system has been accused of instability,[13] and remains open to criticisms from philosophers of a less holistic approach, including those of a more consequentialist tendency.

Another supporter of a holistic or ecocentric approach is John Rodman, whose words well capture one kind of experience of nature:

> I need only to stand in the middle of a clear-cut forest, a strip-mined hillside, a defoliated jungle, or a dammed canyon to feel uneasy with assumptions that could yield the conclusion that no human action can make any difference to the welfare of anything but sentient animals.[14]

Many of us have undergone similar experiences. Yet this evocative passage, penned as a criticism of the sentientism of Peter Singer and others, at best shows that moral standing extends more extensively than just to sentient creatures. (Thus moral standing could belong to all living beings, as biocentrism claims.) It does not show that ecological systems have moral standing as such. Such systems could be valuable not in themselves but because of the living creatures that depend on them.

A reaction to the first, non-anthropocentric, wave of environmental ethicists involved a return to anthropocentrism, present already in Passmore's work, despite his occasional sympathy for sentientism. Characteristic arguments from this school of thought include the claim that since all judgements about right action are human judgements, their criterion must be human interests. But this reasoning is fallacious. Just as each person can judge and act to further the interests of others, and is not restricted to their own alone, so human beings are not restricted to taking into account human interests alone. We can reasonably adhere to what Frederick Ferré has called 'perspectival anthropocentrism' (the view that moral judgements are invariably made from a human perspective),[15] without moving to axiological anthropocentrism (an anthropocentrism of values), the view (rightly rejected by Mary Midgley in the same volume) that only human interests matter, and nothing else.[16]

Another argument deployed by anthropocentrists is that no practical difference is made for policies like wildlife preservation by the adoption of non-anthropocentric values rather than anthropocentric ones, and that since it is easier for environmentalists to secure support for the latter, they should abandon talk of the former.[17] While this is a pragmatic argument, which does not in any case show that the well-being of non-human creatures lacks intrinsic value, it is worth commenting that its premise about policies is mistaken. For if non-human interests add reasons or grounds for action, they will sometimes justify action or policies that would be unjustified otherwise, ranging from legislation against cruelty to animals, via the establishment of seal sanctuaries, to the preservation of species that have no known benefits to humanity.

From an anthropocentric perspective, issues such as cruelty to animals may not appear to be problems at all, for awareness of problems depends on one's value-theory. That is why what makes pollution, deforestation and the rest *problems* could not be considered until now. Armed with a broader value-theory, we are equipped to grasp why these problems are problems, and if necessary to identify new ones, hitherto unrecognized.

Thus there are grounds for recognizing the moral standing not only of human beings (as anthropocentrism does) and of sentient creatures (as sentientism does) but of all living creatures, as does biocentrism, introduced and defended above in the section on Moral Standing, Value and Intrinsic Value. Kenneth Goodpaster's argument, cited in that section, well supports acceptance of the moral standing of whatever has an independent good of its own. That conclusion need not, however, commit us to ecocentrism, if the arguments presented both here and there against the moral standing of species and of ecosystems are accepted. Since future creatures are among those able to be affected by present actions, they too will obviously be included among the bearers of moral standing.

However, biocentrism can be held in deontological, consequentialism and virtue-ethical forms (and possibly even in contractarian ones). So a little thought should now be given to their consistency and tenability.

3. Related theories of normative ethics

Rawlsian contractarianism seems an unpromising framework for an ethics suited to environmental concerns, because of its inescapable anthropocentrism. But, as was mentioned in the section on Animal Ethics, Mark Rowlands has suggested relating it to inter-species ethics as follows. We adjust Rawls' original position so that the participants are unaware not only of their life prospects but also of what species they will belong to, and they have to select rules for inter-species behaviour on this basis.[18] If this thought-experiment could be carried through, contractarianism would have been emancipated from anthropocentrism, and the emergent rules might be ones well-suited to an environmental ethic.

However, it is unclear how sense can be made of individuals who have no idea of what their own good consists in deciding on anything; and yet entities ignorant of what species will be theirs would precisely lack this knowledge. Unfortunately, then, this thought-experiment is an incoherent suggestion, and any coherent form of contractarianism must be regarded as open to the charge of anthropocentrism after all.

Deontology is more promising, and James Sterba has put forward a biocentric version of this kind of approach, the principles of which allow any species to resort to self-defence in certain circumstances.[19] These principles might be more cogent if they recognized the different capacities of different species for responsible action; but deontologists could take this point on board and adjust their principles accordingly. The underlying problem is that the principles are selected on a basis of intuitive reasonableness, but lack the grounding that a consequentialist appeal to the promotion and preservation of value allows.

Virtue ethics is another promising kind of approach. Some of its supporters, such as Thomas Hill, reject the intrinsic value of non-sentient creatures and their flourishing, and locate the wrongness of destroying tracts of nature in the infringement of an ideal of virtuous living, which includes humility, gratitude and sensitivity.[20] However, if there were no such value in the natural creatures preserved from destruction, it is hard to see what makes these virtues virtuous, even when they inspire acts of preservation. Other virtue ethicists, such as Philip Cafaro, recognize intrinsic value in non-sentient life, and can relate the human virtues they commend to living a good human life.[21] The problem with this approach is that we need a concept of rightness independent of what the virtuous person would do (see the section on Virtue Ethics), and that both virtuous dispositions and right actions need to be grounded in the difference they make in terms of what there is reason to promote or preserve, or, in other words, to value.

But this is just what a consequentialist approach to ethics offers. For this approach, the promotion or preservation of value is what underpins the virtues that the virtue ethicist emphasizes, as Dale Jamieson has argued[22] (see the section on Practice-Consequentialism and Virtue-Consequentialism). This approach also facilitates an integrated ethical theory, able to explain rightness independently of virtue, in a manner applicable to inter-human, international and inter-generational dealings, as well as to specifically environmental contexts. So, as long as other problems can be avoided (see the whole chapter on Normative Ethics), a blend of biocentrism and a consequentialism of the Total View variety (see the first section of this chapter) seems the most promising approach.

4. Causes of ecological problems

Several theories have been proposed of the causes of ecological problems, supplementing the implicit reference to technology introduced when these problems were defined as arising from humanity's dealings with natural systems. Having discussed these theories elsewhere,[23] I cannot cover them here. Suffice it to say that theories that ascribe ecological problems to capitalism or population or patriarchy never contrive to explain all the problems, and thus need to be supplemented, whatever initial merits they may have.

In any case, ecological problems seem to have more than one kind of origin. On the one hand, some arise from poverty, and include the pollution of the sewers of many cities of the developing world, and the destruction of nearby forests as poor people are driven to seek firewood for fuel. These are basically problems of under-development, for which sustainable development (see the section on Development Ethics) would be a remedy. On the other hand most arise from high technology, whether in its capitalist form (as when international shipping lanes are invariably infected with massive pollution) or in its Communist form (as when the Aral Sea in central Asia was largely turned into a toxic desert by ill-conceived efforts to irrigate and fertilize cotton plantations nearby). Sustainability is again relevant to rectifying these problems too.

There are also problems involving the rich world exploiting developing countries, as when toxic wastes are deposited in coastal African states, with little or no concern for the resulting health hazards. Here the solution is not sustainability but cessation, brought on by embargos and boycotts of those responsible, if necessary. Generally, consumers in the developed world need to reflect on the practices they are encouraging through what they choose to consume.

There is a widespread myth that ecological problems are due to Judaeo-Christian attitudes and assumptions, a myth originally propagated by Lynn White Jr. in a famous paper in *Science*.[24] If his claims were true, they would be relevant to a book on ethics, since the ethical teachings of Judaism and of Christianity would be put in question (whether as anthropocentric or as heedless of the natural world). In fact, his claims mischaracterize both Judaism and Christianity, besides exaggerating the significance of certain changes of the early Middle Ages in which he finds the origins of the problems.[25] Instead, the longstanding approach in which people are seen as stewards of the world of nature, prevalent among modern Jews, Christians and Muslims too, far from causing the problems, plausibly contributes to their solution.

5. Some related policies

The case for sustainable development has already been presented in the section on Development Ethics. Here it should be added that strong sustainability, which resists the substitution of artificial resources, such as mines and smelters, for natural resources such as forests, will be favoured by biocentrists, rather than weak sustainability, which allows unlimited substitution.[26]

Another key policy, both for nations and for the international community, is the preservation of biological diversity (or biodiversity), that is, efforts to preserve endangered species, sub-species and habitats. Biocentrists will support this policy to ensure that rare species will have living members in the future, but also for the sake of the benefits to humanity of the intactness of wild habitats. Such benefits include the preservation of watersheds, possibilities for finding medicines, and opportunities for recreation and for scientific research.[27]

It should also be added that, since poverty causes population growth and, relatedly, increased pressure on the natural world, the project of preserving tracts of nature is not achievable without ensuring that human beings are fed and their basic needs met.[28] To use a different vocabulary, sustainability requires development, at least in developing countries.

However, both humanity and many other species are increasingly threatened by climate change in the form of global warming, and the principles of almost every ethical system, including those defended in this book, support measures both to mitigate climate change and to adapt to such climate change as is by now inevitable. Adaptation in developing countries such as Bangladesh involves considerable aid and technology transfer on the part of developed countries to avert both flooding and the salination of waterways; it also involves effective international agreements on the sharing of the water of major rivers such as the Ganges and the Brahmaputra. But the underlying problem will remain unaddressed in the absence of measures to arrest or mitigate global warming.

6. Climate change mitigation

By emitting greenhouse gases such as carbon dioxide and methane, humanity is responsible for an alarming increase in levels of carbon dioxide and other greenhouse gases in the atmosphere. The most obvious impact consists in increases of average temperatures above pre-industrial levels, which can only with great difficulty be limited to (at best) 2° centigrade. Even that increase means the melting of large areas of polar ice caps and of many glaciers, rises of sea levels, and threats to the inhabitants of deltas, coastlines and small islands. It also means the spread of diseases like malaria (to higher altitudes and higher latitudes), threats to species whose habitats are lost, and the creation of hundreds of millions of environmental refugees. Freak weather events, such as droughts, wildfires, floods and hurricanes, are already on the increase.[29]

To prevent things becoming worse still, it is vital that greenhouse gas emissions, including crucially carbon emissions, be curtailed. (Even climate change sceptics who admit that there is some reason to believe that global warming is due in part to humanity should endorse this view, in accordance with the Precautionary Principle: see the section on Practice-Consequentialism and Virtue-Consequentialism.) This will involve early and consistent action at individual, local, national and international levels. Reaching a global agreement on emissions mitigation has become indispensable and urgent.

Here is one possible basis for such an agreement. The annual total of permissible emissions is calculated, and emissions entitlements are then shared equally among everyone alive (at a date to be agreed). Entitlements are then allocated to countries in proportion to their population. The total is progressively reduced to ensure that average temperatures rise no more than the agreed target. Countries not using their full entitlement are then allowed to sell it to those requiring an additional entitlement.[30] This system, which is known for obvious reasons as Contraction and Convergence, would redistribute resources, and trading could be limited so that no country can sell emissions required to satisfy the basic needs of its inhabitants.

As Peter Singer has argued, this system can be supported by consequentialists, because of its considerable benefits to humanity and other sentient creatures.[31] Biocentrists can readily endorse this verdict. However, it is more important that there should be a global agreement than that it should adopt this particular shape.

It is also crucial that whatever agreement is reached it is then implemented in each country. We all need to reflect on the contribution of our consumption and our travel to carbon emissions, and as individuals and households to modify our lifestyles accordingly. Such decisions also affect the cultural climate, and make it more feasible for governments to play their part. This is, perhaps, a fitting note on which to conclude our study of environmental ethics.

Study questions

1. What is anthropocentrism, and should it be avoided?
2. Explain and appraise Contraction and Convergence as a basis for an international agreement on global warming.

Notes

1 This is a modified version of the definition given in John Passmore, *Man's Responsibility for Nature*, London: Duckworth, 1974, at p. 43.

2 Intergovernmental Panel on Climate Change (IPCC), *Climate Change 1995: Economic and Social Dimensions of Climate Change*, Cambridge: Cambridge University Press, 1996; IPCC, *Climate Change 2007: The Physical Science Basis*, http://www.ipcc.ch/SPM2feb07.pdf.

3 Aldo Leopold, *A Sand County Almanac and Sketches Here and There*, New York: Oxford University Press, 1949; Rachel Carson, *Silent Spring*, London: Hamish Hamilton, 1963.

4 For Plato, see Passmore, ibid., pp. 175–6; for John Evelyn, see Clarence J. Glacken, *Traces on the Rhodian Shore: Nature and Culture in Western Thought from Ancient Times to the End of the Eighteenth Century*, Berkeley, LA and London: University of California Press, 1967, pp. 485–94.

5 Richard Routley (later Sylvan), 'Is There a Need for a New, an Environmental Ethic?' *Proceedings of the XVth World Congress of Philosophy*, Varna, Bulgaria, 1973, pp. 205–210; reprinted in Robin Attfield (ed.), *The Ethics of the Environment*, Farnham, UK and Burlington, VT, Ashgate: 2008, pp. 3–12; Richard Routley and Val Routley (later Plumwood), 'Human Chauvinism and Environmental Ethics', in Don Mannison, Michael McRobbie and Richard Routley (eds), *Environmental Philosophy*, Canberra: Australian National University, 1980, pp. 96–189.

6 Passmore, ibid., see note 1 above.

7 Holmes Rolston III 'Is There an Ecological Ethic?', *Ethics*, 1975, pp. 93–109; reprinted in Robin Attfield (ed.), *The Ethics of the Environment*, pp. 13–29.

8 Arne Naess, 'The Shallow and the Deep, Long-Range Ecology Movement: A Summary', *Inquiry*, 1973, 95–100.

9 Robin Attfield, *Environmental Ethics: An Overview for the Twenty-First Century*, Cambridge, UK and Malden, MA: Polity, 2003, pp. 192–3.

10 Passmore, op. cit., p. 116.

11 Leopold, op. cit., pp. 224–5.

12 J. Baird Callicott, *In Defense of the Land Ethic, Essays in Environmental Philosophy*, Albany, NY: State University of New York Press, 1989.

13 See Y. S. Lo, 'The Land Ethic and Callicott's Ethical System', *Inquiry*, 44, 2001, pp. 331–58; reprinted in Robin Attfield (ed.), *The Ethics of the Environment*, Farnham, UK and Burlington, VT, Ashgate: 2008, pp. 133–60; Darren Domsky, 'The Inadequacy of Callicott's Communitarianism', *Environmental Ethics*, 28, 2006, pp. 395–412; reprinted in Attfield, ibid., pp. 161–78.

14 John Rodman, 'The Liberation of Nature', *Inquiry*, 20, 1977, pp. 83–145, at p. 89.

15 Frederick Ferré, 'Personalistic Organicism: Paradox or Paradigm', in Robin Attfield and Andrew Belsey (eds), *Philosophy and the Natural Environment*, Cambridge: Cambridge University Press, 1994, pp. 59–73, at p. 72.

16 Mary Midgley, 'The End of Anthropocentrism?', in Attfield and Belsey, ibid., pp. 103–12.

17 Bryan Norton, *Toward Unity Among Environmentalists*, Oxford and New York: Oxford University Press, 1991.

18 Mark Rowlands, *Animal Rights: A Philosophical Defence*, London: Macmillan, 1998.

19 James Sterba, 'A Biocentrist Strikes Back', *Environmental Ethics*, 20, 1998, pp. 361–76; reprinted in Attfield, *Ethics of the Environment*, pp. 301–16.

20 Thomas E. Hill, Jr., 'Ideals of Human Excellence and Preserving Natural Environments', *Environmental Ethics*, 5, 1983, pp. 211–14; reprinted in Attfield, ibid., pp. 319–32.

21 Philip Cafaro, 'Thoreau, Leopold, and Carson: Toward an Environmental Virtue Ethics', in Ronald Sandler and Philip Cafaro (eds), *Environmental Virtue Ethics*, Lanham, MD and Oxford: Rowman & Littlefield, 2005, pp. 31–44.

22 Dale Jamieson, 'When Utilitarians Should Be Virtue Theorists', *Utilitas*, 19.2, 2007, pp. 160–83.

23 Robin Attfield, *Environmental Ethics*, pp. 17–21.

24 Lynn White Jr., 'The Historical Roots of Our Ecological Crisis', *Science*, 155, 37, 1967, pp. 1203–7.

25 Robin Attfield, 'Social History, Religion and Technology: An Interdisciplinary Investigation into White's "Roots"', *Environmental Ethics*, 31, 2009, pp. 31–50.

26 Herman Daly, 'On Wilfred Beckerman's Critique of Sustainable Development', *Environmental Values*, 4, 1995, pp. 49–55.

27 Robin Attfield, *The Ethics of the Global Environment*, Edinburgh: Edinburgh University Press and West Lafayette: Purdue University Press, 1999, chapter 8: 'Biodiversity and Preservation', pp. 133–51.

28 Alan Carter, 'Saving Nature and Feeding People', *Environmental Ethics*, 26, 2004, pp. 339–60; reprinted in Attfield, *Ethics of the Environment*, pp. 543–64.

29 IPCC, *Climate Change 1995*, 1996; *Climate Change 2007*, http://www.ipcc.ch/SPM2feb07.pdf; see note 2 above.

30 Aubrey Meyer, *Contraction and Convergence: The Global Solution to Climate Change*, Totnes, UK: Green Books, 2000.

31 Peter Singer, *One World: The Ethics of Globalization*, 2nd edn, New Haven, CT: Yale University Press, 2004.

References

Attfield, Robin, *The Ethics of the Global Environment*, Edinburgh: Edinburgh University Press and West Lafayette: Purdue University Press, 1999.

—, *Environmental Ethics: An Overview for the Twenty-First Century*, Cambridge, UK and Malden, MA: Polity, 2003.

—, 'Social History, Religion and Technology: An Inter-disciplinary Investigation into White's "Roots"', *Environmental Ethics*, 31, 2009, pp. 31–50.

Cafaro, Philip, 'Thoreau, Leopold, and Carson: Toward an Environmental Virtue Ethics', in Ronald Sandler and Philip Cafaro (eds), *Environmental Virtue Ethics*, Lanham, MD and Oxford: Rowman & Littlefield, 2005, pp. 31–44.

Callicott, J. Baird, *In Defense of the Land Ethic, Essays in Environmental Philosophy*, Albany, NY: State University of New York Press, 1989.

Carson, Rachel, *Silent Spring*, London: Hamish Hamilton, 1963.

Carter, Alan, 'Saving Nature and Feeding People', *Environmental Ethics*, 26, 2004, pp. 339–60.

—, 'Saving Nature and Feeding People', in Attfield (ed.), *Ethics of the Environment*, Farnham, UK and Burlington, VT: Ashgate, 2008, pp. 543–64.

Daly, Herman, 'On Wilfred Beckerman's Critique of Sustainable Development', *Environmental Values*, 4, 1995, pp. 49–55.

Domsky, Darren, 'The Inadequacy of Callicott's Communitarianism', *Environmental Ethics*, 28, 2006, pp. 395–412.

—, 'The Inadequacy of Callicott's Communitarianism', in Robin Attfield, *The Ethics of the Environment*, pp. 161–78.

Ferré, Frederick, 'Personalistic Organicism: Paradox or Paradigm', in Robin Attfield and Andrew Belsey (eds), *Philosophy and the Natural Environment*, Cambridge: Cambridge University Press, 1994, pp. 59–73.

Glacken, Clarence J., *Traces on the Rhodian Shore: Nature and Culture in Western Thought from Ancient Times to the End of the Eighteenth Century*, Berkeley, LA and London: University of California Press, 1967.

Hill, Thomas E., Jr., 'Ideals of Human Excellence and Preserving Natural Environments', *Environmental Ethics*, 5, 1983, pp. 211–14.

—, 'Ideals of Human Excellence and Preserving Natural Environments', in Attfield, *The Ethics of the Environment*, pp. 319–332.

Intergovernmental Panel on Climate Change (IPCC), *Climate Change 1995: Economic and Social Dimensions of Climate Change*, Cambridge: Cambridge University Press, 1996.

IPCC, *Climate Change 2007: The Physical Science Basis*, http://www.ipcc.ch/SPM2feb07.pdf.

Jamieson, Dale, 'When Utilitarians Should Be Virtue Theorists', *Utilitas*, 19.2, 2007, pp. 160–83.

Leopold, Aldo, *A Sand County Almanac and Sketches Here and There*, New York: Oxford University Press, 1949.

Lo, Y. S., 'The Land Ethic and Callicott's Ethical System', in Robin Attfield, *The Ethics of the Environment*, pp. 133–60.

—, 'The Land Ethic and Callicott's Ethical System', *Inquiry*, 44, 2001, pp. 331–58.

Meyer, Aubrey, *Contraction and Convergence: The Global Solution to Climate Change*, Totnes, UK: Green Books, 2000.

Midgley, Mary, 'The End of Anthropocentrism?', in Attfield and Belsey, *Philosophy and the Natural Environment*, pp. 103–12.

Naess, Arne, 'The Shallow and the Deep, Long-Range Ecology Movement: A Summary', *Inquiry*, 1973, pp. 95–100.

Norton, Bryan, *Toward Unity Among Environmentalists*, Oxford and New York: Oxford University Press, 1991.

Passmore, John, *Man's Responsibility for Nature*, London: Duckworth, 1974.

Rodman, John, 'The Liberation of Nature', *Inquiry*, 20, 1977, pp. 83–145.

Rolston, Holmes, III, 'Is There an Ecological Ethic?', *Ethics*, 1975, pp. 93–109.

—, 'Is There an Ecological Ethic?', in Robin Attfield (ed.), *The Ethics of the Environment*, pp. 13–29.

Routley (later Sylvan), Richard, 'Is There a Need for a New, an Environmental Ethic?' in Robin Attfield, *The Ethics of the Environment*, pp. 3–12.

—, 'Is There a Need for a New, an Environmental Ethic?' *Proceedings of the XVth World Congress of Philosophy,* Varna, Bulgaria, 1973, pp. 205–10.

Routley (later Sylvan), Richard, and Val Routley (later Plumwood), 'Human Chauvinism and Environmental Ethics', in Don Mannison, Michael McRobbie and Richard Routley (eds), *Environmental Philosophy*, Canberra: Australian National University, 1980, pp. 96–189.

Rowlands, Mark, *Animal Rights: A Philosophical Defence*, London: Macmillan, 1998.

Singer, Peter, *One World: The Ethics of Globalization*, 2nd edn, New Haven, CT: Yale University Press, 2004.

Sterba, James, 'A Biocentrist Strikes Back', *Environmental Ethics*, 20, 1998, pp. 361–76.

—, 'A Biocentrist Strikes Back', in Robin Attfield, *Ethics of the Environment*, pp. 301–16.

White, Lynn, Jr., 'The Historical Roots of Our Ecological Crisis', *Science*, 155, 37, 1967, pp. 1203–7.

Section 6: The ethics of war

1. Does ethics apply to warfare?

Some reject the applicability of ethics to fighting in wars, citing the adage 'All's fair in love and war.' But if this were true, it would mean that deception and violence were completely unobjectionable in matters of love, and this is clearly unacceptable.

Possibly the argument is that war is a no-holds-barred contest, and that for that reason ethics is irrelevant to its conduct. But if that were the case, there could be no debates about whether the ferocity of war should be mitigated by agreements not to launch acts of deadly violence against civilians, and to respect those who surrender by treating them as prisoners of war. (There would accordingly be no point in the Geneva Conventions on the humanitarian treatment of the victims of war.) And in any case, even if it were true, there would still be room for discussing whether it is ever right to go to war, and whether particular circumstances make doing this justifiable.

So the view that ethics is inapplicable to warfare has to be rejected. It has actually been rejected by a long sequence of ethicists who have debated, since the Middle Ages, when and whether it is right to go to war. Twentieth-century wars have renewed this debate, which resumed among philosophers as a result of the Vietnam War, when many American students found themselves liable to be drafted for military service in Vietnam. Like medical ethics, the ethics of war is thus a field of applied ethics with a longstanding pedigree.

2. Is going to war ever justifiable?

Warfare involves launching deadly violence against one's opponents, and this is not easily justified. Pacifists hold that it is wrong to meet violence with violence, either because non-violence is always the best way to restore peace and reconciliation, or because acts of violence are wrong in themselves.

Jan Narveson criticizes pacifists who claim that non-violence always has better outcomes than resort to violence (a reasonable point), but also claims that pacifism is incoherent. He argues that those who hold that violence is wrong have to believe that everyone has a right not to be a victim of violence, and are therefore inconsistent if they believe it is wrong to take steps to uphold this right.[1] But pacifists need not accept such a right; and those who do affirm it need not believe that there is an obligation to take violent steps to vindicate it. So his case for pacifism being incoherent and for pacifists being confused collapses.

Elizabeth Anscombe objects to pacifism that pacifists reject people's right to self-defence. However, they could instead accept this right, but hold that it is wrong to exercise it. She also objects that pacifism represents all killing as equally wrong, and that this ignores the distinction between killing in a justified war and performing atrocities such as deadly acts of terrorism.[2] Certainly if wars are sometimes justified, we need this distinction, but it remains to be seen whether there are circumstances in which such justifications exist. Besides, pacifists remain free to distinguish between killing in the performance of military 'duty' and unmitigated murder, even if they regard both as wrong.

Yet pacifism becomes problematic if we accept the principle of negative responsibility, and hold that agents are responsible for what happens through their omissions as well as for outcomes of their actions (see the section on Consequentialism). If so, then by refusing to resist violence with violence, we may allow suffering and death for which we bear a large responsibility. This in turn suggests that participation in some wars is justified, even if many or most wars cannot be justified in this way.

A related distinction has been made by Thomas Nagel in the inaugural volume of *Philosophy and Public Affairs*. Arguing on a Kantian basis, Nagel endorses the action of soldiers killing enemy soldiers in self-defence, but cannot accept the bombardment of cities that is characteristic of modern warfare, which is tantamount to massacre, and concludes that modern wars involving indiscriminate violence are morally wrong.[3] This conclusion is, of course, in practice close to pacifism. But it also raises again the issue of whether (and if so, when) wars are justifiable.

3. The just war tradition

Following Augustine, Thomas Aquinas taught that warfare can be just if certain conditions are satisfied. War had to be declared by a legitimate authority; the war had to be fought for a just cause, such as resisting aggression or restoring justice; and the means employed had to be 'moderate', that is, no more savage than necessary for victory.[4]

These conditions have been supplemented by subsequent Catholic writers. Thus seven necessary conditions are set out by Joseph McKenna, and can be summarized as follows. As with Aquinas, the first requirement is declaration of war by a legitimate authority. As for a just cause, the injury to be prevented or rectified must be real and certain; additionally, its seriousness must be proportioned to the harms generated by war. A fourth requirement is that there must be a reasonable hope of success, and a fifth that war must be entered into only as a last resort, after all other remedies have been exhausted. Further, the intentions of the belligerent country must be right; for example, a war of defence must not be conducted with the aim of expansion or expropriation. Finally, the measures used in war must themselves be moral,[5] which in practice requires them both to be proportionate and to involve discrimination between combatants and non-combatants.

All these conditions could be debated, for example by asking whether they are all necessary conditions, and jointly sufficient for a war to be justified. For example, the first condition may be part of a sufficient condition, but can hardly be necessary, as that would prohibit anyone ever going to war against their own government (as when the people of Bangladesh rose up against the oppressive government of Pakistan in 1971). Yet no theory of the ethics of warfare can be satisfactory if it fails to take into account hostilities such as civil wars and revolutions, and the circumstances in which they arise. These conditions in any case often call for interpretation, as over the meaning of 'proportionate'. Besides, in some cases it would be impossible in practice to establish whether they are satisfied or not, as in the case of rightful intentions; this condition, however desirable, will not be discussed further here.

In view of the practice-consequentialist stance adopted in the chapter on Normative Ethics, it is worth asking whether the remaining conditions can be understood in a consequentialist manner. Conseqentialism would require legitimate authorities not to go to war without a declaration, but would not debar all others from taking up arms. It supports the requirement for the injury to be remedied to be real and certain, and can interpret its being proportionate to the evils of war as requiring those evils to be likely to be no greater than that of the injury plus the risks of doing nothing. It can endorse the requirement of a reasonable hope of success, and of war being adopted as a last resort. Like other stances, it cannot usefully interpret 'good intentions', but as for the requirements of discrimination between combatants and non-combatants and of proportionate means, I will argue below that these can be given a consequentialist interpretation and found to be cogent accordingly.

If so, then consequentialists can endorse a version of 'just war' theory and use it to distinguish between justified wars and others. But this does not, of itself, mark them off from other theorists. For, as we have seen, Kantians too can uphold at least some of the proposed conditions, such as discrimination between combatants and non-combatants, and probably most of the others. The same apparently applies to contractarians and to rights-theorists. But there is no telling what conditions particularists would approve; indeed this whole field seems to cry out for the kind of rules that particularists reject, or treat as secondary to intuitive judgements. Much the same applies to most kinds of virtue ethicists.

It can be added that (even if the final condition, which relates to the ethics of conduct within war, is set on one side and considered separately) few wars satisfy the remaining conditions. If these conditions are acceptable, most of the wars of history will have been lacking in justification. A plausible exception was going to war to defend countries that had become victims of Nazi Germany in 1939, and thus the Allies' participation in the Second World War. But even in that war, some of the measures adopted by the victorious Allies (such as saturation bombing) were in breach of requirements such as discrimination between combatants and non-combatants.

4. Individual responsibility

The first six of McKenna's conditions relate to the justifiability of a country going to war (*jus ad bellum*, to use traditional terms). The final condition, however, concerns the ethics of conduct within war (traditionally, *jus in bello*), and the rest of this section considers this issue further.

Starting in 1864, several Geneva Conventions have been agreed to limit the suffering involved in warfare. They have covered issues such as the treatment of injured soldiers and of prisoners of war, and of military personnel at risk after hostilities at sea. (Some of these rules and prohibitions had been advocated by Immanuel Kant in his essay *Perpetual Peace*, in which he argued that a further requirement of a justified war was rejection of conduct incompatible with the war leading to a lasting peace.[6] Kant's impartial cosmopolitanism (see the section on Kantian Themes) is manifested here.) Their international acceptance has given them the status, in international law, of laws of war.

At the Nuremburg War Crimes Tribunals, held shortly after the end of the Second World War, a number of Nazi officers were accused of serious breaches of these Conventions. Their defence often consisted in a plea of 'superior orders'; in other words, they had been acting as instructed by their superiors, and could not be expected to disobey. The issue of whether this was an allowable defence arose again in trials, held in the USA, of American soldiers accused of war crimes during the Vietnam War.

However, the stance of the Nuremburg Tribunals was that appeal to superior orders was no defence, and that military officers carry some degree of individual responsibility for their conduct and for the instructions that they give to subordinates. The prospect of severe retribution for disobeying an order might mitigate an officer's degree of responsibility. But the underlying argument, which was surely a sound one, is that even members of a military hierarchy can exercise some amount of discretion about how and (sometimes) whether orders are carried out. (This does not, of course, detract from the responsibility of superior officers when they issue illegal orders.)

It follows that all military personnel should be trained in the laws of war, to which they are liable to be held answerable, and that military manuals should instruct them to be ready to question or disobey any orders that breach these laws. While this expectation contrasts with the unquestioning obedience widely expected of soldiers and inculcated in them during military training, this remains an obligation of military authorities, who are morally obliged to modify training methods to accommodate it.

5. Non-combatant immunity

The Geneva Convention of 1949 enshrined agreed protections for civilians situated in or around a war zone, and thus upheld the longstanding principle that non-combatants should not be subjected to attack or military violence. However, there is no obvious immediate defence of this principle, since many non-combatants have significant roles in either contributing to their country's war effort, or (in some cases) to leading it, while many combatants are either conscripted or otherwise have little practical choice about finding themselves in military uniform. So treating the latter as being fairly targeted but the former as immune from attack can be represented as unreasonable and unjust.

Thomas Nagel (in the essay cited above: see note 3) defends non-combatant immunity on a Kantian basis. But upholding the distinction between combatants and non-combatants seems inconsistent with consequentialism. George Mavrodes, however, argues that a viable internationally agreed system of respecting non-combatant immunity is the best practical way to mitigate the savagery of war, even though it is based on a convention which is not obviously justifiable in itself.[7]

Consider the alternatives. One would involve war being conducted with uninhibited ferocity, against civilians as well as military personnel; to this, discriminating between combatants and non-combatants is clearly superior. Another might, in theory, be a convention to settle disputes by the outcome of single combat between selected champions of the two parties; but, as Mavrodes remarks, the reported examples of this show that it does not work, since undefeated armies prove unwilling to accept the other side's victory without further hostilities. The convention of non-combatant immunity, by contrast, has proved to receive some degree of compliance in a range of conflicts, and thus has the best prospect of limiting the evils implicit in warfare. Notice that this is a practice-consequentialist defence, which well coheres with the theory of normative ethics presented in the chapter on that topic.

Judith Lichtenberg argues to similar effect, casting considerable doubt on the deontological Doctrine of Double Effect (see the chapter on Normative Ethics), which is sometimes used in support of this kind of discrimination. It is not ultimately people's intentions that justify such policies, she argues, but we can justify a policy of acting *as if* the intention not to attack non-combatants were crucial, albeit because there is an underlying consequentialist justification (as is argued here in the section on Consequentialism). Lichtenberg's essay also raises problems for consequentialism, which cannot be considered here, but its overall tendency is effectively supportive of the findings of Mavrodes.[8] It should be added that the consequentialist case for respect for non-combatant immunity applies not only to international war, but equally to civil wars and revolutions, despite their often indiscriminate nature.

6. Nuclear weapons and nuclear deterrence

The two criteria recognized above as relevant to the justified use of means and measures in time of war, proportionality and discrimination, appear firmly to preclude any use of nuclear weapons, however justified a given war might be. For initiating their use would be disproportionate to any benefits that a war might be thought to bring, and would in most cases be entirely indiscriminate, obliterating combatants and non-combatants alike. Use of 'tactical' nuclear weapons might seem less indiscriminate, but the low prospect of a nuclear exchange remaining limited to tactical weapons makes this an implausible scenario, and the risks of escalation make such use tantamount to the initiation of all-out nuclear warfare.

Further, what goes for initiating a nuclear war goes also for nuclear retaliation. The responsibility for such retaliation would rest with the retaliating party, who could not cogently plead that this responsibility rested with the initiating side; for nuclear retaliation would cause thousands if not millions of avoidable deaths, mutilations and cases of life-long disease or disablement additional to those generated by the initial nuclear attack, together with additional destruction of whole ecosystems. Accordingly, no envisageable use of nuclear weapons is justifiable.

It does not follow from this that nuclear deterrence cannot be justified. For it might be right to threaten to do something, even if this were an action that it would be wrong to perform. Further, it is sometimes argued that making conditional threats of nuclear bombardment is precisely what averts the need to embark on nuclear hostilities. Hence the ethics of nuclear deterrence requires further discussion.

Some theorists, such as Anthony Kenny, uphold deontological principles in this area. Kenny maintains that it is never right to intend to do what it would be wrong to do, and that since nuclear deterrence involves a conditional intention to participate in nuclear warfare, nuclear deterrence is therefore morally impermissible and wrong.[9]

Each of his premises has been contested. R. E. Hare and Carey Joynt, who are consequentialists who support nuclear deterrence, argue that it does not involve the government or the heads of the armed forces having a conditional intention to use nuclear weapons, although it may require military personnel to harbour such an intention.[10] But even it they are right, this seems to supply rather a tenuous basis for something as momentous as nuclear deterrence.

However, Jeff McMahan, who is also a consequentialist, questions the premise that it is never right to intend to do what it would be wrong to do. For if the effects of holding the relevant conditional intention include the prevention of nuclear war, then it could be justified.[11] This would not be an intention to use nuclear weapons, but readiness to use them in the event of (say) an unprovoked attack.

Yet we should not infer that McMahan supports nuclear deterrence. His book concerns Britain's holding nuclear weapons for deterrent purposes, and he in fact argues against this policy that it involves risks of escalation (i.e. of an arms race involving competition to outdo the weaponry of others, escalating into nuclear war), and in particular of proliferation (i.e. of the holding of nuclear weapons being imitated by other states with the necessary economic, scientific and technological capacity), with all the risks that would attach to a world with (say) ten or more powers armed with nuclear weapons. Proliferation has, sadly, ensued since McMahan was writing in 1981, but reversing this trend is far from hopeless; three countries have freely abandoned their nuclear armouries (South Africa, Ukraine and Kazakhstan), although others (Israel, India, Pakistan and North Korea) have now acquired such weapons, and Iran seems poised to do the same.

In the absence of any prospect that British nuclear weapons serve a deterrent function, McMahan's argument from proliferation provides strong support for nuclear disarmament on the part of (at least) the UK, and the same could well hold good for parallel reasons in the cases of France and of the newer nuclear powers. Where the other internationally recognized nuclear powers, the USA, Russia and China, are concerned, the same argument appears to support at least deep cuts in the nuclear armouries of those countries as well.

Study questions

1. How can pacifists reply to the criticisms of Jan Narveson?
2. Can nuclear deterrence be regarded as an ethical policy?
3. Is the principle of discrimination between combatants and non-combatants in situations of war defensible, either on a consequentialist or on some other basis?

Notes

1 Jan Narveson, 'Pacifism: A Philosophical Analysis', *Ethics*, 75, 1965, pp. 259–71.

2 G. E. M. Anscombe, 'War and Murder', in W. Steen (ed.), *Nuclear Weapons: A Catholic Response*, New York: Sheed & Ward, 1962, pp. 43–62.

3 Thomas Nagel, 'War and Massacre', *Philosophy and Public Affairs*, 1, 1971–2, pp. 123–44.

4 Judith Wagner deCew, 'Warfare, Codes Of', in Ruth Chadwick (ed.), *Encyclopedia of Applied Ethics*, San Diego, CA: Academic Press, 1998, vol. 4, pp. 499–505.

5 Joseph C. McKenna, 'Ethics and War: A Catholic View', *American Political Science Review*, 54, 1960, pp. 647–58.

6 Immanuel Kant, *Perpetual Peace, and Other Essays on Politics, History, and Morals*, trans. Ted Humphrey, Indianapolis, IN: Hackett, 1983.

7 George I. Mavrodes, 'Conventions and the Morality of War', *Philosophy and Public Affairs*, 4.2, 1975, pp. 117–31.

8 Judith Lichtenberg, 'War, Innocence and the Doctrine of Double Effect', *Philosophical Studies*, 74, 1994, pp. 347–68.

9 Anthony Kenny, *The Logic of Deterrence*, London: Firethorn Press, 1985.

10 R. E. Hare and Carey B. Joynt, *Ethics and International Affairs*, London: Macmillan, 1982.

11 Jeff McMahan, *British Nuclear Weapons, For and Against*, London: Junction Books, 1981.

References

Anscombe, G. E. M., 'War and Murder', in W. Steen (ed.), *Nuclear Weapons: A Catholic Response*, New York: Sheed & Ward, 1962, pp. 43–62.

deCew, Judith Wagner, 'Warfare, Codes Of', in Ruth Chadwick (ed.), *Encyclopedia of Applied Ethics*, San Diego, CA: Academic Press, 1998, vol. 4, pp. 499–505.

Dower, Nigel, *The Ethics of War and Peace*, Cambridge, UK: Polity, 2010.

Hare, R. E. and Carey B. Joynt, *Ethics and International Affairs*, London: Macmillan, 1982.

Kant, Immanuel, *Perpetual Peace, and Other Essays on Politics, History, and Morals*, trans. Ted Humphrey, Indianapolis, IN: Hackett, 1983.

Kenny, Anthony, *The Logic of Deterrence*, London: Firethorn Press, 1985.

Lichtenberg, Judith, 'War, Innocence and the Doctrine of Double Effect', *Philosophical Studies*, 74, 1994, pp. 347–68.

Mavrodes, George I., 'Conventions and the Morality of War', *Philosophy and Public Affairs*, 4.2, 1975, pp. 117–31.

McKenna, Joseph C., 'Ethics and War: A Catholic View', *American Political Science Review*, 54, 1960, pp. 647–58.

McMahan, Jeff, *British Nuclear Weapons, For and Against*, London: Junction Books, 1981.

Nagel, Thomas, 'War and Massacre', *Philosophy and Public Affairs*, 1, 1971–2, pp. 123–44.

Narveson, Jan, 'Pacifism: A Philosophical Analysis', *Ethics*, 75, 1965, pp. 259–71.

5

Meta-Ethics

Chapter Outline

Section 1: Non-cognitivism, projectivism and prescriptivism

1. The 'naturalistic fallacy'

Meta-ethics is the study of the status and meaning of moral talk or discourse. In 1903, it took a new turn when G. E. Moore argued in *Principia Ethica* that a fallacy is committed when people attempt to reason from facts to moral claims, and thus (explicitly or implicitly) attempt to define moral terms such as 'good'. This fallacy he called 'the naturalistic fallacy', and it is a fallacy because 'good' is indefinable (or so he thought).[1]

To show that 'good' is indefinable, he deployed the Open Question argument. Take any suggested definition of 'good'; it does not matter which one we select. Examples might be 'pleasant', 'approved by us', 'more evolved' or 'commanded by God'. Let us call the suggested defining phrase 'C'. Then if the definition were successful, the question 'Are things which are C good?' would be a closed question (the answer being 'Unquestionably, yes'). But in fact, whenever questions of this kind are asked, they prove to be open questions, with no unquestionable answer. It follows that no definition of 'good' is successful.

For several decades, most philosophers were persuaded by Moore's reasoning, and, because 'ought' seems to belong in the same camp as 'good', they often adopted slogans such as: 'From "Is" to "Ought", No Road' echoing a theme of Hume (see Chapter 1, Section 2), and holding that otherwise the naturalistic fallacy is committed. Even if this is granted, they could tell themselves, the language of 'good' and 'ought' might still convey truths, as Moore continued to hold (see below), and allow of knowledge.

But problems arose about how we could ever know such truths. On the one hand, they cannot be grounded in reasoning from facts (see the same slogan). On the other hand, if, as Moore also held, 'good' is not a natural property that can be studied by any of the natural sciences, then we cannot observe its presence, in the way that we can detect natural properties which happen also to be indefinable. (Moore's example of one of these is 'yellow'.) So there seems no way at all in which we can know such truths, unless, like Moore, we take the view that we can know them by intuition, being naturally equipped to recognize goodness when we come across it. But this view raises numerous problems, such as how children could ever learn to recognize goodness (in the complete absence of any methods or clues). So it is not surprising that some philosophers who accepted Moore's reasoning came to doubt that moral language conveys truths, or involves statements, at all. The view that there are no moral truths or statements (and thus no moral knowledge) is called 'Moral non-cognitivism'.

But perhaps we should not be too readily persuaded by Moore's reasoning after all. Let 'C' once again be a suggested definition of 'good'. One of Moore's premises is that questions such as 'Are things which are C good' is always an open question, and never a closed one. But how does he know *this*? To know this, he would need to know beforehand that good is indefinable. But that is his conclusion, which he therefore cannot assume if he is to rely on the premise just mentioned. (Indeed if a successful definition of 'good' were produced, something that he cannot exclude beforehand, the question 'Are things that are C good?' would be an open one after all, and his premise would collapse. This makes it clear that Moore was assuming that no successful definition will ever be produced, and was thus actually assuming his own conclusion on the way to reaching it.) In other words, Moore's Open Question argument begs the question that it claims to resolve.[2]

While others have put forward further arguments to replace Moore's Open Question argument, such arguments have proved to be vulnerable to similar problems. Thus the argument that originally inspired some of Moore's disciples to become non-cognitivists turns out to be fallacious itself. Non-cognitivism could still be correct, but would need other considerations to support it. To express the matter in different language, moral discourse might still fail to be 'truth-apt', that is, capable of being either true or false; for that is what moral non-cognitivists are really saying. But they would need arguments to persuade the rest of us that no one knows anything in the area of morality (including the difference between right and wrong).

As hinted above, Moore's own view was a form of moral cognitivism. Moral cognitivists hold that there are moral truths (about what is good or what ought to be done: see the section on Cognitivism and Realism). Yet he denied that terms such as 'good' and 'ought' can be translated into natural characteristics or properties (holding that this would involve the naturalistic fallacy). So the relevant truths are of a non-natural character, discerned ultimately by intuition. But this stance eventually became regarded as an unstable one, for the kind of reasons indicated above. Rather than challenge Moore's critique of naturalism, *non*-cognitivism seemed to many to be the way forward. (For a discussion of ethical naturalism, see the final section of this chapter.)

2. Non-cognitivism and emotivism

The idea that moral discourse does not make statements but expresses feelings was probably first presented by David Hume. As we have seen in the section on Hobbes and Hume, he probably reasoned as follows. The language of 'oughts' is *practical* language, capable of stirring either the speaker or the hearers to action. But reason is incapable of motivating action or stirring us towards it. Nothing but passions has this capacity. Therefore 'ought'-language, rather than being based on reason, must express passions (emotions, that is). Implicitly, it is neither true nor false (or not, in contemporary terms, 'truth-apt'), and certainly not derivable from facts. Several problems with this reasoning were also presented in that section. But the philosophers of the early twentieth century who adopted non-cognitivist stances were more concerned to develop a theory of moral language that avoided the naturalistic fallacy than to appropriate or defend the ideas of Hume.

However, they shared with Hume the view that moral language has a dynamic role that guides action, and the conclusion that it therefore cannot be emotionally or motivationally inert, as they took fact-stating language to be. Rather, it either expresses the emotions of its speaker, or it galvanizes its hearers into relevant emotions and action (and sometimes it has both these roles). Its primary meaning is accordingly to be understood not as conveying facts but as consisting in emotive meaning (its tendencies, that is, either to express or to generate emotions). Indeed the presence of emotive meaning was supposed to explain why 'oughts' cannot be derived from factual language; for factual language (surely) lacks emotive meaning. Therefore 'ought'-language, in which such meaning is present, cannot possibly be derived from it. This overall position became known as 'emotivism'.

A sophisticated version of emotivism was presented by Charles L. Stevenson, first in the journal *Mind*, and then in his book *Ethics and Language*.[3] However, Stevenson sometimes allowed that ethical claims could be said to be true, a view that casts doubt on whether his position was genuinely a kind of non-cognitivism. More uncompromising and clearer defences of emotivism are to be found in some earlier works, Ogden and Richards' book, *The Meaning of Meaning* (1923), and in A. J. Ayer's even more celebrated book, *Language Truth and Logic* (1936).[4] According to Ayer, ethical claims do not even express propositions at all, but only 'pseudo-propositions'; they are literally meaningless, but still have emotive meaning because of their capacity to stir up emotions, attitudes and action.

One central problem with emotivism was that it provides insufficient scope for moral reasoning. A great deal of moral reasoning does actually take place (as all the sections of the chapter on Applied Ethics bear out). Yet a theory which represents moral judgements as primarily expressions or evocations of emotion simply fails to capture the way in which such reasoning moves from (sometimes) relevant grounds to (sometimes) well-grounded conclusions about desirability, rightness or even obligation. Indeed if emotivism were correct, then any emotionally expressive or evocative judgement would apparently be no less tenable than any other, as long as sufficient impacts on people's emotions are made.

This brings in a second problem. The question of whether impacts on emotions or attitudes are made, and even the question of whether they tend (or are prone) to be made are issues dependent on factors beyond the meaning of the language used and often beyond the control of the speaker. The action of stirring up emotions is not, in J. L. Austin's terms, an 'illocutionary' act (such as stating or asking), necessarily performed *in* uttering the relevant sentence, but a 'perlocutionary' act, performed *through* making such an utterance (like persuading someone, or starting a riot).[5] But perlocutionary acts are no more than contingently related to the meaning of the language used. Hence this part of emotivism is out-of-place as a theory of the meaning of moral language, and seems (contrary to fact) to make the meaning vary either with actual effects or with causal tendencies.

There is also a third problem. The second problem is no problem for the remaining part of the theory, the part which detects the meaning of moral language in the expression of the speaker's feelings. Expressing feelings is, admittedly, an illocutionary act. But this part of the theory implies that the meaning of 'keeping promises is obligatory' is different when it expresses feelings (however strong) and when it is uttered or written dispassionately (as it often is). Yet the implications of these utterances remain the same (e.g. for *my* promises), as, surely, does the meaning. This, then, is the third problem for emotivism. Meaning does not always vary with differences of the illocutionary act(s) performed, and in particular does not always vary with the illocutionary acts of expressing various feelings that emotivism makes it turn on.

Hence, if non-cognitivism was to become a defensible stance, then some more coherent theory was going to be needed. Philosophers who recognized the force of (at least) the first of the above problems now sought refuge in Richard Hare's theory of prescriptivism.

3. Prescriptivism

One of the strengths of Richard Hare's position was his claim that moral judgements are implicitly universal, and that those who make them are obliged to judge similar cases alike. Whatever particularists may say to the contrary (see the section on Virtue Ethics), this claim amounted to real progress, not least because it explained how there can be moral reasoning based on the requirement of consistency. Hare was not saying, like Kant, that rightness involves the possibility of everyone acting alike (solidarity), but that each similar case must be judged alike, whether as right or wrong (universalizability).

However, what made Hare's position non-cognitivist was his prescriptivism: his view that a judgement is moral if and only if subscription to it entails that the utterer performs an action of the kind she or he explicitly or implicitly prescribes when there is an opportunity to do so (Hare's prescriptivity requirement). Because judgements are implicitly universal, anyone's judgements about someone else apply to themselves when in the same situation. If they fail to act accordingly, then their language was not properly moral language in the first place, except in an 'off-colour' sense, but was insincere. Thus the primary meaning of moral language is prescriptive, and (because factual language is not such) moral language is never entailed by facts alone.[6]

But in cases of moral weakness (when people fail to do that they believe they ought to do), the moral beliefs of the person concerned would often still be said to be sincere. Such non-performance is not restricted to cases of what Hare calls 'physical or psychological impossibility'; it can also be due to inadvertence, laziness, preoccupation or apathy. Thus Hare's prescriptivity requirement is too strong, and fails to supply a necessary condition of judgements being moral ones. Despite the fact that moral judgements have the role of guiding behaviour, the relation between moral beliefs and action are not always as close as this requirement suggests, and cannot be represented as turning on the very meaning of the former.

What of Hare's view that the combination of prescriptivity and universalizability forms a sufficient condition of judgements being moral ones? One longstanding objection to this view is that it allows moral judgements to have any content whatever, as long as the utterer is prepared to stand by them consistently. But morality seems to have a content that requires more than consistency plus commitment; for example, not all the judgements of fanatics (such as Nazis) are recognizably moral judgements.

Hare struggled valiantly to respond to the problem of fanatics. A fanatic, he held, is a person who holds an ideal which overrides both her or his own interests and those she or he would have if in the situation of others. But this disregard for their own interests (actual or hypothetical) means that the fanatics are using moral language irrationally, and should not be regarded as a problem for universal prescriptivism. However, this response seems to make everyone prepared to die for a principle or a cause into a fanatic, and thus to claim too easy a victory. Eventually Hare took the view that not even the fanatic could consistently and rationally resist judgements based on universalizing their own interests. But this still leaves the problem that universal prescriptivism counts as moral judgements ones that, while possibly being irrational, are held with the appropriate kind of consistency and commitment, even if their content is not related to the good or harm of anyone or anything; and this implication counts strongly against the theory that implies it.

In his later works, Hare claimed that universal prescriptivism supported a form of utilitarianism (preference-utilitarianism), the verdicts of which were rational or objectively correct, although he remained a non-cognitivist.[7] This phase of his work is discussed in the section on 'The Re-emergence of Applied Ethics'. These claims brought in their train problems about whether Hare's meta-ethic really does support utilitarianism, as well as problems about the adequacy of a normative theory that turns entirely on preferences.[8]

Further, Hare's suggestion that there were correct and objective answers to ethical questions seemed to undermine most if not all of the usual motivation for adhering to non-cognitivism. For if correct answers could be reached by reasoning from interests, then the gulf between 'is' and 'ought' seemed to have been bridged, and the conclusions of this reasoning appeared to have the status of nothing short of knowledge.

4. Projectivism

Recently, an influential variety of non-cognitivism has been projectivism. According to projectivists such as Simon Blackburn, moral judgements result from people projecting emotions and attitudes onto situations or features of the world, such that there seem to be objective properties like rightness or impermissibility belonging to those features. Like Stevenson, Blackburn holds that moral judgements can be said to be 'true' (at least in some minimal sense of 'true'), and the judgements can be believed to be true. But there would be no such truths, he would add, if it were not for the projection of emotions.[9]

Such a form of non-cognitivism encounters some of the same problems as emotivism (mentioned above). It avoids the second problem, as it does not attempt to relate the meaning of moral judgements to the generation of emotions in others. But it has to tackle the first, and provide a convincing account of moral reasoning, while at the same time regarding moral properties as no more than projections of speakers' or thinkers' feelings; and it also has to address the third, since the meaning of moral properties seems no different when they are used to express emotions and when they are employed dispassionately. It also has to defend the view that there would be no value if there were no human valuers (as issue discussed in the section on 'Moral Standing, Value and Intrinsic Value', particularly in the sub-section on 'Value, Valuation and Valuers').[10]

Blackburn combines being a projectivist with being a moral quasi-realist. According to moral realists, there are moral properties which are independent of the states or properties of moral valuers and appraisers. Blackburn, as we have seen, rejects this view, and is thus a moral anti-realist. But as a quasi-realist, he claims that all the language that seems to belong to moral realism is available to the anti-realist and to the projectivist too, language such as 'If stealing is wrong, then getting your little brother to steal is also wrong'.[11] (Examples such as this one have often been presented as a problem for non-cognitivists, since they can figure in apparently valid deductive arguments, and thus supply evidence for 'stealing is wrong' being significantly truth-apt. They also suggest that 'wrong' has the same meaning in 'if' clauses as in assertions, even though 'if' clauses seem not to express either emotions or, come to that, prescriptions, contrary to what non-cognitivism seems to imply.) Quasi-realism has to provide an account of how *all* this language can be reconciled with anti-realism and projectivism, and of how accepting the premises and rejecting the conclusions of valid deductive ethical arguments is inconsistent even for a projectivist, an arduous undertaking on any account.

What if the project of quasi-realism were to succeed, and all realist language were to be satisfactorily accounted for (including 'Stealing would still be wrong regardless of anyone's perceptions of it')? If so, then realist claims such as the claim that wrongness is a moral property independent of the states of valuers and appraisers would also have been explained and accepted. But by this stage, realism would itself be beyond objection, and quasi-realism would have collapsed entirely into realism.[12]

5. Conclusion

Some of the work of non-cognitivists, such as Hare's theory of the universalizability of moral judgements, is valuable. But none of the most prominent kinds of non-cognitivism (emotivism, prescriptivism, projectivism) turns out to be persuasive, or immune from serious problems. Non-cognitivism was in any case motivated originally by an insecure argument (Moore's argument for the naturalistic fallacy), and no arguments put forward subsequently seem to make it more secure. And this is important, because if people's moral judgements and principles consisted in prescriptions, approvals or expressions of emotions *and nothing more*, they could hardly be taken as seriously as we usually assume to be necessary.

Accordingly, we shall shortly reconsider the case for realism, for cognitivism, and for naturalism. But first we should return to the meaning of 'good' and of 'ought'.

Study questions

1. Is there a naturalistic fallacy?
2. Does the action-guiding role of moral language require a non-cognitivist theory?
3. How cogent is the universal prescriptivism of Richard Hare?

Notes

1 G. E. Moore, *Principia Ethica*, Cambridge, UK: Cambridge University Press, 1903.

2 Dorothy Mitchell, 'Must We Talk About "Is" and "Ought"?', *Mind*, 77, 1968, pp. 543–9.

3 C. L. Stevenson, 'The Emotive Meaning of Ethical Terms', *Mind*, 1937, pp. 14–31; 'Ethical Judgements and Avoidability', *Mind*, 47, 1938, pp. 45–57; 'Persuasive Definitions', *Mind*, 47, 1938, pp. 331–50; *Ethics and Language*, New Haven, CT: Yale University Press, 1944.

4 C. K. Ogden and I. A. Richards, *The Meaning of Meaning: A Study of the Influence of Language upon Thought and of the Science of Symbolism*, London: Routledge & Kegan Paul, 1923; A. J. Ayer, *Language, Truth and Logic* (1936), London: Gollancz, 1967. For a more recent attempt to defend emotivism, see J. O. Urmson, *The Emotive Theory of Ethics*, London: Hutchinson University Library, 1968.

5 J. L. Austin, *How to Do Things with Words*, Oxford: Clarendon Press, 1962.

6 R. M. Hare, *The Language of Morals*, Oxford: Clarendon Press, 1952; *Freedom and Reason*, Oxford: Clarendon Press, 1963.

7 See, for example, R. M. Hare, *Moral Thinking: Its Levels, Method and Point*, Oxford: Clarendon Press, 1981.

8 See Robin Attfield, *Value, Obligation and Meta-Ethics*, Amsterdam and Atlanta, GA: Éditions Rodopi, 1995, pp. 205–12.

9 Simon Blackburn, *Spreading the Word*, Oxford: Clarendon Press, 1984; *Ruling Passions*, Oxford: Oxford University Press, 1998.

10 See further Robin Attfield, 'Unprojected Value, Unfathomed Caves and Unspent Nature: Reply to an Editorial', *Environmental Values*, 14, 2005, pp. 513–18; also *Value, Obligation and Meta-Ethics*, pp. 40–2, 201–5.

11 Simon Blackburn, *Essays in Quasi-Realism,* Oxford: Oxford University Press, 1993.

12 Richard Joyce, 'Supplement to Anti-Realism: Projectivism and Quasi-Realism', http://www.seop.leeds.ac.uk/entries/moral anti-realism/projectivism-anti-realism.html, accessed 29/7/2010.

References

Attfield, Robin, *Value, Obligation and Meta-Ethics*, Amsterdam and Atlanta, GA: Éditions Rodopi, 1995.

—, 'Unprojected Value, Unfathomed Caves and Unspent Nature: Reply to an Editorial', *Environmental Values*, 14, 2005, pp. 513–18.

Austin, J. L., *How to Do Things with Words*, Oxford: Clarendon Press, 1962.

Ayer, A. J., *Language, Truth and Logic* (1936), London: Gollancz, 1967.

Blackburn, Simon, *Spreading the Word*, Oxford: Clarendon Press, 1984.

—, *Essays in Quasi-Realism*, Oxford: Oxford University Press, 1993.

—, *Ruling Passions*, Oxford: Oxford University Press, 1998.

Hare, R. M., *The Language of Morals*, Oxford: Clarendon Press, 1952.

—, *Freedom and Reason*, Oxford: Clarendon Press, 1963.

—, *Moral Thinking: Its Levels, Method and Point*, Oxford: Clarendon Press, 1981.

Joyce, Richard, 'Supplement to Anti-Realism: Projectivism and Quasi-Realism', http://www.seop.leeds.ac.uk/entries/moral anti-realism/projectivism-anti-realism.html, accessed 29/7/2010.

Mitchell, Dorothy, 'Must We Talk About "Is" and "Ought"?', *Mind*, 77, 1968, pp. 543–9.

Moore, G. E., *Principia Ethica*, Cambridge, UK: Cambridge University Press, 1903.

Ogden, C. K. and I. A. Richards, *The Meaning of Meaning: A Study of the Influence of Language upon Thought and of the Science of Symbolism*, London: Routledge & Kegan Paul, 1923.

Stevenson, C. L., 'The Emotive Meaning of Ethical Terms', *Mind*, 1937, pp. 14–31.

—, 'Ethical Judgements and Avoidability', *Mind*, 47, 1938, pp. 45–57.

—, 'Persuasive Definitions', *Mind*, 47, 1938, pp. 331–50.

—, *Ethics and Language*, New Haven, CT: Yale University Press, 1944.

Urmson, J. O., *The Emotive Theory of Ethics*, London: Hutchinson University Library, 1968.

Section 2: 'Good', 'ought' and morality

1. Introduction

One ground for resisting a realist and cognitivist understanding of moral discourse is the view that ethical language is 'evaluative' in some sense involving its not being derivable from facts and conceptual truths. Some people suppose that such language conveys choices or commendations rather than being truth-apt, and cite as evidence the lack of clear criteria for the use of terms such as 'good' and 'ought'. So it is time to investigate the meaning of these terms more closely.

No one can deny that ethical language is used to evaluate actions, policies, traits of character and sometimes agents themselves. But it does not follow from language being used to evaluate that it is 'evaluative' in the sense just mentioned. Indeed *most* language can be used in making evaluations. Yet nothing follows from this about such language (e.g. 'she beat the record', 'he outdid his competitors') not being derivable from facts and conceptual truths. On the contrary, these claims can readily be derived from truths about meaning plus the facts of the matter.

We turn first to the meaning of 'good', which is sometimes held to be primarily an expression of the commendation or the choice of the speaker who uses it. This view has been well contested by Peter Geach and by Philippa Foot.

2. The meaning of 'good'

The main reason why the criteria of goodness are so varied is that the meaning of 'a good *x*' depends on what kind of thing is being depicted as good, and thus on the meaning of the relevant '*x*'. We do not look for the same qualities in good cars/automobiles and good cucumbers, or in good fuel, good foxgloves and good friends. But exactly the same is true of terms such as 'large', 'small', 'short' and 'tall'. A large flea is not a large animal, nor is a small elephant a small animal. Otherwise, as Geach remarks, we could validly argue: 'This is a small elephant. But all elephants are animals. Therefore this is a small animal.' The reason why we cannot validly reason like this is that 'small' has different meanings in the first premise and in the conclusion, because of the different sortal terms ('elephant' in the first case, and 'animal' in the second) with which it is linked.[1] And much the same applies to 'good'.

Geach here suggests some helpful terminology. He borrows from grammatical classifications of adjectives the distinction between *attributive* adjectives (like 'green' in 'the green tree') and *predicative* adjectives (like 'green' in 'The tree is green.'). Then he adapts this distinction to make the *logical* distinction between adjectives (and other epithets) of which the meaning hinges on the sortal term to which they are attached (he calls these 'logically attributive adjectives'), and other adjectives etc. the meaning of which is more or less constant whatever kind of thing they are used of ('logically predicative adjectives'). Using this new terminology, we find that 'good' and 'bad' resemble 'large', 'small', 'short' and 'tall' in being *logically attributive.* By contrast, colour-terms (like 'green') and shape-terms (like 'triangular') are logically predicative.[2] See Table 5.1.

Table 5.1 Table of Geach's distinction between logically attributive and logically predicative terms

Grammatically attributive adjectives: 'Green' as in 'the green grass'	**Grammatically predicative adjectives:** 'Green' as in 'The grass is green'
Logically attributive adjectives: 'Large', 'small', 'tall', 'short', 'good', 'bad', 'real'	**Logically predicative adjectives:** Colour-terms and shape-terms

This being so, we need to use the logically attributive character of most uses of 'good' in explaining the diversity of the meanings of goodness. Good cactuses are good as cactuses, whereas we do not look for the same qualities in good calculations or, there again, in good cars. In order to explain the variety of criteria of goodness, we have no need to hypothesize that the primary or central meaning of 'good' is some kind of 'evaluative' or 'prescriptive' meaning, as if there were no constant relation between being an *x* and being a good *x*. If the central meaning were such an evaluative meaning, then whether something was good or not would depend on the speaker's attitude. But in fact, speakers sometimes call things good of their kind even when they deplore or detest all or most things of that kind. Thus policemen or federal agents can say of attempts to get round the law 'That is a good ruse', and arachnophobes – haters of spiders – can still say of a good specimen 'that is a good spider'.

Indeed, as Philippa Foot has explained, being chosen or commended is neither necessary nor sufficient for a thing being good of its kind.[3] It is not sufficient because a speaker may have eccentric standards or requirements, diverging from the usual public standards (e.g. in wallpaper or furnishings), and thus what they commend may be not good but hideous. And it is not necessary, since a speaker could choose or commend (in their own interests) teeth or tusks that are fragile or brittle rather than functional (and thus good) organs of a flourishing beast.

What, then, is the common relation between being an *x* and being a good *x*? Dorothy Mitchell suggests that good *x*s are ones that satisfy the most usual interest in *x*s[4]; and this formula seems to work well for resources and artefacts, but not so well for organs and organisms. (As Foot implies, good claws belonging to wild predators seldom serve the interest of those who could become their prey.[5]) The formula 'performing its/her/his function well' works for organs like eyes and for human role-holders like judges, as well as for resources like coal and artefacts like chairs, but works for organisms only if we are willing to accept, with Aristotle, that flourishing ones perform their function well. Otherwise we probably need two accounts of an entity being a good *x*, performing the relevant function well as an *x*, and flourishing as an *x*; to be a good *x* (when no specific perspective or point of view is in the picture), something has to satisfy one or the other. But if we believe that not everything has a function, the duality of this account need not surprise us.

This account should be refined to cope with cases where the criteria of being good as an *x* are explicitly or implicitly whatever makes something a good *x* from a specific point of view. Sometimes when we say 'That was a good day', we assume some perspective, such as that of farmers or of bookmakers. In such cases, the full meaning is not clear unless the claim can be expounded as 'That was good as an *x* (e.g. as a day) from the *y* point of view'.[6] As will be seen below, the moral perspective or point of view is one that has to be borne in mind if moral uses of 'good' are to be properly understood. But this refinement in no way undermines the above account, and in many cases there will be no need to specify any point of view other than whatever is the standard one.

If some such generic account of what makes good *x*s good is correct, then the apparent need to appeal to 'good' having an evaluative or prescriptive meaning disappears, and ascriptions of goodness can be readily seen to be potentially grounded in the facts plus the meanings of 'good' and of the sortal term in question (plus sometimes the criteria brought to bear by one or another specific point of view). Judgement, no doubt, will often be required in applying the implicit standards of being a good *x* to the case in point; but that does not mean that the goodness of whatever is under discussion depends on the attitudes of the speaker.

However, 'good' is not always used attributively. For there are cases where 'good' is used, for example, of pleasure or of friendship, to say that they have *intrinsic* value or goodness. Recognizing this involves a qualification to Geach's attributive theory.[7] Yet this recognition need not undermine the account offered above. What is common to these cases and to those where 'good' is used attributively is that 'good' means 'desirable' or 'such as there is reason to want'. In cases such as 'Pleasure is good', 'good' is short for 'intrinsically desirable' (see the section on Value), while in the generality of cases 'good' is short for 'desirable as an *x*' (or desirable as an *x* from the *y* point of view), and what makes things desirable as an *x* (etc.) will then be explicable by the above account.

It could, however, be asked whether all this applies to the moral uses of 'good'. Some have been briefly covered here (like the use of 'good' with role-terms such as 'judge'), and I will later be claiming that it also applies to the others. But much turns on the sense of 'morally', which colours many such uses of 'good', and that remains to be considered. However, before it is considered, it is convenient to reflect on another apparently problematic term, namely 'ought'.

3. The meaning of 'ought'

The reason why the criteria of 'ought' are so diverse may be that 'ought' is an incomplete or shorthand expression.[8] As we have seen in the section on Hobbes and Hume, Thomas Hobbes assumed that it was short for 'ought in the interests of the person concerned', or 'prudentially ought'. But as we have also seen, 'ought' is sometimes short (instead) for 'legally ought' or 'technically ought' or 'aesthetically ought' or 'morally ought'. Further, because each of these expansions of 'ought' has different criteria, the meaning of 'ought' is only to be expected to vary accordingly, even if 'ought' itself just means, in effect, 'has reason to' (as it surely does).

But once it is clear which kind of 'ought' is in use, it becomes possible to reason from the facts and the relevant criteria to 'ought' conclusions. This is why it was claimed in the same section that Hobbes implicitly showed how to reason from 'is' to 'ought', well before David Hume suggested that doing this was problematic. Unfortunately, however, Hobbes assumed that 'oughts' are always prudential, and so his reasoning is open to the objection that the moral 'ought' is either disregarded or misrepresented.

The meaning of the moral 'ought' is yet to be discussed. But just say it can be expounded in the way suggested in that same section, and amounts to: 'ought insofar as contributing to the wellbeing of all the affected parties is concerned'. If so, and if informal appraisals of contributions to well-being are possible, then it really would be possible to reason from the facts of the matter via these criteria to 'ought' conclusions of the moral 'ought' kind. Such 'oughts' would at the same time supply reasons for action to anyone who cared about moral considerations; and so there would be no need to introduce theories about 'ought' language carrying 'evaluative' or 'prescriptive' meaning to explain its tendency to influence people's behaviour.

While this account of the moral 'ought' will be slightly modified below, the above findings will not be significantly affected. The language of 'ought' may seem mysterious, but, like the language of 'good', it is capable of being clarified in a way consistent with the moral conclusions sometimes expressed in such language being truth-apt and being known.

4. Defining morality

What is needed here is a definition of 'moral' as in 'moral principle' or 'moral judgement' (and thus as in 'morally good' and 'morally ought'). We are not seeking a definition of 'morally right', or of 'moral' as opposed to 'immoral', but rather of the sphere of the moral, as opposed to the sphere of the prudential, or, come to that, of the technical or the aesthetic. The question concerns what is moral rather than non-moral.

What is needed is a specification of the kind of justification relevant to such principles and judgements. We cannot require that such a justification would always be given by relevant speakers and thinkers, because such justifications might never cross the minds of adherents of relevant principles or makers of relevant judgements. But we could require that such a justification either would *or could* be given for such judgements and principles.

The appropriate kind of justification will be one that relates a principle or judgement to states, experiences or actions of intrinsic value, either because the acts, traits or policies subject to these principles or judgements generate such value or perhaps because they instantiate it. (Intrinsic value, we may recall, of itself involves impersonal reasons for action, and the range of its application extends to all the bearers of moral standing.) If no justification involving such impersonal reasons for action is available, then the principle or judgement can hardly be a moral one. However, principles or judgements that are believed to involve such value can be understood as moral, even if the belief is mistaken; and this brings into the sphere of the moral those beliefs and judgements (such as, perhaps, those of Nietzsche) that relate to what is good for humanity, but involve an arguably defective view of human well-being.[9]

What agents morally ought to do will then be deeds that would or could be justified by reference to intrinsic value generated or exemplified by those deeds; and, when more than one action is thus justifiable, then whichever is best justifiable in this way. (This account is compatible with the interpretation of the moral 'ought' suggested above as what ought to be done 'insofar as contributing to the wellbeing of all the affected parties is concerned', as long as well-being is agreed to have intrinsic value.) But the best course of action will often consist in compliance with a rule or practice or quality with this kind of justification, as was argued in the chapter on Normative Ethics. Further, qualities and traits of this kind turn out to be morally good, as do their bearers, the people who manifest such qualities and traits.

5. 'Morally good' and 'morally ought'

It remains to ask what makes morally good traits and agents good, and what explains the 'ought' attaching to actions that morally ought to be done, and to moral principles and judgements relating to actions of this kind. The same issue arises in part if it is asked how the above account of the meaning of 'good' fits moral uses of 'good' and 'goodness'; while there is a parallel issue concerning the above account of the meaning of 'ought' and its application to moral 'oughts'. The above account of the meaning of 'moral' can now be related to these issues.

The above account of the meaning of 'good' suggests that a morally good *x* is an *x* which is good or desirable as an *x* from the moral point of view. Where traits or qualities are concerned, this fits dispositions the overall tendency of which is optimific (or productive of intrinsic value), and thus the virtues. And since motives often carry the same names as qualities of character, this account allows us to grasp what makes good motives good, and to distinguish between being motivated by compassion, a good motive, and by fear, usually a bad motive. At other times, motives are characterized in terms like: 'She acted from a desire to . . .'; whether such motives are good, bad or indifferent will turn on the overall tendencies of acting from this kind of desire.

We next need to reflect on how this all fits 'a good agent' or 'a good person', where 'good' is short for 'morally good'. Once again, 'a good person' will be one who behaves, reacts, feels and thinks in ways that are desirable from the moral point of view, ways that either have intrinsic value themselves or which generate such value overall. Such a person will have virtues like kindness, courage and fairness. They may not always do what is right, because (for example) they may not notice some of the circumstances or impacts of action; but we do not require an agent to do what is right all the time as a condition of calling them a good person. Sometimes, admittedly, there are quite different criteria for a person being a good person, but this is where a different perspective is contextually implied, such as that of good craftsmanship or good sportsmanship. But where no such special perspective is implicit, the moral point of view is usually assumed to be the relevant point of view, and the above theory of what is morally good is (I suggest) in place.

What explains the 'ought' attaching to actions that morally ought to be done has partly been explained above. But it can be added that if 'ought' is equivalent to 'what there is reason to do', and 'morally ought' to 'what there is reason to do from the moral point of view', then our account of the moral point of view helps complete the explanation. Principles or judgements are moral ones, it was suggested above, because the acts, traits or policies subject to these principles or judgements generate intrinsic value or because they instantiate it, and 'oughts' are moral 'oughts' when they would or could be justified by reference to intrinsic value generated or exemplified by the deeds in question. Not all justifications are successful ones, and thus not all moral judgements will be sound ones; but what is needed here is not an account of sound moral judgements but of what makes the issues addressed by 'ought' questions to be moral ones in the first place.

Sometimes, of course, 'oughts' will embody a specialist perspective other than that of morality, whether legal, technical or aesthetic. But where no specialist context is implicit, which might have suggested that a legal, technical or aesthetic 'ought' was underlyingly in question, 'oughts' will usually be moral ones, and the account just given, I suggest, may well be regarded as spelling out what will on those occasions be meant by 'ought'.

If the above account (or something close to it) is correct, then the language of 'ought', of 'good' and of morality turns out to be much less mysterious and much more comprehensible than is often supposed, and moral claims will often be decidable on the strength of facts and meanings. This would have a bearing on the acceptability of cognitivism and of realism (and thus on whether moral claims can be truth-apt and can be known), but that is a matter for the coming section.

Study questions

1. Explain the stance of Peter Geach about the meaning of 'good'. To what extent does he persuade you of his case?
2. Is the puzzling nature of 'ought'-language best explained by understanding uses of 'ought' as incomplete expressions, short for 'prudentially ought', 'morally ought', 'legally ought', etc.?

Notes

1 Peter Geach, 'Good and Evil', *Analysis*, 17, 1956, pp. 33–42; also in Philippa Foot (ed.), *Theories of Ethics*, Oxford: Oxford University Press, 1967, pp. 64–73.

2 Geach, ibid.

3 Philippa Foot, 'Goodness and Choice', *Proceedings of the Aristotelian Society Supplementary Volume*, 35, 1961, pp. 45–60; also in Philippa Foot, *Virtues and Vices*, Oxford: Basil Blackwell, 1978, pp. 132–47.

4 Dorothy Mitchell, 'Must We Talk About "Is" and "Ought"?', *Mind*, 77, 1968, pp. 543–9.

5 Foot, op. cit.

6 Robin Attfield, *Value, Obligation and Meta-Ethics*, Amsterdam and Atlanta, GA: Éditions Rodopi, 1995, p. 237.

7 Michael J. Zimmerman, 'In Defense of the Concept of Intrinsic Value', *Canadian Journal of Philosophy*, 29, 1999, pp. 389–410.

8 Aaron Sloman, '"Ought" and "Better"', *Mind*, 79, 1970, pp. 385–94.

9 Robin Attfield, *Value, Obligation and Meta-Ethics*, Amsterdam and Atlanta, GA: Éditions Rodopi, 1995, pp. 238–42.

References

Attfield, Robin, *Value, Obligation and Meta-Ethics*, Amsterdam and Atlanta, GA: Éditions Rodopi, 1995.

Foot, Philippa, 'Goodness and Choice', *Proceedings of the Aristotelian Society Supplementary Volume*, 35, 1961, pp. 45–60; also in Philippa Foot, *Virtues and Vices*, Oxford: Basil Blackwell, 1978, pp. 132–47.

Geach, Peter, 'Good and Evil', *Analysis*, 17, 1956, pp. 33–42; also in Philippa Foot (ed.), *Theories of Ethics*, Oxford: Oxford University Press, 1967, pp. 64–73.

Mitchell, Dorothy, 'Must We Talk About "Is" and "Ought"?', *Mind*, 77, 1968, pp. 543–9.

Sloman, Aaron, '"Ought" and "Better"', *Mind*, 79, 1970, pp. 385–94.

Zimmerman, Michael J., 'In Defense of the Concept of Intrinsic Value', *Canadian Journal of Philosophy*, 29, 1999, pp. 389–410.

Section 3: Cognitivism and realism

1. Introduction: realism and cognitivism

While moral cognitivism maintains that moral claims can be known, moral realism holds (among other things) that they can be true or false, and are thus truth-apt. But realism says more than this, because it implicitly rejects the error theory and also subjectivism.

According to the error theory, moral claims purport to be true but fail (one and all), and are all false.[1] By contrast, realism holds that at least some of them are true. Obviously, cognitivism holds this too.

Subjectivists say that there are moral truths, but they are truths about the attitudes or approvals of the speakers or the believers in those truths. Actions are right when (and because) they are approved either by me (a relevant speaker or thinker) or by the moral community to which I belong. Realists, by contrast, hold that there is more to rightness than this; moral properties, as well as being real, are independent, they say, of the states of mind of the people who ascribe these properties to actions or agents.

In this respect, moral realism resembles realism in general, including realism about science, mathematics, history and religion. Generic realism holds that reality is independent of us, and also of our conceptions of it.[2] By contrast, generic anti-realism holds that our conceptions do not just structure reality, but constitute it, and that it is not independent of us at all. But there is no need here to trace how the debate between realism and anti-realism applies to science, mathematics, history or religion.[3] The key claim of moral realists is the independent reality of moral properties. This claim goes with (and supplements) the view that some moral beliefs are true.

Even if anti-realism is mistaken about science, mathematics, history and religion, it could in theory be correct about morality. One ground (discussed below) is the extent of disagreement within moral discourse. However, the stance of common sense supports moral realism. It is usually held that some actions really are right, and others wrong, whatever people may think about them.[4] Indeed it is usually held that most people know the difference between right and wrong, or, in other words, can tell which actions are which. So common sense supports moral cognitivism too. But common sense could possibly be wrong.

We shall first review the various theories that clash with realism, and then some of the grounds for questioning it (and thus for doubting cognitivism too). Then we return to the case for moral cognitivism and moral realism.

2. Non-cognitivism, error theory, subjectivism

Perhaps the most obvious theory for opponents of realism to adopt is the theory that moral claims do not involve statements, and are not truth-apt, because they have an entirely different character, such as expressing emotions or prescriptions. When moral judgements are made, or principles presented, the speech act is not one of conveying information, but expresses either the speaker's feelings or attitudes or motivations, or her or his commands or guidance to others (if not both); or so moral non-cognitivists suggest.

But, as we have seen in the section on Non-cognitivism, none of the most prominent kinds of non-cognitivism (emotivism, prescriptivism, projectivism) turns out to be persuasive, or immune from serious problems. One of the arguments often considered supportive of non-cognitivism, the link between moral language and motivation, will be discussed further in the section on

Internalism and Externalism, but has already been briefly countered in the section on Hobbes and Hume (see the part on Hume). (This topic is also touched on below in connection with John Mackie's 'argument from queerness'.)

Here it is worth mentioning that another argument often held to give non-cognitivism the edge over cognitivism (arguing from the link between moral language and action, which is sometimes thought to differentiate moral language from statements of fact, and make it closer to prescriptions) does not succeed. For many statements of fact have the capacity to guide action no less than prescriptions do: examples include 'There is a bull in that field', and 'Smoking can damage your health'. Besides, moral utterances usually supply moral reasons for action, and this may be sufficient to account for the fact that moral language and action are closely linked.[5] Thus non-cognitivism seems an unnecessary and unpromising approach, quite apart from the arguments of the previous section, which suggest that such language can often be validly derived from facts, and must therefore carry a truth-value (contrary to the claims of non-cognitivists).

Realism can alternatively be avoided by adopting the error theory of moral language, which suggests that all moral claims are false. This view is sometimes supported by the argument from the link between moral language and action, discussed in the previous paragraph, but found to be inconclusive. (For a fuller discussion, see the section on Internalism and Externalism.) But it is also a profoundly paradoxical theory. People who take morality seriously are usually regarded as seeking the truth about what is right or ought to be done, and yet the error theory claims that belief in such a truth is an illusion. Thus the error theory strikes at some of the very practices that, as a theory of moral philosophy, it is seeking to interpret. This counts significantly against it.

The remaining stance opposed to realism is subjectivism, which relates moral properties to the appraisals (usually approvals or disapprovals) of relevant subjects or societies. Moral claims on this view have truth-values (contrary to the emotivist view), and represent moral properties as real but as dependent on people's states of mind (which they implicitly report). Many have found this a tempting view. But it cannot withstand a version of Moore's Open Question argument. Let us construe subjectivism as holding that 'right' means 'approved by S (a subject or subjects)'. If we now ask whether things approved by S (or by any given subject) are right, this question is invariably an open question (with answers such as 'It all depends'), except possibly when asked by S, rather than the closed question that it would have to be if the subjectivist analysis of 'right' were correct.[6] And this is evidence for the realist view that moral properties are real properties, independent of the states of mind of people who ascribe them, and against subjectivism. (Which is unsurprising, for 'morally right' means, in part, what there is moral reason to do, and not just what people in fact approve.)

Realism, then, turns out to be (so far) more cogent than its rivals: non-cognitivism, the error theory and subjectivism. We should now investigate how well it fares in face of objections.

3. Disagreement

The extent of moral disagreement is often used as evidence that here are no moral facts, or that if there are such facts they merely convey the (divergent) attitudes of subjects or of speakers. People persistently disagree about the morality of abortion (see the section on Medical Ethics) and of euthanasia (see the section on Worthwhile Life), and that of monogamy and polygamy, about issues of war and peace and about countless other issues besides. These disputes seem irresolvable, and are sometimes taken to suggest that there is no truth of the matter about which they turn.

The mere fact of disagreement does not of itself suggest that there are no facts of the matter in question. Thus there are plenty of disagreements in the fields of science and in history, without the quest for truth being abandoned or the view that no truth is attainable being widely adopted. It is rather the radical nature of moral disagreement that gives rise to such sceptical suggestions. Could moral disagreements merely reflect clashes of emotions, of interests, or of cultures, and have no bearing on truth whatever?

Yet realists (and cognitivists) can utilize the factors of differences in emotions and in interests as part of their explanation of persistent disagreement. People's judgements are prone to be coloured and often skewed by their emotions and their interests, and to fail to understand others' judgements for these reasons. People are also prone, whether for these reasons or for others, to argue past each other, without fully recognizing the range of circumstances relevant to the case and adduced by others. Even persistent disagreement is consistent with realism (and with cognitivism), as long as explanations of such disagreement (which can include cultural factors) can be consistently supplied.[7]

David Hume maintained that there is more to moral disagreement than the resources of reason can handle. 'But after every circumstance, every relation is known, the understanding has no further room to operate, nor any object on which it could employ itself.' What remains when moral judgements are made is a matter not for reason but for 'active feeling and sentiment'.[8] Yet as we have seen in the section on Hume, that philosopher had an unduly narrow conception of the scope of reason, and there can be reasoning not only involving deduction, observation and experiment, but also about desirability. Indeed there can even be reasoning, it was argued in the previous section, about what ought to be done. Thus there is no need to infer that moral judgements are just either reports of our feelings (as subjectivists claim) or expressions of them (as emotivists and projectivists maintain). While attitudes or emotions are often expressed, moral judgements make interpersonal claims, capable of both support and of scrutiny through reason and argument.

No termination of the processes of reason and argument can be foreseen or predicted in advance, since many factors can prolong disagreement and frustrate or impede those processes. It is here that realists and cognitivists can appeal to the many factors (psychological, economic, ideological and religious ones included) that help explain the persistent nature of moral disagreements.[9] This appeal, however, is consistent with the possibility of eventual moral agreement, with moral judgements being truth-apt (or what could the agreement or the disagreement be about?), and with their sometimes amounting to moral knowledge.

4. Some other objections to moral realism

Besides the objection concerning radical disagreement, further objections to moral realism are sometimes made. Some have already been covered in the section on Value, which considered subjectivist and other sceptical challenges to that concept and its applications.

One challenge will be mentioned here but discussed in the section on Internalism. John Mackie, writing in 1966, called this challenge 'the argument from queerness'. Moral properties of the kind affirmed by the moral realist, he maintained, have to be both objective and at the same time motivationally compelling. But such properties would be unprecedented and unique (or 'queer' in the old-fashioned sense of that word), and are not to be found, and so the realists are wrong and all their claims are false. This argument appears to pitch the strength of motivation required of moral properties at too demanding a level; a parallel point was argued in connection with prescriptivism, in the section on Non-cognitivism. But whether realists can satisfactorily cope with moral motivation, or it is their opponents who present implausibly strong requirements in this field, are questions needing to be considered separately (see the next section).

There are also a cluster of issues surrounding naturalism (in G. E. Moore's sense of the term: see section on Non-cognitivism). For if ethical naturalism involves a fallacy (the one labelled by Moore 'the naturalistic fallacy') then the moral facts that realism acknowledges cannot be derived from (say) scientific facts, not even ones about health, danger or injury. But even if (as was argued in the same section) Moore failed to clinch the case for there being such a fallacy, issues can still be raised about how moral truths can be vindicated or justified,[10] and how (if cognitivism is right) this grounding can be secure enough for them to be known. However, these are issues rather than objections, and will be further discussed in a separate section on Naturalism and Non-naturalism, as well as initially in the last part of the current section.

5. Moral knowledge

Perhaps the best way to argue for realism (and at the same time for cognitivism) is to present one or more examples of moral knowledge. If they are more securely known than the various grounds on which they might be doubted, then the case for cognitivism is itself secure, as long as the problems mentioned above can be satisfactorily resolved.

In this spirit, Renford Bambrough puts forward the following example. 'We know that this child who is about to undergo what would otherwise be painful surgery should be given an anaesthetic before the operation. Therefore we know at least one moral proposition to be true'.[11] Bambrough's view is that this is known more securely than any fact or principle that might be used to question it.

Some might hesitate before agreeing. We would also need to know that safe and effective anaesthetics are available; that the child does not have a condition that would make the administration of an anaesthetic hazardous; and that the hospital or clinic is run along professional lines, with staff committed to beneficence and non-maleficence, and is not a corrupt or careless institution. Bambrough seems to assume all this. But let us allow him these assumptions, and build them into his story. This granted, many would say that he has presented a genuine example of moral knowledge.

Joel Kupperman presents several examples for the same purpose; here is his first one.

> Jones has been taught since early childhood that it is in general wrong to steal. He assents, and when questioned says that theft is in general wrong. He has an excellent opportunity to steal an art object which he greatly covets, under conditions in which it is virtually certain that he would escape detection. But he clenches his teeth, looks for a moment like Immanuel Kant, and does not do the deed. (Jones knows that he should not steal the art object.)[12]

Kupperman comments that in this scenario it is not only clear that Jones believes that stealing the art work would be wrong, but also that the other elements normally expected of knowledge are satisfied, the belief being (surely) true, and what is more being justified. The justification hangs not only on the social teaching to which Jones assents, but on the implicit case in its favour that general observance of the rules for respecting others' property is socially beneficial, and that although under some conditions there are legitimate exceptions to these rules, those conditions are not remotely present in the current case. (Once again, a longer story could be told, such as that there are no lives that Jones can save through a timely theft; but if the justification of which Jones is aware really holds up, then it is also clear that no such life-saving possibilities are in prospect, nor anything else that would make this case one to which the general rule does not apply.)

Nor does the claim of some anarchists that property is theft cast doubt on Jones' knowledge or on Kupperman's example. For this slogan itself relies on recognition of the concept of theft and on theft's general wrongness; and so critics of at least this particular stripe presuppose the very social teaching on which Jones' knowledge and thus Kupperman's example depend.

If Kupperman's case is accepted here, then his discussion supplements Bambrough's vindication of moral knowledge by showing that such knowledge satisfies the normal expectations that knowledge should comprise justified true belief, and is thus closely comparable to knowledge of other kinds, for example, scientific knowledge, historical knowledge or mathematical knowledge. And while we would probably not regard all justified true belief as knowledge, our finding that claims that are candidates for comprising knowledge (such as this one) amount to justified true belief suggests that the necessary conditions for knowledge are satisfied (which is reassuring, at least for cognitivists).

While further examples (such as Kupperman's) could be rehearsed, enough have been presented for present purposes. It can be added that it is only to be expected that there are such examples, granted that we often talk about people knowing the difference between right and wrong. For there would have to be actual examples of knowledge if talk of that kind is coherent. I am not suggesting that moral knowledge is readily accessible. But plausibly it is actually widespread.

However, moral knowledge would not be possible unless moral realists are correct in holding that at least some moral claims are true. Yet the possibility of moral knowledge is of the utmost importance for our everyday moral practice. While the case for moral realism presented here – and against non-cognitivism, the error theory and subjectivism – strengthens the case for moral cognitivism, the case for the latter from actual examples serves to confirm that for moral realism. Yet the case for neither is complete until the issue of internalism and externalism has been investigated, a task to be undertaken in the coming section.

Study questions

1. How cogent is Renford Bambrough's suggested example (the child who needs an anaesthetic) of moral knowledge? (See the section on Moral Realism of his book *Moral Scepticism and Moral Knowledge*, London and Henley: Routledge & Kegan Paul, 1979. If possible, see also Bambrough's chapter 'Proof' (same book), pp. 11–36. This chapter is reprinted in Russ Shafer-Landau, *Ethical Theory: An Anthology*, Oxford, UK and Malden, MA: Blackwell, 2007, pp. 103–10.)
2. Compare the merits of moral realism and any one rival theory.

Notes

1 J. L. Mackie, *Ethics: Inventing Right and Wrong*, Harmondsworth, UK: Penguin, 1966.

2 Martin Warner, 'Introduction', in Martin Warner (ed.), *Religion and Philosophy*, Cambridge: Cambridge University Press, 1992, pp. 1–21.

3 I have discussed the debate between generic realism and anti-realism in Robin Attfield, *Creation, Evolution and Meaning*, Aldershot, UK and Burlington, VT: Ashgate, 2006, chapter 2. For discussion of how this general debate relates to moral realism, see David O. Brink, *Moral Realism and the Foundations of Ethics*, Cambridge, UK: Cambridge University Press, 1989.

4 See Geoffrey Sayre-McCord, 'Moral Realism', in *Stanford Encyclopedia of Philosophy*, http://www.seop.leeds.ac.uk/entries/moral-realism (accessed 16 August 2010); Brink, pp. 7–8.

5 Robin Attfield, *Value, Obligation and Meta-Ethics*, Amsterdam and Atlanta, GA: Éditions Rodopi, 1995, pp. 203–5; David Hume, *Enquiries Concerning Human Understanding and Concerning the Principles of Morals*, ed. P. H. Nidditch, 3rd edn, Oxford: Clarendon Press, 1975.

6 See further Robin Attfield, *Value, Obligation and Meta-Ethics*, pp. 200–3.

7 Renford Bambrough, *Moral Scepticism and Moral Knowledge*, London and Henley: Routledge & Kegan Paul, 1979, pp. 18–19 and 72–4.

8 David Hume, *An Inquiry Concerning the Principles of Morals*, Appendix 1; available in David Hume, *Enquiries Concerning Human Understanding and Concerning the Principles of Morals*, ed. P. H. Nidditch, 3rd edn, Oxford: Clarendon Press, 1975, p. 290.

9 Attfield, *Value, Obligation and Meta-Ethics*, pp. 250–2.

10 Thus Geoffrey Sayre-McCord, 'Moral Realism', in *Stanford Encyclopedia of Philosophy*, http://www.seop.leeds.ac.uk/entries/moral-realism (accessed 20 August 2010).

11 Bambrough, op. cit., p. 15.

12 Joel J. Kupperman, *Ethical Knowledge*, London: Allen & Unwin and New York: Humanities Press, 1970, pp. 130–1.

13 See further Attfield, *Value, Obligation and Meta-Ethics*, pp. 193–8.

References

Attfield, Robin, *Value, Obligation and Meta-Ethics*, Amsterdam and Atlanta, GA: Éditions Rodopi, 1995

—, *Creation, Evolution and Meaning*, Aldershot, UK and Burlington, VT: Ashgate, 2006.

Bambrough, Renford, *Moral Scepticism and Moral Knowledge*, London and Henley: Routledge & Kegan Paul, 1979.

—, 'Proof', reprinted in Russ Shafer-Landau, *Ethical Theory: An Anthology*, Oxford, UK and Malden, MA: Blackwell, 2007, pp. 103–10.

Brink, David O., *Moral Realism and the Foundations of Ethics*, Cambridge, UK: Cambridge University Press, 1989.

Hume, David, *Enquiries Concerning Human Understanding and Concerning the Principles of Morals*, ed. P. H. Nidditch, 3rd edn, Oxford: Clarendon Press, 1975.

Kupperman, Joel J., *Ethical Knowledge*, London: Allen & Unwin and New York: Humanities Press, 1970.

Mackie, J. L., *Ethics: Inventing Right and Wrong*, Harmondsworth, UK: Penguin, 1977.

Sayre-McCord, Geoffrey, 'Moral Realism', in *Stanford Encyclopedia of Philosophy*, http://www.seop.leeds.ac.uk/entries/moral-realism.

Warner, Martin, 'Introduction', in Martin Warner (ed.), *Religion and Philosophy*, Cambridge: Cambridge University Press, 1992, pp. 1–21.

Section 4: Internalism, externalism and practicality

1. Introduction: realism and practicality

While there is, as we have seen, a strong case for realism, moral language has another feature which many have considered to point towards anti-realism instead. For moral language, far from being inert, motivates action in line with moral judgements and principles, and at the same time provides reasons for such action. These characteristics of moral language have often been held necessary to moral language and to the very concept of morality. The stance that credits this necessary connection is called 'internalism'.

But internalism has been argued to conflict with realism. One reason is that language of which internalism holds good can arguably motivate or provide reasons for action only if it touches (or expresses) our desires, something that factual language seems unable to do. Factual language informs us, but seems to lack the dynamic quality that of itself instigates action, the 'practicality' (as we might call it) of moral language.[1] The nature and implications of this practicality are discussed in this section.

Some philosophers, however, maintain that the connection between moral language and motivation and/or providing reasons for action is not a necessary one, as internalists hold, but contingent. Moral judgements and principles do not necessarily or invariably motivate action, they claim, and do not necessarily or invariably supply reasons for action either. This is the stance of 'externalism', and externalism is widely recognized to raise no problems for realism, as it coheres with moral claims being claims about how things are. This section will also consider whether we should be internalists or externalists.

However, there is more than one kind of internalism and externalism, and some are more plausible than others. The issue becomes in the end which blend of internalism and externalism we should favour, and whether the more plausible kinds of internalism can be reconciled with realism. I will suggest that they can, and that the kinds that cannot were never plausible in the first place.

2. The debate about motivation

We should first consider internalism about motivation, which holds that moral considerations necessarily motivate the relevant people. The relevant people could be either relevant agents or else appraisers holding relevant moral beliefs, and we should consider these possibilities in turn. Nearly everyone (including externalists) would agree that in general moral considerations motivate people (or at least adults), but is this a matter of conceptual necessity?

First, we should reflect on agent internalism, which maintains that moral obligations necessarily motivate the agents to whom they apply. But this theory clashes with our commonsense belief that certain obligations (such as promise-keeping) apply to every moral agent regardless of their desires. For agent internalism implies that people who have no desire to perform such obligations (and are thus not motivated to do so) do not even have such obligations at all, and that the obligations that we ordinarily consider to belong to all moral agents (such as promise-keeping) really belong only to those who have the desire to perform them. But these are unacceptable implications, which would allow people successfully to disown obligations simply because they do not care about them in the least. These implications strongly suggest the conclusion that agent internalism must be rejected.[2]

It is in any case implausible for another reason: many people would seem to have obligations without being aware of them, and most of these people are unlikely to be motivated to act as if they were aware of these unrecognized obligations. For example, many people in developed countries have not noticed that they have obligations to limit their carbon emissions, and relatedly show no signs of attempting to do so (although they often could if they thought about the matter). Hence the view that simply being subject to a moral obligation motivates the agent in question to act accordingly proves to be unacceptable.

This brings us to appraiser internalism about motives, which maintains that holding moral beliefs necessarily motivates those holding these beliefs to act accordingly when the opportunity arises. A version of this view was considered in the section on Non-cognitivism, in connection with the prescriptivism of Richard Hare. The problem, once again, is that this kind of internalist holds that it is impossible for anyone to hold a moral belief and not to be motivated by it. This view, however, implies that people who hold moral beliefs and have no inclination to act accordingly (amoralists) do not and cannot exist.

These are not people whose wish to act in line with their beliefs is overwhelmed by other desires (such as the comfort of a quiet life), although these people too pose a problem for Hare's very strong version of motivation internalism. They are the smaller set of people with no such wish at all. Yet, although they are probably few in number, they do seem to exist, and their existence should not be regarded as inconceivable (as this kind of internalist has to regard them). This being so, appraiser internalism about motives seems to conflict with the facts, and thus to be unacceptable itself.[3]

Accordingly, both agent internalism and appraiser internalism about motives seem misguided views, and neither of them succeeds in capturing the dynamic, action-instigating property of moral language, or its practicality (which we shall shortly investigate further). Indeed where motives are concerned, externalism (which 'makes the motivational force of moral considerations a matter of contingent psychological fact, depending on the beliefs and desires agents happen to have'[4]) seems a preferable view of the relation between morality and motivation.

We are now in a position to return to one interpretation of the argument of J. L. Mackie against moral realism, mentioned in the previous section.

Moral properties of the kind affirmed by the moral realist, Mackie can be interpreted as holding, have to be both objective and at the same time motivationally compelling; but such properties are not to be found; hence all claims involving them are false, and realism is to be rejected.[5] This argument, however, itself relies on internalism about the motivational force of moral language. For moral properties such as moral rightness need not be motivationally compelling, either on the realist view or on any other (except for some forms of internalism). Indeed this argument, like internalism about motives in general, exaggerates and distorts the relation between motivation and morality, and thereby invents a problem for realism that proves to be imaginary. For internalism about motives has been shown to be misguided.

However, both internalism and Mackie's argument too can be understood instead as concerning not motives but reasons for action. It is reasons for action, the internalist can claim, that are necessarily related to moral considerations. To the debate raised by this kind of internalism we now turn.

3. The debate about reasons for action

We should now consider internalism about reasons for action, which holds that moral considerations necessarily supply reasons for action to relevant people. This seems a plausible theory, and would pose a problem for realism if a realist interpretation of moral claims conflicted with, or failed to explain, this property of moral discourse.

However, the plausibility of this kind of internalism depends on the sense of 'reason' in use. One route for the anti-realist to take is to appeal to the Humean view of reasons as desires, which are reasons because (for this approach) they are needed to explain actions and thus give us the reasons for those actions. Reasons at any rate involve desires, according to this approach, even if they consist in more than desires and involve some kind of conscious mental state as well.

Mendel F. Cohen has well expressed the relevant principle: 'Nothing constitutes a reason for an individual to act or refrain from acting unless it is related to his [or her] sentiments or passions'.[6] And, as Cohen goes on to remark, this is plausible for one sense of 'reason'. However, as he goes on to say, it also clashes with the key tenet that 'moral principles constitute reasons to do or refrain no matter what an individual's wants, desires, sentiments or passions may be'.[7] But this is the sense of 'reason' that is needed, because this is the sense in which moral considerations provide reasons (or a reason) for action. Moral considerations, for example, supply reasons (in this sense) against adultery for those who endorse them, but often still fail to supply reasons against adultery in the sense of desire or inclination.

So we need to distinguish between two senses of 'reason for action'. One of these is the Humean sense of explanatory reason (where reasons either are or necessarily involve desires); and this is the sense that begins to make the above anti-realist argument from reasons for action look plausible. The other is the un-Humean sense of justificatory reason; but this is the only sense in which it is plausible that moral considerations always provide reasons for action.[8] However, relevant agents will often lack reasons in the first sense, through lacking any inclination or motivation to behave in accordance with moral principles or considerations. Thus moral considerations give them reasons (in the second sense) for behaving accordingly whether they have matching desires or not, and sometimes they do not.

The argument against realism from an internalist view of reasons for action trades on this ambiguity. Implicitly focusing on appraisers, and thus on people who believe in and are committed to moral judgements or principles, it argues that their moral beliefs give them reasons for action, and interprets this as implying that they invariably have matching desires, given that they have these beliefs at all. But reasoning of this kind assumes that amoralists do not and cannot exist, and that people cannot hold moral beliefs without their behaviour being affected. Even if it is granted that moral considerations confer reasons for action on their adherents, and necessarily at that, these cannot be reasons for action in the Humean sense. The reasons conferred would have to be reasons in the sense of justifying reasons, rather than explanatory reasons. The argument against realism seems to succeed only because it shifts in mid-stream from the first to the second sense of 'reasons for action'.

This suggests in turn that we should avoid adherence to internalism about reasons for action in the Humean sense of reasons involving related desires. For moral considerations do not invariably or necessarily supply reasons for action in this sense. Where this sense is in use, we should be externalists, accepting (as before) that moral considerations supply reasons (in this sense) contingently, and only where agents are not disinclined to be motivated accordingly. Let us defer for a moment consideration of whether we should be internalists about reasons for action in the un-Humean sense of justificatory reasons.

We are now in a position to consider Mackie's argument against realism, interpreted as grounded not in motivations but in reasons for action. Moral properties of the kind affirmed by the moral realist, Mackie can this time be interpreted as holding, both are objective and at the same time necessarily provide reasons for action; but such properties are not to be found; hence realism is to be rejected. But this argument assumes both an internalist view of the relation of morality and reasons for action, and at the same time a Humean view of what reasons for action are; for this is the likely basis for claiming that reasons, understood as involving desires to act in line with moral considerations, are not (or not always) to be found. But where this sense of 'reasons' is in use, as we have just seen, internalism is implausible, and so the argument fails.

If, however, reasons for action are understood as justifying reasons, it is much less clear that such reasons are not to be found. Mackie probably considered that no facts could embody such reasons, and might also have wanted to deny that the desirability of anything can ever be a fact (or be known or discovered). Yet sceptics such as Mackie seem to have no difficulty with the notion of credibility, or thus with *reasons for belief* (which they would ascribe, for example, to their own conclusions), and this is surely a parallel case to *reasons for action*. So if (in the case of reasons for belief) there is such a property as credibility or what we might call 'to-be-believedness', there should be no objection (in the case of reasons for action) to there being a property of desirability or what we might call 'to-be-desiredness' or 'to-be-doneness'.[9] Accordingly the claim that the properties that realists talk about are not to be found has not been vindicated, and the anti-realist argument fails again.

4. Moral commitments

It is time to return to consideration of whether we should be internalists about reasons for action in the sense of justificatory reasons. *Must* people who adhere to moral judgements have reasons for action in this sense?

Take the simple case of someone who holds that people should keep their promises. Let us ignore the exceptions that they might make to this, and ask about reasons for action relevant to cases that are not exceptional. Let us also assume that this person is aware that she has made a promise. This being so, then she must judge that she should keep her promise. We cannot predict that she will actually do so, but logic and consistency require her to make this judgement about herself. Much the same applies to her judgements about other people whom she knows to have made promises, at least where there are no exceptional circumstances.

Thus a person who adheres to moral judgements involving a 'should' or an 'ought' must make corresponding 'should' or 'ought' judgements about relevant particular cases, including their own case;[10] and since such an 'ought' judgment about oneself involves a reason for action, we can conclude that adherence to such moral judgements necessarily supplies reasons for action (in the sense of justifying reasons), in conjunction with relevant beliefs about particular cases. But to accept this is to accept a form of internalism about reasons for action in the sense of justifying reasons. (The same reasoning applies to other forms of 'ought' judgements, such as prudential judgements, but that is not our current concern.) The person may omit to act accordingly, and they would even be justified in acting otherwise, if there were (justifying) reasons that supersede the reason to keep the promise, although such reasons would only arise if there were exceptional circumstances after all. But they cannot in any case deny that they ought (other things being equal) to keep the promise, and this is to have a reason for action.

The commitments of people who adhere to moral principles or judgements need (strictly speaking) go no further than this. Very often, they will be motivated to act in line with their moral beliefs, because they will want the goods that those beliefs uphold, such as the maintenance of trust between people, the good of others or the good of society. But where the question concerns the necessary connection of moral judgements to reasons for action, nothing more than the very limited form of internalism commended here needs to be recognized.

This form of internalism, it should be added, raises no problems for realists. Even if moral judgements are truth-apt and their truth is not dependent on people's mental states, they will still have implications for particular cases, and when those implications are recognized to concern oneself, they will still involve reasons for action. There are no implications here about motivation, and thus no problems raised by any necessary relation of moral judgements to motivation. The necessary connection to reasons for action is, as we have seen, of a different kind, but one which may be enough to explain both the practicality of moral judgements and the intuitive attractiveness of internalism.

5. Realists and reasons for action

Realists, then, can be unashamedly externalist about the relation of moral judgements to motivation, and also about the relation of moral judgements to reasons for action, in the sense of explanatory reasons. None of this in any way undermines their realism; indeed it immunizes them from anti-realist arguments grounded in the corresponding kinds of internalism, which we have seen to be misguided. They should be internalists only with regard to the relation of moral beliefs to reasons for action in the sense of justifying reasons, as argued above.

In this sense, moral considerations do necessarily supply reasons for action to relevant people. As mentioned above, there would be a problem for realism if a realist interpretation of moral claims conflicted with, or failed to explain, this property of moral discourse. But as we have seen, it does not conflict with this property. However, can realists explain it?

Here we are trying to explain why people who adhere to moral judgements necessarily have reasons to act accordingly, in the sense of justifying reasons, and thus why moral language should be regarded as action-guiding in this sense. Realism explains this by claiming that moral judgements aspire to being true, and adding that if they are true, then the implications they have in conjunction with other truths about particular cases will also be true (and thus usually important too). If I recognize that it is true that I ought to behave in a certain way, and this in turn conveys that acting in this way truly has or promotes value,[11] then no further explanation is required for my having a (justifying) reason for action, or thus for the practicality of my 'ought' judgement. There could be a problem here for anti-realists, because if 'oughts' consist in nothing more than prescriptions or approvals or reports of subjective states, there could be room to doubt whether they really involve value or constitute reasons for action at all. For realists, however, there is no such problem.

Hence the objection to moral realism based on practicality turns out to be no objection. Granted the positive case for realism and the replies to other objections presented in the previous section, there are good grounds to reject moral anti-realism in all its forms, and instead accept realism.

Study questions

1. Can people have obligations to act in ways that they have no inclination to act?
2. Does the practicality of moral language require an anti-realist theory of such language?
3. Explain and appraise John Mackie's anti-realist argument.

Notes

1 See Michael Smith, 'Realism', in Russ Shafer-Landau (ed.), *Ethical Theory*, Oxford and Malden, MA: Blackwell, 2007, pp. 72–6; also in Peter Singer (ed.), *A Companion to Ethics*, Oxford and Cambridge, MA: Blackwell, 1993, pp. 399–410.

2 See David O. Brink, *Moral Realism and the Foundations of Ethics*, Cambridge and New York: Cambridge University Press, 1989, p. 45.

3 Brink, op. cit., pp. 45–8.

4 Brink, op. cit., p. 49.

5 J. L. Mackie, *Ethics: Inventing Right and Wrong*, Harmondsworth, UK: Penguin, 1966.

6 Mendel F. Cohen, 'The Practicality of Moral Reasoning', *Mind*, 78, 1969, pp. 534–49; see p. 544.

7 Cohen, op. cit., p. 546.

8 For this distinction, see Brink, op. cit., p. 39. See also James Lenman, 'Reasons for Action: Justification versus Explanation', in *Stanford Encyclopedia of Philosophy*, http://www.seop.leeds.ac.uk/entries/reasons-just-vs-expl/ (accessed 7 September 2010).

9 See further Robin Attfield, *Value, Obligation and Meta-Ethics*, Amsterdam and Atlanta, GA: Éditions Rodopi, 1995, pp. 30–1.

10 See Cohen, op. cit., pp. 546–9.

11 Brink, op. cit., pp. 78–9.

References

Attfield, Robin, *Value, Obligation and Meta-Ethics*, Amsterdam and Atlanta, GA: Éditions Rodopi, 1995.

Brink, David O., *Moral Realism and the Foundations of Ethics*, Cambridge and New York: Cambridge University Press, 1989.

Cohen, Mendel F., 'The Practicality of Moral Reasoning', *Mind*, 78, 1969, pp. 534–49.

Lenman, James, 'Reasons for Action: Justification versus Explanation', in *Stanford Encyclopedia of Philosophy*, http://www.seop.leeds.ac.uk/entries/reasons-just-vs-expl/.

Mackie, J. L., *Ethics: Inventing Right and Wrong*, Harmondsworth, UK: Penguin, 1966.

Smith, Michael, 'Realism', in Peter Singer (ed.), *A Companion to Ethics*, Oxford and Cambridge, MA: Blackwell, 1993, pp. 399–410.

—, 'Realism', in Russ Shafer-Landau (ed.), *Ethical Theory*, Oxford and Malden, MA: Blackwell, 2007, pp. 72–6.

Section 5: Naturalism and non-naturalism

1. Introduction: justifications for ethical truth

As was mentioned in the section on Realism, issues remain about how moral truths can be justified, and how (if cognitivism is right) this grounding can be secure enough for them to be known. Such issues are explored in this section.

Realism and cognitivism imply one or other of two bases for ethical truths. They may either be derivable from facts such as those within the purview of science (roughly, the kind of 'naturalism' rejected by G. E. Moore), or they may be truths of an entirely different kind, known not on the basis of experience and related reasoning but intuitively (a stance that Moore favoured and named 'non-naturalism').

But non-naturalism faces large problems. If, as Moore held, ethical terms cannot be defined, and ethical truths cannot be derived from facts of experience, it is far from easy to explain how anyone can ever learn to use these terms and recognize these truths. (See the section on Non-cognitivism.) Yet non-naturalism at least provides scope for reasoning about what is right (from, for example, what is good, as argued by Moore in *Ethics*[1]). And perhaps we have the ability to intuit what is good.

However, the problems of non-naturalism, together with the question-begging nature of Moore's argument against naturalism (see again the section on Non-cognitivism), suggest that the cogency of ethical naturalism should be further considered here. But before we can embark on this inquiry, we need to reflect on the meanings (for there are several) of the word 'naturalism'.

2. Senses of 'naturalism'

Besides the kind of naturalism that Moore rejected (let us continue to call this kind 'ethical naturalism'), the term 'naturalism' is also used in philosophy for a range of stances about ontology and about methodology.[2]

Ontological naturalism is prone to claim that the only facts are facts studied by science, plus facts that supervene on or are constituted by these facts (as when, for example, 'being made of water' supervenes on 'being H_2O'). Sometimes it also includes appeals to the best explanation of these facts, which might invoke God's role as cosmic creator, but more often it precludes such appeals. (Strangely, Moore included in 'naturalism' definitions of ethical concepts invoking facts about God, calling this 'metaphysical naturalism', and considered this equally subject to the 'naturalistic fallacy' as empirical definitions.[3] For present purposes this just serves to show how distant his sense of 'naturalism' was from the other senses of 'naturalism', whether ontological or methodological, covered here.)

Methodological naturalism holds rather that progress in both science and philosophy can only be made by appealing to the facts studied by science, plus relevant concepts. Like ontological naturalism, this stance is in conflict with Moorean non-naturalism.

Both ontological naturalism and naturalism of the methodological kind are, however, consistent with ethical naturalism, as long as they provide for supervenience. For ethical facts may supervene on, or be underpinned by, natural (empirical) ones. If, as is plausible, two identical situations necessarily result in the presence of the same ethical properties, then these properties can be said to 'supervene' on the natural ones. For example, with activities such as administering an anaesthetic to a child about to undergo an otherwise painful operation, as in Bambrough's example[4] (see the section on Realism), the ethical property of rightness supervenes. While non-naturalists will perforce find great difficulty in recognizing such ethical supervenience, it poses no problem for ethical naturalists.

In their more restrictive versions, both ontological and methodological naturalism conflict with ethical naturalism, and hold that there are no facts about desirability, rightness or obligation. But as we have seen in the section on Internalism and Externalism, it is plausible that there are such facts, facts which thus supply reasons for action (in the sense of justifying reasons). We can thus disregard these more restrictive kinds of naturalism (whether ontological or methodological), and the issues that they raise. And since the less restrictive kinds (whether true or false) leave room for ethical naturalism, we can now return to naturalism in that sense, and investigate which kinds of facts might underpin ethical ones.

3. Foot, harm and supervenience

As Philippa Foot argued, in articles of the 1950s, not just anything can be adduced as evidence for ethical conclusions, and considerations of human good and harm cannot be counted as irrelevant to moral deliberation.[5] Besides, there are facts about what comprises (say) harm, and what causes it (facts that are pivotal to, for example, the science of medicine).

Human welfare and harm are certainly not the only morally relevant considerations. Thus the well-being of other living creatures is relevant too (see the section on 'Moral Standing, Value and Intrinsic Value'), and so are injuries and harms to such creatures. (Further, there are facts about the flourishing of creatures, and about what harms them, pivotal to the science of biology.) Besides, the quality of life of future generations is also widely held to be morally relevant, even though most of their members cannot strictly be benefited or harmed by present actions (because the possibility of harm depends on that of existing in more than one future, which probably does not fit most future individuals). But, while we cannot define moral rightness in terms of human welfare and harm alone, there are still conceptual connections between generating human welfare or harm and moral rightness and wrongness respectively, and between generating human welfare or harm and what ought or ought not (respectively) to be done (see the section on 'Good', 'Ought' and Morality).

The rediscovery of these connections proved influential when moral philosophy began to be applied once again to issues of public life in the 1960s and 1970s; see the section on 'The Re-emergence of Applied Ethics'. Thus when other considerations are either absent or equal, the harmfulness of a course of action necessarily counts decisively against it. But this is just the kind of necessary connection between facts and moral conclusions that ethical naturalism leads us to expect. Besides, if we try asking a Moorean question along the lines: 'This action is avoidable, and harmful to someone, and there are no countervailing considerations, but is it wrong?', this proves not to be an open question, as Moore's stance would lead us to believe, but a closed one.

All this gives us a better grip on supervenience. Supervenience does not of itself imply naturalism. (Indeed some non-cognitivists recognize the supervenience of ethical properties on natural ones.) But naturalists can explain supervenience, through the necessary connections between facts about nature and ethical conclusions, or between natural properties and ethical ones. This is why identical activities or situations result in and underpin identical ethical properties (supervenience). If so, then supervenience is no contingency; it could not fail to be the case, granted naturalism.[6] So if naturalism is correct, supervenience fits neatly into place.

Not every form of naturalism is vindicated by these considerations. Thus the kind of naturalism that attempts to define ethical properties in theological terms (what Brink calls 'supernaturalism'[7]) seems to remain subject to a form of Moore's Open Question argument. For the question 'Is what God wills good?' appears to remain an open one (unless God is defined as 'good' in the first place). Besides, only if it is an open question can believers praise God for his goodness. Thus the relation between God and goodness is best regarded as a contingent one. But the naturalist need not be committed to all the many suggested conceptual connections between facts and ethical conclusions. Naturalism will be correct as long as some such conceptual connections exist. The connection between causing harm and moral wrongness seems sufficient to clinch this case.

4. Searle and institutions

A quite different way of arguing validly from facts to an 'ought'-conclusion, and thus (we might add) of vindicating ethical naturalism, has been presented by John R. Searle. Searle's argument opens with one man (Jones) saying to another (Smith) 'I promise to pay you five dollars'. We also understand that Jones is not acting or jesting, and that he and Smith each know that both are competent speakers of English. The conclusion is that Jones is under an obligation to pay Smith five dollars, and that, as far as his obligation is concerned, he ought to pay Smith this amount.[8] He might, in theory, also have clashing obligations, but if not, then he really ought to pay, all things considered. (Searle's argument is further considered in the section on 'The Re-emergence of Applied Ethics'.)

If this reasoning is valid, as Searle recognized, it is because of the institution of promising. The institution of promising makes it a necessary truth that anyone who utters words such as 'I promise' (or one of its equivalents in other languages) in circumstances where there is no play-acting or joking going on, and all parties speak the same language and know this, actually makes a promise, and therefore undertakes a related obligation. Opponents suggested that this is not a valid deduction because we can choose whether or not to accept the institution of promising. But Searle could respond that this institution is needed in every society, and that anyone who questions whether uttering words like 'I promise' in circumstances such as these generates an obligation does not understand the meaning of those words. For no one can use those words in those circumstances without accepting the related commitments. Playing along and then disowning one's responsibility is not an option.

We certainly cannot argue that since the conclusion embodies an 'ought' it cannot be validly derived from the premises; for this is just what Searle's reasoning manages to show to be possible. Indeed if we choose to call the conclusion an 'evaluative' conclusion, then Searle seems to have shown that at least some evaluative conclusions can be validly derived from facts and conceptual truths alone. (So, as Searle implies, we must avoid defining 'evaluative' conclusions as ones that cannot be thus derived.[9]) However, someone could question whether the 'ought' of this conclusion is actually a moral 'ought'.

Philippa Foot raised this question in her 'Introduction' to *Theories of Ethics*. She grants that Searle shows how an 'ought' can be validly derived, but holds that his premises are the wrong ones for reaching a moral 'ought'. This, she suggests, would require premises 'which referred to such things as injury, freedom and happiness, i.e. to things that count in the scale of human good and harm'.[10] She suggests that this becomes clearer if we ask whether verbal engagement in a bad institution such as duelling would generate a moral obligation to shoot someone; we might reasonably hold that it would not,[11] even if it generated some other sort of obligation (which we might call an 'institutional' obligation).

Be that as it may, the institution of promising could readily be defended as itself tending to enhance human well-being, and thus to promote something of intrinsic value, and its rules thereby satisfy the definition of moral principles argued for in the above section on 'Good', 'Ought' and Morality. (With the rules of duelling, by contrast, this is much less plausible.) This suggests that the 'ought' of Searle's conclusion really is a moral one (contrary to Foot's view), but that to reach it he needs to invoke the principle that keeping promises is morally obligatory, which is itself grounded in and justified by human good. If so, then Searle's own premises do not serve to vindicate ethical naturalism as they stand, for doing this would involve making their tacit appeal to human well-being explicit. But that very appeal, with its valid move from the promotion of human well-being to the principles of promising, would itself be entirely consistent with the naturalist case.

However, Foot appears to take too narrow a view in requiring the grounds of ethical conclusions to consist in human good and harm, for there are other intrinsic goods and evils such as the flourishing or the suffering of non-human animals (see the previous sub-section). But if we reject Foot's restriction on the range of the grounds of moral 'oughts', this means that there are yet broader possibilities for valid derivations of moral 'oughts' from natural facts than she seems to have supposed. Or in other words, moral properties such as rightness are realizable on the basis of several kinds of natural facts (or 'multiply realizable', in philosophers' jargon). So the narrowness of Foot's approach is not in any way a problem for ethical naturalism.

5. Non-naturalism

Nevertheless, people who accept moral realism but find ethical naturalism unacceptable may find themselves favouring non-naturalism. Non-naturalism continues to have its champions, including Russ Shafer-Landau.[12]

People could find themselves driven towards non-naturalism, despite its various problems, by reasoning as follows. Realists are correct in holding that there are truths about desirability and about actions that there are moral reasons to perform. But naturalism appears to deny all this, or at least that these facts can be regarded as natural. So these truths should be regarded as non-natural ones, and moral realists should therefore be non-naturalists.[13]

The vulnerable step in this reasoning is the claim that naturalism denies that there are truths about desirability and about actions that there are moral reasons to perform. Certainly the more restrictive kinds of ontological and methodological naturalism are prone to make these denials. But that is a reason for adopting less restrictive versions, if one adopts naturalism of these sorts at all. In any case ethical naturalism has no need to endorse these denials, and naturalistic philosophers like Philippa Foot and David O. Brink have no tendency to go along with them. Ethical naturalism, in other words, can recognize truths about desirability and about reasons for action (see above). So those who recognize such truths have no need to reject naturalism and adopt non-naturalism instead.

6. Naturalism, intrinsic value and moral 'oughts'

It is time to relate the ethical naturalism supported here to other themes from elsewhere in this chapter and this book.

Ethical claims, it was argued in the section on Realism and Cognitivism, are truth-apt, aspire to be true, and can sometimes be known. All this clashes with non-cognitivism, discussed in the section with that title, which rejects ethical truth and knowledge. But what makes ethical truths true?

According to ethical naturalism, they result from and are underpinned by natural facts, such as facts about human harm and well-being, and the relevant facts are necessarily connected to the corresponding ethical truths, and constitute them. Facts of other kinds can also be relevant, such as facts about animal welfare and suffering. Other relevant facts include ones with a bearing on whether one or another agent could or could have acted otherwise; for when the facts show that she or he could not so act, it follows that she or he is not responsible for relevant actions, and that a whole range of possible judgements become inapplicable (see the chapter on Free Will).

Among the facts relevant to ethical claims are ones relating to intrinsic value, whether through disclosing its presence (such as facts about pleasure), or describing actions that promote or frustrate it (such as facts about the impacts of action on welfare or misery). Intrinsically valuable states of affairs are ones that there is reason to promote or cherish, and confer value on actions that either exemplify or produce (or tend to produce) them (see the section on Moral Standing, Value and Intrinsic Value). Since morally right actions embody reasons for action, in the sense of justifying reasons (see the section on Internalism and Externalism), this all helps explain why some facts rather than others can underpin ethical judgements and constitute the truths that they sometimes express.

Moral rightness and moral obligation are clearly conceptually related to what there is reason to do (see the section on Moral Standing, Value, Rights and Rightness), and this adds to the explanation for facts that present reasons for action being central among those that underpin and constitute moral truths. Besides, if the sections on Consequentialism and on Deontology make their case, then right actions either comply with optimific (good-making) practices or generate the best foreseeable balance of value over disvalue. This being so, facts that present the contributions made to valuable outcomes are just the ones needed to underpin sound moral conclusions. Facts relevant to instrumental and other kinds of non-intrinsic value are included in this, as well as facts relevant to intrinsic value, as agents often need to discover the best means as well as the most desirable ends.

Other moral judgements concern goodness and the various virtues. The relevant kind of goodness is moral goodness, and on this subject the section on 'Good', 'Ought' and Morality argues that a morally good *x* is an *x* which is good or desirable as an *x* from the moral point of view. If so, it becomes clear why certain kinds of facts will underpin judgements of this sort. Further, if that section and the one on Virtue-Consequentialism are correct, then the virtues are dispositions the overall tendency of which is optimific (or productive of intrinsic value). And if so, a range of facts about dispositions and their tendencies will be needed to underpin judgements about one or another virtue.

What has just been said needs refinement for particular situations. For example, habits not resulting from choices may be ones that a relevant agent cannot help, and will not be virtuous, however beneficial they may be; and further facts, about the genesis of such habits, will need to be taken into account before moral praise or blame could even begin to be in place. But my aim here is not to explain the grounds of all the kinds of moral judgements, but to relate some of the more central kinds (and some of the other themes of this book) to the ethical naturalism expounded in this section, and thus illustrate some of the ways in which this kind of naturalism underpins and explains the realism and the cognitivism defended in earlier sections, and thus coheres with the conclusions reached about normative and applied ethics in other chapters.

Delving in this way into the justification for such moral knowledge is important, since the case for realism and cognitivism could be regarded as incomplete and gap-ridden unless such a justification is available. Besides, as we have seen, the case for realism and for cognitivism is vital to our moral practice. Enough, however, has probably been said for present purposes to plug this gap and make good any appearance of incompleteness. While our moral practice is undoubtedly often ill-informed, partial or otherwise defective, it turns out not to be altogether lacking in grounds or foundations or reasons for action.

Study questions

1. To what extent does Philippa Foot succeed in showing that moral judgements have conceptual limits and can be derived from facts?
2. Does John R. Searle succeed in deriving a moral 'ought' from an 'is'?

Notes

1 G. E. Moore, *Ethics* (1912), London: Oxford University Press, 1966.

2 David Papineau, 'Naturalism', *Stanford Encyclopedia of Philosophy*, http://www.seop.leeds.ac.uk/entries/naturalism/ (accessed 13 September 2010).

3 G. E. Moore, *Principia Ethica* (1903), Cambridge: Cambridge University Press, 1968, p. 39.

4 Renford Bambrough, *Moral Scepticism and Moral Knowledge*, London and Henley: Routledge & Kegan Paul, 1979, p. 15.

5 Philippa Foot, 'Moral Beliefs', *Proceedings of the Aristotelian Society*, 59, 1958–9, pp. 83–104; reprinted in Foot (ed.), *Theories of Ethics*, London: Oxford University Press, 1967, pp. 83–100; 'Moral Arguments', *Mind*, 67, 1958, pp. 502–13; reprinted in G. Wallace and A. D. M. Walker (eds), *The Definition of Morality*, London: Methuen, 1970, pp. 174–87.

6 David O. Brink, *Moral Realism and the Foundations of Ethics*, Cambridge: Cambridge University Press, 1989, p. 160; Robin Attfield, *Value, Obligation and Meta-Ethics*, Amsterdam and Atlanta, GA: Éditions Rodopi, 1995, pp. 232–6.

7 Brink, ibid., pp. 22 and 91.

8 John Searle, 'How to Derive "Ought" from "Is"', *Philosophical Review*, 73, 1964, pp. 43–58; reprinted in Philippa Foot (ed.), *Theories of Ethics* (see note 5), pp. 101–14.

9 Searle, ibid., in Foot, p. 114.

10 Philippa Foot, 'Introduction', in Foot (ed.), *Theories of Ethics*, pp. 1–15, at p. 12.

11 Foot, ibid., p. 11.

12 Russ Shafer-Landau, 'Ethics as Philosophy: A Defense of Ethical Nonnaturalism', in Russ Shafer-Landau (ed.), *Ethical Theory: An Anthology*, Malden, MA and Oxford: Blackwell, 2007, pp. 62–71.

13 Shafer-Landau, pp. 68–70.

References

Attfield, Robin, *Value, Obligation and Meta-Ethics*, Amsterdam and Atlanta, GA: Éditions Rodopi, 1995.

Bambrough, Renford, *Moral Scepticism and Moral Knowledge*, London and Henley: Routledge & Kegan Paul, 1979.

Brink, David O., *Moral Realism and the Foundations of Ethics*, Cambridge: Cambridge University Press, 1989.

Foot, Philippa, 'Moral Beliefs', *Proceedings of the Aristotelian Society*, 59, 1958–9, pp. 83–104; reprinted in Foot (ed.), *Theories of Ethics*, London: Oxford University Press, 1967, pp. 83–100.

—, 'Moral Arguments', *Mind*, 67, 1958, pp. 502–13; reprinted in G. Wallace and A. D. M. Walker (eds), *The Definition of Morality*, London: Methuen, 1970, pp. 174–87.

—, 'Introduction', in Foot (ed.), *Theories of Ethics*, London: Oxford University Press, 1967, pp. 1–15.

Moore, G. E., *Principia Ethica* (1903), Cambridge: Cambridge University Press, 1968.

—, *Ethics* (1912), London: Oxford University Press, 1966.

Papineau, David, 'Naturalism', *Stanford Encyclopedia of Philosophy*, http://www.seop.leeds.ac.uk/entries/naturalism/.

Searle, John, 'How to Derive "Ought" from "Is"', *Philosophical Review*, 73, 1964, pp. 43–58; reprinted in Philippa Foot (ed.), *Theories of Ethics*, pp. 101–14.

Shafer-Landau, Russ, 'Ethics as Philosophy: A Defense of Ethical Nonnaturalism', in Russ Shafer-Landau (ed.), *Ethical Theory: An Anthology*, Malden, MA and Oxford: Blackwell, 2007, pp. 62–71.

6

Free Will and Responsibility

Chapter Outline

Section 1: Responsibility, character and determinism

1. Introduction

This chapter asks whether and when we are responsible for our actions, focusing on ethics-related aspects of these questions, and glancing at metaphysical aspects only when necessary. In the opening section, we invoke Aristotle's help to discover when action is either unfree or excusable, that of Epicurus to recognize a problem about endorsing both freely chosen action and determinism, and that of the Stoics who attempted to reconcile these beliefs. While the problem noticed by Epicurus was arguably not recognized by Aristotle, Aristotle's account of responsible action appears the best of those here considered.

2. Aristotle on voluntariness, coercion and ignorance

Aristotle did some valuable pioneering work about responsibility through investigating when actions are voluntary. As was mentioned in the section on

Aristotle, he explains that voluntary actions are ones that result neither from coercion nor from ignorance, and that it is only voluntary actions that qualify for praise or blame (*Nicomachean Ethics*, Book III, chapter 1).

If someone is holding a gun to your head, or, in terms that would apply equally well in Aristotle's day, a knife to your throat, then you have little or no choice about what you do. There again, if a contrary wind blows a ship off course, the captain has no choice about steering where it sends him. In such cases, says Aristotle, the cause of the action is external to the agent.

But he is concerned not to extend such 'compulsory' actions to cases where the so-called compulsion consists in our reasons or feelings. Here, claims that we are left with no choice are unfounded, and the resort (we might say) of hypocrites, gangsters or bullies. In a play of Euripides, Alcmaeon kills his mother to avenge his father's death, and pleads that he was 'compelled' by these reasons; as Aristotle says, such 'compulsion' can be resisted, and such behaviour remains blameworthy. Otherwise, he adds, every action would be compulsory. Less securely, he comments that when the movement of the limbs that leads to an action originates in the agent himself, it is in the agent's power to act or not to act. We return below to some problems with this view.

Aristotle now turns to actions performed through ignorance, remarking that these actions are not voluntary, but are not always involuntary. We have noted in the section on Kant that the same action can take different descriptions, even when there is no problem about ignorance. The agent, however, could be unaware of one or more true descriptions of an action, including (as Aristotle says) the nature of the act, the object of the act (or who is 'in the firing line'), the instrument used, its effect and even its style or manner (such as whether it is performed gently or roughly).

Aristotle further suggests that actions are involuntary only if the agent regrets them afterwards; but this seems to assume that they are in some way unfortunate or bad, and passes over the possibility of ignorantly doing good, like those praised in the biblical parable of the Sheep and the Goats (Matthew 25:34-40). But he may have been wisely taking precautions against people contriving to be conveniently ignorant of what they were doing.

He also draws a useful distinction between acting *in consequence of* ignorance and acting *in* ignorance. When someone acts unawares because of being drunk or in a passion, he (Aristotle had male citizens in mind) is acting *in* ignorance, but his deeds result not *from* ignorance but from one or other of these conditions, for which he may well be responsible, perhaps because of a vicious disposition, itself generated by past choices. So it is not a general ignorance of the good that exculpates, but the particular kinds of ignorance listed above. While this is a helpful distinction, it does also assume that people are always responsible for their character, an assumption that will be revisited below, and again in the final section of this chapter.

As was mentioned in the section on Aristotle, he proceeds to discuss the subset of voluntary actions that are deliberate or chosen, which importantly differentiates many voluntary human actions from those of animals. But first he attempts a definition of a voluntary act as an act 'of which the origin or efficient cause lies in the agent, he knowing the particular circumstances in which he is acting'.[1] Once again, we will need to return (in later sections) to the view that when an agent originates an action with full knowledge of the circumstances, that action is voluntary.

3. Aristotle on character

Rather than return to Aristotle's discussion of choice and of deliberation (covered already in the section on Aristotle), we should briefly consider his views in Book III, chapters 4 and 5, on whether our characters are always to our credit or discredit. By this stage, he has explained that our virtues and vices result from habits of choice formed in the past, and that, while they cannot be changed at will, they are voluntary because of the voluntary nature of the choices that led to them. The problem arising is the possibility that the end or the vision of the good that animated these choices might itself be defective or mistaken, or even beyond our control. As was mentioned in the section on Aristotle, he holds that we are likely to begin making good choices if we are well brought up. But what about those who are badly brought up?

One answer open to Aristotle is that their characters still result from choices, and choices are voluntary. But with regard to those whose choices were skewed, this answer appears unconvincing. Perhaps they had choice (as he says) about means, but not effectively about ends or principles. Aristotle certainly regards deliberation as open to all normal human beings, but considers it confined to choices of means, rather than of principles (Book III, chapter 3). If he had allowed a wider scope for deliberation, his problem might have been less intractable. For we can, in the course of deliberation, reflect on values and on principles, as well as on what to do next. Maybe, then, we have more control over our principles than Aristotle felt able to claim.

Aristotle's stance is, as mentioned above, that our virtues and vices, and our principles too, are adopted gradually through our choices, each of which is voluntary. Maybe he is too ready to conclude that actions that society considers voluntary really are so, and that social practices of rewarding and punishing are rational accordingly. But when he contemplates the possibility that we are not responsible for our own characters, but that they are rather a gift of nature, he is able to respond that this would mean that virtue and vice are not voluntary at all, an unacceptable implication. However, when he allows that nature (rather than ourselves) may conceivably endow us with 'the end' (and thus our understanding of the good), he accidentally makes room for doubts about his conclusions, doubts that are only partly countered by his robust remarks about the way in which we all contribute something to the formation of our own characters (Book III, chapter 5).

Aristotle's analysis of voluntariness and of choice is a paradigm of ordinary language philosophy. Largely we do use 'voluntary' of actions that are neither coerced nor performed because of ignorance, and 'virtues' of salutary characteristics that result from past choices. But ordinary language analysis cannot resolve all the issues, as was noticed in the next generation by the philosopher Epicurus.

4. Epicurus and the problem of determinism

Epicurus (341–271 BCE), who lived soon after Aristotle, took over from the earlier philosopher Democritus (a contemporary of Plato) both the belief that everything is made of atoms and of void, and (in large part) the determinism that seemed implicit in this belief.[2] The kind of determinism upheld by Democritus claims that every event is in principle predictable by reference to natural forces and earlier states of affairs. Since neither natural forces nor past states of affairs are within our control, an implication of this, as Epicurus noticed, was that living creatures such as ourselves have no real choice about what we do, since whatever we do is determined by factors and forces beyond our control.

But this implication was unacceptable to Epicurus, whose central aim was to teach an ethic, based on seeking pleasure, avoiding pain and aiming at a life of tranquillity and self-sufficiency. Anyone who teaches an ethic needs to be able to claim that a difference is made by the adoption of that ethic, and by people's acting accordingly; there would seemingly be no point in such teaching if human behaviour were believed to be fully predictable and determined already. Besides, the teaching of philosophers like Democritus appeared quite generally to make no provision for human choice whatever. As Epicurus (despite his opposition to conventional religion) put it:

> it would be better to follow the mythology about gods than to be a slave to the 'fate' of the natural philosophers: the former at least hints at the hope of begging the gods off by means of worship, whereas the latter involves an inexorable necessity.[3]

For this reason, Epicurus modified Democritus's metaphysical teachings, to make room for human freedom, voluntariness and spontaneity. Atoms, he held, have a tendency to deviate or swerve randomly from the trajectory that they would otherwise have followed; hence the behaviour of human beings and animals is not entirely predictable. Precisely how this tendency of atoms to swerve is supposed to make free choices possible is unclear, and the interpretation of Epicurus' theory continues to be debated, particularly as random motion seems as likely to generate random behaviour as behaviour that is freely and rationally chosen. But there is no need to take this debate further here.

What is important for present purposes is the fact that Epicurus noticed the problem of reconciling determinism and belief in freely chosen action, and also that he took the view that these beliefs were incompatible, and that believers in freely chosen action have to reject determinism. To put things another way, he implicitly perceived that belief in freely chosen action (and in voluntary action in general) presupposes that at the moment of action more than one future is possible, and that this conflicts with the implication of determinism that at any given time only one future is possible.[4] In other words again, determinism embodies a threat to belief in people's responsibility for their actions. Although Aristotle was struggling with related problems, he never makes this problem fully explicit.

The Epicureans (as Epicurus' followers were called) taught and defended Epicurus' version of physics, metaphysics and ethics for eight hundred years, stressing the freedom of the will at the heart of their message. (We have one comprehensive statement of this position, in the form of the Latin poem of Lucretius, *On The Nature of The Universe*.[5]) But issues surrounding determinism and human freedom can be better traced if we turn now to the philosophy of their contemporary opponents, the Stoics.

5. Stoicism, determinism and character

Stoics have always held that the good of a person consists simply in virtue, and that the attainment of virtue fulfils a person's nature and is entirely within their control. Thus they are strongly committed to the beliefs that virtue is voluntary and to a person's credit, and that people are in general responsible for what they do.

At the same time, they also held that whatever happens is determined by fate. The universe is entirely material and also designed in every particular for the best; everything that happens unfolds (as Gottlieb puts it) 'in an inexorable chain of cause and effect'.[6] But if so, then apparently nothing whatever is within our control.

Accordingly, opponents of Stoicism (including Plato's successors at the Academy) used to claim that the Stoics could not consistently teach virtue or offer a path to happiness, since no one has any freedom if their teachings are right. One such criticism consisted in 'the lazy argument'. If you are ill, there is no point in calling a doctor, granted the Stoic belief in fate; for if you are fated to recover, a doctor will not help, and if you are fated not to recover, then calling a doctor is futile.

To this Chrysippus, a leading Stoic of the third century BCE, replied that the agency of the doctor may be what would cause a difference, and may be fated to cure you. So there is a point in calling a doctor after all.[7] Hence the effort of making decisions and taking action may be justified, even if it is fated; and the same would apply to the actions of the Stoics themselves in teaching virtue. Chrysippus in this way avoided the charge, frequently made against fatalism (the view that whatever happens is bound to happen), that it seems to make effort pointless.

However, this still leaves a problem about responsibility; for Stoic beliefs in fate and in the supposed inexorable chain of cause and effect apparently leave no room for actions being to anyone's credit or discredit. To this Chrysippus replies that your actions may well be due to your character, and thus to your credit or discredit, just as a cylinder's rolling down a hill is not entirely due to outside forces, but partly due to its nature as a cylinder. If it had had a different character, more like that of a rectangular lump of marble, then it would not roll at all. What you do is as much due to internal factors as to external ones. So responsibility supposedly remains intact, despite Stoic determinism.

But this reply, as Gottlieb says, does not really work. For your character is as it is, according to Stoicism, due to factors over which you have no control, and ultimately to factors in being before your birth.[8] Nothing is achieved by distinguishing internal factors from external ones, if the internal ones are no more within your control than the others. Thus no one can fairly be praised or blamed for the actions that their character gives rise to, given Stoic assumptions. Punishments and rewards may modify behaviour, but Stoic beliefs imply that no one deserves either, contrary to what the Stoics actually taught. This is a profound embarrassment for a philosophy centrally concerned to advocate virtue.

6. Compatibilism and incompatibilism

The attempt of the Stoics to reconcile determinism with belief in human responsibility and free will (the belief that some actions are freely chosen) is an early example of compatibilism, or the claim that determinism and human responsibility may both be the case. (Belief in free will amounts, more precisely, to the belief that 'human beings (and possibly other animals), faced with choices between two or more mutually incompatible courses of action, frequently have it in their power to (or can) carry out each of them'.[9]) Or in other words, that there need be no contradiction in holding both of these beliefs simultaneously. However, Chrysippus's failure to make his case indicates that better arguments than his would be needed to make compatibilism defensible. Otherwise, at least one of these beliefs would have to be abandoned.

By contrast, the stance of the Epicureans, requiring abandonment of determinism with a view to upholding belief in free will, comprises an early example of incompatibilism, or the denial of compatibilism. Incompatibilists maintain (to use other words) that there is a contradiction in adhering both to determinism and belief in free will, and that this combination of beliefs is necessarily false. As well as the Epicureans, the Platonist critics of Chrysippus seem also to have been incompatibilists (except that their scepticism may have deterred them from adopting any position at all, apart from a critical stance towards others).

Thus the incompatibilism of the Epicureans gained some support among their contemporaries. But their attempt to explain and justify their belief in human freedom by reference to the doctrine of the swerve was less successful. Their overall position was thus less than satisfactory.

Aristotle, by contrast, cannot be characterized either as compatibilist or as incompatibilist, as he did not directly address the topic of determinism (although he did discuss in *Categories* whether future events are all inevitable). However, in rejecting the view that all our actions are 'compulsory', he may have been hinting that not everything that we do is done out of necessity, and in accepting that what we do because of ignorance is not voluntary, he avoided falling into the trap of holding that all actions that are not due to external factors are performed voluntarily.

Further, Aristotle's account of character as dispositions resulting from past choices could have been used to supplement Chrysippus's remarks about the internal nature of character. Chrysippus was in no position to deploy this analysis to defend his general stance, because of his belief that our past choices are themselves determined by fate. But if, as Aristotle held, they are genuinely voluntary (rather than fated), and sequences of them generate our characters, then our characters can defensibly be held to be (to some extent) within our control, and we to be (to some degree) responsible for them.

Thus, despite not explicitly addressing the issue of determinism, Aristotle's overall position seems to have been more defensible than either that of the Epicureans or that of the Stoics. Whether his beliefs about voluntariness, choice and character can actually still be sustained is a different matter, but they remain at least an option. To consider this further, we need to consider the philosophy of a later age, when materialism and determinism were raised again, in conjunction with laws of nature (as is done in the coming section).

Study questions

1. Which factors mitigate or nullify moral responsibility? Was Aristotle right about this?
2. How satisfactory was the Epicureans' treatment of human freedom, granted their acceptance of atomism?

Notes

1 Aristotle, *Nicomachean Ethics*, III: I; translated by J. A. K. Thomson as *The Ethics of Aristotle*, Harmondsworth, UK and Baltimore, MD: Penguin, 1953; see p. 81.

2 For Epicurus, see Anthony Gottlieb, *The Dream of Reason: A History of Western Philosophy from the Greeks to the Renaissance*, London: Penguin, 2001, pp. 283–309.

3 Epicurus, *Letter to Menoeceus*; quoted at Gottlieb, p. 304.

4 See Peter van Inwagen, *An Essay on Free Will*, Oxford: Clarendon Press, 1983, p. 8.

5 Lucretius (Titus Lucretius Carus), *The Nature of the Universe*, trans. R. E. Latham, Harmondsworth, UK: Penguin, 1951.

6 Gottlieb, op. cit., p. 311.

7 Gottlieb, ibid., p. 318.

8 Gottlieb, ibid., p. 319.

9 van Inwagen, op. cit., p. 8.

References

Aristotle, *The Ethics of Aristotle*, trans. J. A. K. Thomson, Harmondsworth, UK and Baltimore, MD: Penguin, 1953.

Gottlieb, Anthony, *The Dream of Reason: A History of Western Philosophy from the Greeks to the Renaissance*, London: Penguin, 2001.

Lucretius (Titus Lucretius Carus), *The Nature of the Universe*, trans. R. E. Latham, Harmondsworth, UK: Penguin, 1951.

van Inwagen, Peter, *An Essay on Free Will*, Oxford: Clarendon Press, 1983.

Section 2: Laws of nature, 'ought' and 'can'

1. Thomas Hobbes and laws of nature

Many thinkers of the Early Modern period (1600–1800) newly attempted to explain the natural world by appeal to 'laws of nature', laws of the form that in specified circumstances events of a certain specific kind invariably occur. If every event is subject to laws of nature, then every event will be necessitated by the circumstances and antecedent events; and if human actions are included among events, then human actions too will be necessitated. This new approach gave rise to vigorous discussion of whether there was still room for belief in the freedom of the will and in moral responsibility. This section will review its bearing both on determinism and on some of these debates.

One of the early adherents of such necessitarianism (the view that all events are necessary, and none could have happened otherwise) was Thomas Hobbes (1588–1679), whose psychological egoism and contractarianism have been discussed above in Chapter 1. Hobbes was not himself a scientist (or natural philosopher, to use the term then current), but was firmly committed to the view that all change is due to the impact of one body upon another, and thus to mechanical factors. Human desires themselves are mechanically generated and propel agents to forming 'volitions' (or intentions) and to performing actions in a mechanical manner; the freedom of the will consists in the unimpeded operation of our volitions, generated by our desires and expressed in bodily movements. None of these movements could have assumed a different form in the particular prevailing circumstances.

Hobbes' version of necessitarianism amounts to a new form of determinism, grounded in laws of nature. The determinism of Democritus was presented in the previous section as the belief that every event is in principle predictable by reference to natural forces and earlier states of affairs. With laws of nature in the picture, determinism can be redefined as the belief that every event is in principle predictable by reference to laws of nature and antecedent states of the world. Since laws of nature are beyond our control, and earlier states of the world are by now irreversible, such determinism all the more clearly poses a problem for belief in the human ability to choose on occasion between more than one courses of action, and the ability in some situations to act or to refrain from acting at all. It also poses a problem for moral responsibility, which we investigate further below. Nevertheless Hobbes combined with his determinism a form of compatibilism (see the previous section for the meaning of this term), for he claimed to be able to reconcile belief in the freedom of the will (interpreted in his own way) with his necessitarianism.

2. Responses to Hobbes

This set of beliefs, as expressed in *Leviathan* (1651) and in *Of Liberty and Necessity* (1654), together with Hobbes' psychological and ethical egoism, stirred up whole swarms of criticism during the seventeenth and eighteenth centuries from defenders of traditional morality and of more robust versions of belief in human freedom. We cannot chronicle their many stances here; some of the best known have been assembled, together with relevant writings of Hobbes, in David Daiches Raphael's reader, *The British Moralists*.[1] Characteristic responses involved claims, such as that of Ralph Cudworth (1617–88), that human freedom amounts to more than Hobbes allows. But, as we shall see, specifying the nature of this ampler freedom proved far from easy. (Cudworth also shrewdly recognizes that Hobbes' necessitarianism broadly echoes that of the Stoics.)

Cudworth rightly stresses (against earlier respondents to Hobbes) that what is free is not some faculty or component of the mind or soul, as if the will might be in competition with our understanding or even with our desires; it is the soul or, as we would say, the person as a whole that exercises freedom. But this freedom consists in more than the absence of external obstacles, as Hobbes seemed to suggest. There is a genuine capacity for 'not doing or doing this or that', in the very same circumstances.[2] Cudworth did not want to represent this capacity as 'an indifferency', as if we were free to leap into one or another course of action for no reason or randomly (a problem for some accounts of free will that is still debated today), but eventually comes down in favour of people having the ability to act in different ways, despite their love of the good, through deliberating better or less well, without any of this being determined by antecedent factors.[3]

But this suggests that free will is only operative in certain deliberate choices, and not in the broad range of voluntary human actions. It also suggests that it is possible for human beings (above the age of infancy) alone, and certainly not for non-human animals. These conclusions cohere with Cudworth's beliefs about the soul, but clash with Aristotle's view that voluntariness (as opposed to deliberation and choice) often belongs to children and animals as well as to adult humans. Yet voluntariness itself implies the ability to do otherwise. So either Aristotle was wrong in ascribing it to children and animals, or the ability to do otherwise has a much wider scope than Cudworth recognized.

Gottfried Wilhelm Leibniz (1646–1716) likewise held that defences of human freedom should avoid doctrines of 'liberty of indifference',[4] which supplied no scope for praise or blame. We make our choices not in a vacuum of indifference, but in the light of reasons and motives. However, 'motives incline without necessitating',[5] for agents are able to appraise both reasons and motives, and are not condemned to move in accordance with the mechanical resultant of their combined strength. Some of the other themes of Leibniz, such as that of the unfolding of each person's life from the complete concept of the person concerned, give little help to those reflecting on freedom and responsibility. But this observation about motives illuminates an otherwise overcast and confusing scene.

3. Hume, laws of nature and compatibilism

In the eighteenth century, David Hume (1711–76) supplied his own account of necessity and of causation.

> Our idea, therefore, of necessity and of causation arises entirely from the uniformity observable in the operations of nature, where similar objects are constantly conjoined together, and the mind is determined by custom to infer the one from the appearance of the other.. . . Beyond the constant *conjunction* of similar objects, and the consequent inference from one to the other, we have no notion of any necessity or connexion.[6]

Whether this is an account of actual causes, of our idea of causes, or of both, can be left for others to interpret. But Hume is clear that there is no more to the idea of causal necessity than experience of the constant conjunction of two kinds of phenomena, and the consequent association of ideas in human minds. So if such a conjunction can be found in matters of free and voluntary action, there will be no question of incompatibility between belief in liberty and in necessity.

After a long (and contentious) excursus on the uniformity of human nature at all times and places, Hume goes on to claim that 'the conjunction between motives and voluntary action is as regular and uniform as that between cause and effect in any part of nature',[7] and that no one has ever doubted this. Thus the doctrine of necessity applies to humanity as much as to the rest of nature, and is in no way at odds with belief in human liberty. By 'liberty' we 'mean *a power of acting or not acting, according to the determinations of the will*; that is, if we choose to remain at rest, we may; if we choose to move, we also may'. And 'this hypothetical liberty is universally allowed to belong to everyone who is not a prisoner and in chains'.[8] So the project of reconciling liberty and necessity is supposedly complete.

However, both limbs of Hume's reconciliation strategy are open to question. Many have questioned whether his account of necessity accounts for relations such as implication (or, similarly, of x being a sufficient condition of y), and whether his account of causes adequately captures the powers that talk of causation ascribes. One specific problem is that his account implies that no cause is ever unprecedented or unique of its kind (and no effect either), which would make talk of the Big Bang impossible, and equally talk of the cause of human evolution.

But here it is more apposite to problematize his account of liberty, because it fails to address whether human agents are free in the same circumstances to choose to move or not to move, irrespective of the antecedents of such a choice. Hume's account of necessity suggests that, given the antecedents of choice and given the relevant laws of nature, only one of these two choices is possible. But his definition of 'liberty' suggests that both options remain possibilities. This being so, his project of reconciliation is neither complete nor successful. Hume's compatibilism is more subtle than that of Hobbes, but just as unpersuasive.

4. Kant, 'ought' and 'can'

Immanuel Kant (1724–1804) held that our intuitive awareness of the moral law requires us to believe, *inter alia*, in human freedom. But this freedom is located not in the realm of phenomena, where causal determination holds good, but in that of 'noumena', or things in themselves.[9] Those who are unable to accept this division of reality into the phenomenal and the noumenal realms have to look to other writers for help in reconciling necessity and freedom.

However, one of Kant's claims (made in several works of his) is more helpful, the claim that '"Ought" implies "can"'.[10] For talk of responsible agency often involves the belief that the agent ought to do otherwise or ought to have done otherwise. But this kind of belief is only credible if the agent can do otherwise or could have done otherwise. This, indeed, is probably part of what Kant was suggesting. Further, the interpretation of 'can do otherwise' and of 'could do otherwise' has continued to play a central part in debates about human freedom and responsibility from the time of Kant onwards. (See the coming section.)

Besides, the relation between 'ought' and 'can' seems to comply with what is required for the former to imply the latter. For it would apparently never be the case both that someone ought to do something, and that they cannot. (Maybe there are exceptions to this, as when someone ought to manage a certain athletic achievement soon, and is in training, but cannot manage it yet. But if so, what they ought to do is, more accurately, to try to achieve it.)

On the other hand, it is also true to say that if someone ought not to do something, then they can do it (unless it is so distasteful that they cannot bring themselves to do it). But when both a given proposition and its contradictory are true only if another proposition is true, then the first one does not strictly speaking imply the second, but presupposes it. However, this may be misleading in turn, because the contradictory of 'X ought' is not 'X ought not', but 'It is not the case that X ought' (so to act), and the latter would be true when X cannot so act, as well as (sometimes) when X can so act. Accordingly it is best to stick with the slogan that 'ought' implies 'can' (rather than 'ought' presupposes 'can') after all.

This slogan has recently been interpreted to imply that there are limits to what we ought to do, limits set by our limited capacities. For example, in debates about internalism it is sometimes argued by one kind of internalist that agents who lack desires to act in certain ways cannot be obligated so to act. Externalists, however, are prone to reply that people's obligations cannot be supposed to depend on their desires, and stand or fall independently of what the agents in question happen to want. Indeed this reply is endorsed in the relevant section of this book, the section on Internalism, Externalism and Practicality.

In any case, recently Robert Stern has argued persuasively that Kant did not adhere to this 'strong' interpretation of '"ought" implies "can"'. Rather, he used it to argue from the moral law, which is often intuitively clear, to our capacities, which can be argued often to be greater than we realize.[11] We cannot, of course, infer from this that claims about the extent of obligations are never exaggerated, much less that arguments from absence of capacities to absence of obligations always fail. But where Kant's support is being claimed, it is best to confine our interpretations of '"ought" implies "can"' to the claim that if someone ought to act or ought to have acted otherwise, then it must be that they can or could have acted otherwise. Whether this means that they could have acted otherwise in exactly the same circumstances or not must for the present be left open. If it does, then the plausibility of compatibilism begins to recede.

5. Thomas Reid and agent-causation

Thomas Reid (1710–96) was unconvinced by the argument of Hume, his fellow-Scot, that actions are either determined by their agents' motives, or, if lacking in motives, then inexplicable.[12] Unlike mechanical causes, motives (he held) are not efficient causes but are subject to agents' consideration; it is not they that cause actions, but the agents themselves.

In reply to the necessitarian claim that agents are propelled into action by 'the strongest motive', Reid questions whether we have any grasp of this concept except when it means the motive actually acted on. Prior to the making of a decision about how to act, our motives cannot be represented as irresistible forces, but should be thought of as like advocates in a law court, where it is not they but the judge that gives the verdict. Hence we cannot reliably infer people's actions just from knowledge of their motives.[13] Thus we need to distinguish between motives in the sense of inclinations antecedent to decisions about action, and motives in the sense of the desires from which actions on which we have decided are performed, and which thus explain the actions. Motives in the second sense can always be found for deliberate actions, but are not antecedents of the relevant decisions; it is motives in the first sense to which necessitarians need to appeal, but these, while antecedent to action, lack the status of being its determinants. For, as Reid says, people have the ability to resist them, and to do what there is the strongest motive in the sense of the greatest reason (whether of morality or of prudence) to do.

At the same time, through explaining that actions performed from a single desire can still be free (because if we had exerted ourselves we could have acted differently), Reid's account affirms the wide scope of free and voluntary action. This scope is not restricted to deliberate choices, as Cudworth's writings had suggested, but (I would suggest) to all the areas of activity to which adverbs like 'whole-heartedly', 'spontaneously', 'reluctantly', 'hesitantly' and even 'grudgingly' are applicable.

Reid's view that voluntary actions are not uncaused but are caused by their agents makes him the modern progenitor of theories of agent-causation. Timothy O'Connor argues that such theories are much more cogent than those theories of indeterminism (affirmations of freely chosen action that reject determinism) which represent voluntary actions as having no cause or causes at all (*mere* indeterminism, as we might call them). Theories of agent-causation depend on agents having capacities of self-determination and of initiating actions in ways that are not themselves determined, and on the causal activity of such agents co-existing in the same world with the kind of efficient causes studied by natural science.[14] This belief about the world we live in may initially seem problematic; but agent-causation theorists can insist that our concepts of person and of agent are more basic and more unshakeable than even our concepts of cause and effect, and that in our beliefs about agency, we all presuppose nothing less (whatever theories we may consciously embrace). Nor need human agents be conceived as the sole examples of agency in the universe; for many non-human animals are standardly regarded as (other) conscious initiators of voluntary action.

While Reid was probably the originator of modern theories of agent-causation, his ideas were anticipated in part by Aristotle. It was Aristotle who defined voluntary acts as ones 'of which the origin or efficient cause lies in the agent, he knowing the particular circumstances in which he is acting'.[15] Reid, however, should have the credit for reverting to such a view in response to the challenges of determinism and to the kind of compatibilism advocated by Hume. Nor is the resemblance between Aristotle and Reid limited to adherence to this view. For both of them did their philosophy through examination of ordinary language and the analysis of concepts such as 'voluntary', 'choice', 'motive' and 'free', and both were concerned to be able to defend ethical beliefs about responsibility, virtue and right conduct. Of the two philosophers, at least Reid regarded belief in determinism as potentially undermining traditional morality; it seems not unlikely that Aristotle would have adopted the same view. If his lost works are one day rediscovered, it may become possible to vindicate this interpretation.

Study questions

1. How successful was Thomas Hobbes in seeking to show that determinism is compatible with belief in free will?
2. How successful was David Hume in his efforts to show that determinism and belief in free will are compatible?
3. Do you agree with Immanuel Kant that 'ought' implies 'can', and what is it about this claim that makes it an important one?

Notes

1 D. D. Raphael (ed.), *British Moralists 1650–1800* (2 vols), Oxford: Clarendon Press, 1969.

2 Ralph Cudworth, *A Treatise of Freewill* (1688 or earlier), in Raphael, pp. 126–7.

3 Cudworth, in Raphael, p. 153. See further Samuel I. Mintz, *The Hunting of Leviathan: Seventeenth-Century Reactions to the Materialism and Moral Philosophy of Thomas Hobbes*, Cambridge: Cambridge University Press, 1962, pp. 126–33.

4 G. W. Leibniz, *Theodicy*, trans. E. M. Huggard, ed. A. M. Farrer, London: Routledge & Kegan Paul, 1952, p. 112.

5 Leibniz, *Correspondence with Clarke, Fifth Paper*, 9, in Leibniz, *Leibniz: Philosophical Writings*, ed. G. H. R. Parkinson, Everyman Classics, London and Melbourne: Dent, 1972, p. 222.

6 David Hume, *Enquiry Concerning Human Understanding* (1748), in David Hume, *Enquiries Concerning Human Understanding and Concerning the Principles of Morals*, ed. P. H. Nidditch, 3rd edn, Oxford: Clarendon Press, 1975, p. 82. Also available at www.earlymoderntexts.com.

7 Hume, ibid., p. 88.

8 Hume, ibid., p. 95.

9 I. Kant, *Groundwork for the Metaphysics of Morals*, trans. Thomas K. Abbott, ed. Lara Denis, Orchard Park, NY: Broadview, 2005, Third Section.

10 Robert Stern, 'Does "Ought" Imply "Can"? And Did Kant Think It Does?', *Utilitas*, 16, 2004, pp. 42–61; also available at: http://eprints.whiterose.ac.uk/298/1/sternr1.pdf.

11 Stern, ibid.

12 Hume, *Enquiry Concerning Human Understanding* (see note 6), Section VIII, Part II.

13 Thomas Reid, *Essays on the Active Powers of Man*, Essay IV, chapter IV; reprinted in Raphael (ed.), *British Moralists* (vol. 2), pp. 276–82.

14 Timothy O'Connor, *Persons and Causes: The Metaphysics of Free Will*, Oxford: Oxford University Press, 2000.

15 Aristotle, *Nicomachean Ethics*, III: I.

References

Aristotle, *Nicomachean Ethics*, trans. J. A. K. Thomson as *The Ethics of Aristotle*, Harmondsworth, UK and Baltimore, MD: Penguin, 1953.

Cudworth, Ralph, *A Treatise of Freewill* (1688 or earlier); selection reprinted in Raphael, D. D. (ed.), *British Moralists* (vol. 1: see below.).

Hobbes, Thomas, *Leviathan* (1651); selection reprinted in Raphael, D. D. (ed.), *British Moralists* (vol. 1).

—, *Of Liberty and Necessity* (1654); reprinted in Raphael, D. D. (ed.), *British Moralists* (vol. 1).

Hume, David, *Enquiry Concerning Human Understanding* (1748), in David Hume, *Enquiries Concerning Human Understanding and Concerning the Principles of Morals*, ed. P. H. Nidditch, 3rd edn, Oxford: Clarendon Press, 1975.

—, *Enquiry Concerning Human Understanding* (1748), available at http://www.earlymoderntexts.com.

Kant, Immanuel, *Groundwork for the Metaphysics of Morals*, trans. Thomas K. Abbott, ed. Lara Denis, Orchard Park, NY: Broadview, 2005.

—, *Groundwork for the Metaphysics of Morals*, trans. Jonathan Bennett, available at http://www.earlymoderntexts.com.

Leibniz, G. W., *Theodicy*, trans. E. M. Huggard, ed. A. M. Farrer, London: Routledge & Kegan Paul, 1952.

Mintz, Samuel I., *The Hunting of Leviathan: Seventeenth-Century Reactions to the Materialism and Moral Philosophy of Thomas Hobbes*, Cambridge: Cambridge University Press, 1962.

O'Connor, Timothy, *Persons and Causes: The Metaphysics of Free Will*, Oxford: Oxford University Press, 2000.

Raphael, D. D. (ed.), *British Moralists 1650–1800* (2 vols), Oxford: Clarendon Press, 1969.

Reid, Thomas, *Essays on the Active Powers of Man*; selection reprinted in Raphael, D. D. (ed.), *British Moralists* (vol. 2), pp. 276–82.

—, *Essays on the Active Powers of Man*, available at http://www.earlymoderntexts.com.

Stern, Robert, 'Does "Ought" Imply "Can"? And Did Kant Think It Does?', *Utilitas*, 16, 2004, pp. 42–61; also available at: http://eprints.whiterose.ac.uk/298/1/sternr1.pdf.

Section 3: Evolution, randomness, 'could' and 'would'

1. Darwinism, deterministic or non-deterministic

In this section, some selected nineteenth- and twentieth-century contributions to debates about determinism, indeterminism and compatibilism are reviewed. (The first two of these terms are defined in the previous section; 'compatibilism' is defined below.) As in the two previous sections of this chapter, no continuous narrative or general survey of these debates can be offered. Indeed the nineteenth century is represented simply by the key contribution made by Charles Darwin (1809–82) with his theory of evolution.

Some key critical discussions of determinism and compatibilism and debate about problems for indeterminism represent the twentieth century.

Darwin's theory concerning the evolution of all living creatures by natural selection was first published in his *Origin of Species* (1859).[1] This theory was combined several decades later with the genetic theories of Darwin's contemporary, Gregor Mendel, into the widely accepted synthesis known as 'Darwinism', which explains that our own species, as well as all others currently alive, gradually evolved from earlier species through the differential survival of those living beings best suited to thrive and to leave thriving descendants, and that creatures' various traits and faculties (including our own) were largely selected in this way. (For a helpful guide to the implications of Darwinism for human motives and for ethics, see Mary Midgley's *The Ethical Primate*,[2] which is discussed further in the coming section.)

Darwin did not adopt any explicit stance about the question of whether evolution was a deterministic process. Significantly, he often wrote of choice not only among humans but also among other animals.[3] But one of his remarks suggests that he feared that his theory might have unwelcome deterministic implications.

> With me the horrid doubt always arises whether the convictions of man's mind, which has been developed from the mind of the lower animals, are of any value or at all trustworthy. Would anyone trust in the convictions of a monkey's mind, if there are any convictions in such a mind?[4]

In other words, his theory of evolution may imply that, given natural selection, the human mind could not have been otherwise, and its beliefs could have no other form or content, and thus may lack the value normally ascribed to them when they are considered to be autonomously formed. (Alvin Plantinga has named this worry 'Darwin's Doubt'.[5]) Our ethical beliefs and convictions (as well as all our choices) would be subject to the same verdict. Yet Darwin did not form this view about the value of his own convictions, which suggests that he may not have been wholly committed to determinism.

The apparent problem became more intense when the role of genes in evolution came to be recognized. Here is how Richard Dawkins has expounded (in *The Selfish Gene*[6]) the relation between people and genes, which build people as their 'survival machines'. The genes now:

> swarm in huge colonies, safe inside gigantic lumbering robots . . . you and me; . . . they created us, body and mind, [and] . . . manipulat(e) by remote control. (p. 21)

Indeed

> all life evolves by the differential survival of replicating entities; . . . the gene . . . happens to be the replicating entity which prevails on our own planet. (p. 206)

Thus when Dawkins eventually declares that human beings (alone among life forms) have the power to rebel against these (supposedly) selfish manipulators, he seems too deeply immersed in genetic determinism for this power of resistance to appear credible. Dawkins' version of Darwinism has become all-but-committed to determinism.

Dawkins' interpretation of Darwinism is, however, controversial, appearing as it does to remove agency from people altogether and transfer it to genes. Darwinists could instead say that genes predispose people to certain forms of behaviour, or enable them to be performed, without the people concerned being manipulated or controlled, or losing their freedom of action.

A quite different interpretation of Darwinism has been put forward by Keith Ward.[7] Ward accepts that 'human beings have descended by a process of mutation and adaptation from other and simpler forms of organic life over millions of years', and that natural selection is 'the main but possibly not the only driving force of evolutionary change' (p. 261). Yet he also holds that human beings have (what he calls) 'libertarian freedom':

> Libertarian freedom is that property of a rational agent by which, on at least some occasions, no prior physical state, even with the addition of a set of general laws of nature, entails one specific outcome of a given situation. There are real alternative possible futures, and only the agent's uncompelled decision decides which future is realized. (p. 263)

Such freedom seems, in any case, compatible with Darwinism, and also, given Kant's teaching that 'ought' implies 'can', a necessary condition of moral responsibility.

However, some other Darwinists, such as Daniel Dennett, continue to present a deterministic interpretation of Darwinism, together with compatibilist interpretations of human freedom and of phrases such as 'she could have done otherwise'.[8] While it is not clear that Darwinism must be regarded as intrinsically deterministic (see the following section), it is to some twentieth-century problems for determinism and to some new defences of compatibilism that we now turn.

2. Quantum indeterminacy

Until 1905, physics was assumed on all sides to be deterministic. But in that year Albert Einstein published a paper which showed that light behaves both as a wave and as a particle, and that the pathways of individual electrons are unpredictable. From that stage, 'quantum indeterminacy' became an accepted part of physics, quanta (literally 'amounts') being the fixed packages in which light is emitted.[9]

Some writers claim that determinism is thus shown to collapse, while others say that our changed understanding of sub-atomic events makes no difference to events at an everyday, macroscopic level, since this invisibly small-scale unpredictability probably evens out, leaving middle-sized and larger objects unaffected. An intermediate view is that quantum indeterminacy implies the possibility of limits to predictability at the level of animal and human agents, without making such limits likely or even likelier; we can no longer assume that determinism applies universally, but maybe we do not know either that it does not apply to ourselves (although J. R. Lucas has ingeniously argued to contrary effect[10]).

In the circumstances, it seems best to continue to take determinism seriously, and therewith issues about its compatibility (or otherwise) with belief in free will, as if nothing had definitively changed. At the same time, the truth of determinism should not be taken for granted.

3. Twentieth-century defences of compatibilism

We have already encountered, in the two previous sections, attempts to defend compatibilism (the claim that determinism and belief in free will are compatible) on the part of the Stoics, of Thomas Hobbes and of David Hume. In the twentieth century, new efforts of these kinds were advanced by G. E. Moore and by Patrick Nowell-Smith, in each case in books entitled *Ethics*.[11] Thus both were seeking to make room for such practices as ethical praise and blame within a deterministic framework, and both used the method of linguistic analysis to clinch their point.

Moore presents two suggestions about the key phrase of believers in free will, 'could have done otherwise'. His first suggestion is that 'could have' is an incomplete expression, and that 'could have done otherwise' is short for 'could have done otherwise if he/she had chosen'. His second suggestion is that 'could have done otherwise' is better to be construed as 'would have done otherwise if he/she had chosen'. Moore considered that determinists can happily endorse 'could have' if this is what it means, for they can accept that the relevant agent could or would have acted differently if the world had been different through their making a different choice, which would have caused a different action.

Later, Nowell-Smith attempted to improve on Moore's approach by presenting a general analysis of 'could' and of 'can', and thus of 'could do otherwise' and of 'can do otherwise'. 'Could' means 'would . . . if . . . ' and 'can' means 'will . . . if . . .'. Specifically, to use J. L. Austin's paraphrase, 'Smith can run a mile' means 'If Smith has the opportunity to run a mile, and a preponderant motive for running it, he will run it'.[12] (We should notice here the language of the strongest or predominant motive, advanced by Hume and criticized by Reid: see the previous section.) Once again, the suggestion is that determinists can go along with claims that an agent 'could have done otherwise', thus interpreted, because it simply means that the agent would have done otherwise if the world had been different with regard to the agent having or lacking a suitable opportunity or motive.

Austin replies to Moore that people are tempted to construe 'could have' as in need of completion with an 'if' clause only because 'could' happens sometimes to mean 'would be able'. But it is also the ordinary past tense of 'can', meaning 'was able' (indicative), and this is what it always means in 'could have done otherwise, if he/she had chosen'. (Other languages, he remarks, use different words for these different senses of 'could'.) So there is nothing incomplete about 'could' in 'could have done otherwise' and thus no need for completion through an 'if' clause; 'could have' simply tells us what an agent was able to do. He adds that 'if he/she had chosen otherwise' does not in any case express a causal condition, for 'he/she could have done otherwise if he/she had chosen' is actually compatible with 'he/she could have done otherwise whether or not he/she had chosen'. (So the determinist cannot treat this 'if' clause as depicting a causally different world; the 'if' is not a causal 'if', but more like an 'if' of hesitation or doubt.) Besides, 'could have done otherwise if he had chosen' means nothing like 'would have done otherwise if he had chosen', and so a different argument is needed if the latter is supposed to be an analysis of 'could have done otherwise'.

Just such an analysis, however, is part of what Nowell-Smith suggests. His claim is partly that 'could have' is always a conditional, and thus in need of an 'if'; but this claim, as Austin has already shown, rests on a confusion. However, Nowell-Smith also argues in favour of his analysis of 'could' and of 'can', in each case as requiring one or another conditional 'if' clause. The suggestion is that 'He/she could run a mile' means 'he/she would run a mile, if he/she has/had the opportunity and a preponderant motive' (and similarly for 'can' and 'will').

But, as Austin replies, whether or not someone would or will run a mile if certain conditions are satisfied takes us away from the issue of what they could do, and thus of their actual abilities (or, sometimes, of their actual opportunities). For even if the conditional claim, made of a person with these abilities, happens to be true, it does not follow either that it expresses the meaning of 'could' (any more than any of the many other implications of claims involving 'could' contrive to do), or that 'could' requires a conditional analysis at all. Thus 'Smith can run a mile' has not been shown to *mean* 'If Smith has the opportunity to run a mile, and a preponderant motive for running it, he will run it' (which is surely another matter); nor should we construe 'can' in general as meaning 'will . . . , if . . .', nor 'could' as 'would . . . , if . . .'. Nowell-Smith, then, fails to establish his determinism-friendly analysis of 'could have done otherwise' as involving abilities or tendencies conditional on a different world from that of what was actually done, and his failure suggests that 'could have done otherwise' tells us not about a different world but about abilities present in the actual one. Or, as Austin puts it, 'determinism . . . appears not consistent with what we ordinarily say, and presumably think'.[13]

So the prospects for compatibilism appear slender, and it begins to look as if incompatibilism should be preferred. But incompatibilism can take either of two forms, both of which may also seem unpromising. In one, we go along with B. F. Skinner, who (in *Beyond Freedom and Dignity*[14]) argues that we should endorse determinism and for that reason discard belief in free will, responsibility and related human capacities; but this seems like a last resort, since it involves discarding the notion of human agency, on which ethics is grounded. The other involves rejecting determinism in favour of belief in the kind of libertarian freedom portrayed above in the passage from Ward. But whatever the merits of rejecting determinism, the absence of causes for human actions (in the sense of sufficient conditions of those actions being performed) might seem to make them random, rather than free or rational. It is the problem of randomness that we now need to consider.

4. Indeterminism and randomness

Some forms of indeterminism claim (as we have seen in the previous section) that free actions are uncaused and even inexplicable and unpredictable. This approach has generated the response that if free action is neither explicable nor predictable, then it is also random and irrational behaviour, and the very antithesis of action that is responsible, for the agent is beyond control. Action of this kind, to quote A. J. Ayer, is the action of a lunatic.[15] To rescue responsibility, this response continues, we must forsake indeterminism.

This response seems in place as a response to Sartre's existentialist advocacy of unconstrained freedom, involving choices uninfluenced either by causes (external or internal) or by recognized values. For such choices seem completely unintelligible.

However, not all forms of indeterminism are subject to this criticism. The kind of libertarian freedom portrayed by Ward need not be inexplicable, nor need the free actions that theorists of action-causation explain by human agency. For, as John Lucas has argued,[16] action that is unexplained in terms of sufficient antecedent physical conditions may be far from random where explanations in terms of the agent's reasons are concerned. There are more than one kinds of explanation, and what is unexplained and random with regard to one kind can be readily explicable (and thus not random at all) through a rational explanation (which explains an action by reference to the agent's reason or reasons). So the absence of causes in the sense of sufficient antecedent conditions does not mean that an action is irrational, inexplicable, random or irresponsible.

Thomas Reid, who was mentioned in the previous section, two hundred years earlier presented his response to the 'randomness' objection, which he expresses in the words: 'if men are not necessarily determined by motives, all their actions must be capricious'.[17] His reply is that resisting what might be considered our strongest motives 'when duty requires, is so far from being capricious, that it is, in the highest degree, wise and virtuous. And we hope this is often done by good men'.[18] In other words, the objection only seems to work in the abstract, but as soon as we think of actual examples, such as conflicts between passion and duty, its misguidedness becomes both clear and important. But, as Reid would agree, the scope of voluntary action is much wider than that of conflicts between duties and desires.

Further (to return to the topic of sorts of explanation), as Lucas goes on to argue, only behaviour that is under-determined in terms of causal explanation is open to explanation by the agent's reasons.[19] While there will usually if not always be necessary causal conditions for an action (such as the Earth's gravitational pull on the agent), yet if there were sufficient causal conditions, then there would be nothing left to be explained, for the sufficiency of the sufficient causal conditions would mean that the action is already guaranteed, and would-be explanations in terms of the agent's reasons would be superfluous and redundant. Thus explanations of this kind work as explanations only because relevant causal explanations are (or are at least considered to be) incomplete. This, Lucas suggests, is the fundamental problem for compatibilism, which is committed to there being two explanations for each free action, both of them having genuine explanatory power. Accordingly believers in free will (or, in other words, in some human actions being voluntary and some of those being freely chosen) should abandon compatibilism, and adopt one or another form of incompatibilist indeterminism or libertarianism ('libertarianism' being the kind of position presented above by Ward, or, for some writers, simply another name for indeterminism).

They would not have to say that agents have control of the circumstances in which they act, much less over the relevant laws of nature. Nature and society, through both hereditary and environmental factors, can be recognized both to shape and to constrain people's scope for freedom. Yet if we sometimes have genuine options when we act (and could act otherwise), then more than one future is open to us; and if so, the use of ethical language about human action remains anything but futile.

Study questions

1. Can 'could have done otherwise' be interpreted in a sense compatible with determinism and at the same time expressing the freedom of human agents?
2. Are causally undetermined actions random and/or capricious as such?

Notes

1 Charles Darwin, *On the Origin of Species by Means of Natural Selection, or the Preservation of Favoured Races in the Struggle for Life*, London: John Murray, 1859.

2 Mary Midgley, *The Ethical Primate: Humans, Freedom and Morality*, London and New York: Routledge, 1994.

3 Alan Holland, 'Darwin and the Meaning of Life', *Environmental Values*, 18.4, 2009, pp. 503–18, at p. 505.

4 Charles Darwin, letter to William Graham, Down, 3 July 1881, in Francis Darwin (ed.), *The Life and Letters of Charles Darwin Including an Autobiographical Chapter*, London: John Murray, 1887, 1, pp. 315–16.

5 Alvin Plantinga, *Warrant and Proper Function*, New York and Oxford: Oxford University Press, 1993, pp. 216–37.

6 Richard Dawkins, *The Selfish Gene*, Oxford: Oxford University Press, 1976.

7 Keith Ward, 'Theistic Evolution', in William A. Dembski and Michael Ruse, *Debating Design: From Darwin to DNA*, Cambridge and New York: Cambridge University Press, 2004, pp. 261–74.

8 Daniel Dennett, *Elbow Room: The Varieties of Free Will Worth Wanting*, Oxford: Oxford University Press, 1984.

9 Kenneth R. Miller, *Finding Darwin's God: A Scientist's Search for Common Ground Between God and Evolution*, New York: HarperCollins, 1999, pp. 198–204.

10 J. R. Lucas, *The Freedom of the Will*, Clarendon Press: Oxford, 1970, pp. 107–72.

11 G. E. Moore, *Ethics* (1912), London: Oxford University Press, 1966; Patrick Nowell-Smith, *Ethics*, Harmondsworth, UK: Penguin, 1954.

12 J. L. Austin, 'Ifs and Cans', in J. L. Austin, *Philosophical Papers*, ed. J. O. Urmson and G. J. Warnock, London and New York: Oxford University Press, 1961, pp. 205–32, at p. 226.

13 Austin, ibid., p. 231.

14 B. F. Skinner, *Beyond Freedom and Dignity*, Harmondsworth: Penguin, 1973.

15 A. J. Ayer, 'Freedom and Necessity', *Philosophical Essays*, New York: Bedford/St. Martin's Press, 1969, pp. 271–84; reprinted in Russ Shafer-Landau (ed.), *Ethical Theory: An Anthology*, Malden, MA: Blackwell, 2007, pp. 349–54, where the relevant passage is at p. 350.

16 J. R. Lucas, 'Freedom and Prediction', *Proceedings of the Aristotelian Society, Supplementary Volume* XLI, 1967, pp. 163–72, at pp. 170f.; *The Freedom of the Will*, p. 58.

17 Thomas Reid, *Essays on the Active Powers of Man*, Essay IV, chapter IV; reprinted in Raphael (ed.), *British Moralists* (vol. 2), pp. 276–82, at p. 281.

18 Reid, ibid.

19 Lucas, 'Freedom and Prediction', pp. 170f.; *The Freedom of the Will*, pp. 47–50.

References

Austin, J. L., 'Ifs and Cans', in J. L. Austin, *Philosophical Papers*, ed. J. O. Urmson and G. J. Warnock, London and New York: Oxford University Press, 1961, pp. 205–32.

Ayer, A. J., 'Freedom and Necessity', *Philosophical Essays*, New York: Bedford/St. Martin's Press, 1969, pp. 271–84.

—, 'Freedom and Necessity', reprinted in Russ Shafer-Landau (ed.), *Ethical Theory: An Anthology*, Malden, MA: Blackwell, 2007, pp. 349–54.

Darwin, Charles, *On the Origin of Species by Means of Natural Selection, or the Preservation of Favoured Races in the Struggle for Life*, London: John Murray, 1859.

Darwin, Francis (ed.), *The Life and Letters of Charles Darwin Including an Autobiographical Chapter*, London: John Murray, 1887.

Dawkins, Richard, *The Selfish Gene*, Oxford: Oxford University Press, 1976.

Dennett, Daniel, *Elbow Room: The Varieties of Free Will Worth Wanting*, Oxford: Oxford University Press, 1984.

Holland, Alan, 'Darwin and the Meaning of Life', *Environmental Values*, 18.4, 2009, pp. 503–18.
Lucas, J. R., 'Freedom and Prediction', *Proceedings of the Aristotelian Society, Supplementary Volume* XLI, 1967, pp. 163–72.
—, *The Freedom of the Will*, Clarendon Press: Oxford, 1970.
Midgley, Mary, *The Ethical Primate: Humans, Freedom and Morality*, London and New York: Routledge, 1994.
Miller, Kenneth R., *Finding Darwin's God: A Scientist's Search for Common Ground Between God and Evolution*, New York: HarperCollins, 1999.
Moore, G. E., *Ethics* (1912), London: Oxford University Press, 1966.
Nowell-Smith, Patrick, *Ethics*, Harmondsworth, UK: Penguin, 1954.
Plantinga, Alvin, *Warrant and Proper Function*, New York and Oxford: Oxford University Press, 1993.
Reid, Thomas, *Essays on the Active Powers of Man*; reprinted in D. D. Raphael (ed.), *British Moralists* (vol. 2), pp. 276–82.
Skinner, B. F., *Beyond Freedom and Dignity*, Harmondsworth: Penguin, 1973.
Ward, Keith, 'Theistic Evolution', in William A. Dembski and Michael Ruse, *Debating Design: From Darwin to DNA*, Cambridge and New York: Cambridge University Press, 2004, pp. 261–74.

Section 4: The future is open

1. Three stances

The three previous sections have focused on issues relating to free will and determinism from three historical periods, the ancient world, the Early Modern period and the more recent period. This section surveys these issues for themselves, rather than historically, and seeks to draw some relevant conclusions.

The first requirement is to make clear the rival stances in this field. Determinism has all along claimed that every event is in principle predictable by reference to natural forces and earlier states of affairs, and in the language of laws of nature that every event is in principle predictable by reference to antecedent states of the world and laws of nature. It thus implies that at any given time only one future is physically possible. Belief in free will, however, holds that (in the words of Peter van Inwagen) 'human beings (and possibly other animals), faced with choices between two or more mutually incompatible courses of action, frequently have it in their power (or can) carry out each of them'.[1] The problem is that this belief seems to conflict with only one future being physically possible, and the rival stances are responses to this problem.

One stance endorses determinism and rejects belief in free will. This stance is often called 'hard determinism', and is a form of incompatibilism, or the view that determinism and belief in free will are incompatible. This stance involves abandonment of belief in human responsibility, and in what we usually mean by 'human agency'.

Table 6.1

Hard Determinism	Compatibilism, usually held in the form of Soft Determinism	Indeterminism, sometimes known as 'Libertarianism'
Determinism is true and incompatible with belief in free will, which is false, as is belief in moral responsibility.	Determinism and belief in free will are compatible and (a/c Soft Determinism) both are true. So free actions are determined.	Determinism and belief in free will are incompatible. The former is false and the latter is true. Free actions are not determined.

A second stance claims that determinism and belief in free will are compatible, and is called 'compatibilism', which seeks to supply determinism-friendly interpretations of phrases like 'free' and 'could have done otherwise'. Compatibilists need not accept determinism, but when they do their stance is known as 'soft determinism', to distinguish it from that of determinists of an incompatibilist tendency. Compatibilists also attempt to find room within a determinist framework for human responsibility.

The third major stance is another form of incompatibilism, but, unlike hard determinism, it rejects determinism in favour of belief in free will. Usually, as in this chapter, it is called 'indeterminism', but some people also call it 'libertarianism'. People who reject compatibilism need to discard either free will or determinism, and indeterminists abandon the latter. Their critics claim that indeterminism makes undetermined actions random and their agents out of control, but in the previous section we saw how this criticism proves unsuccessful. The three stances can be portrayed as in Table 6.1.

2. Encountering problems

Besides making sense of the language of voluntariness, freedom and choice, any acceptable theory needs to be able to provide for there being degrees of responsibility. For our attitudes to agency include not only exculpation, which removes responsibility, but also mitigation, which diminishes it. Phrases used to mitigate responsibility include 'impulsively', 'reluctantly', 'half-heartedly' and 'inadvertently'. Hard determinism makes no attempt to respect these distinctions, which it has to regard as illusory. While some forms of indeterminism, holding that freedom is an all-or-nothing matter, are equally unhelpful, others can recognize that the scope for and extent of freedom varies both between agents and between situations.

Soft determinists can attempt to say the same, but have to accept the handicap that in their view in no situation is any other outcome physically possible in any case. The scope for freedom must if so concern the extent to which different desires on the agent's part would have generated different outcomes. But this seems less than we mean when we talk of voluntary actions and of free choices. Besides, as we saw in the previous section, there are formidable problems for the claim of compatibilism that free actions have two independent explanations, both of which make an explanatory difference.

Perhaps the most cogent form of compatibilism turns on the claim that free actions are caused by the agent's character (a move that we have encountered earlier on the part of the Stoic Chrysippus). Of itself, this claim is a plausible one, although it may still be mistaken, since actions that are out-of-character sometimes happen, and, impulsive as they may often be, some of them seem to be freely chosen.

However, even if we grant that free actions are generally caused by the agent's character, can this claim be harnessed to a determinist account of action? For the very concept of character concerns dispositions to choose in certain ways (see the sections on Aristotle, on Virtue Ethics and on Responsibility), and so this approach implicitly appeals to the agent's choices. Besides, if Aristotle and his many followers are right, character necessarily originates through an agent making the kinds of choice that later give shape to her character. This may not be the full story, but while it is arguable that in some cases character is as much shaped by an adverse or precarious social environment, it is implausible that an agent's choices play no part at all in character-formation. So this appeal to character implicitly appeals twice over to choices on the agent's part, and at that to choices where (short of some compatibilist analysis being accepted) more than one outcome is possible. Accordingly appeals to character (which are actually all but appeals to agent-causation) fail to advance the compatibilist case.

Granted also the inadequacy of compatibilist analyses of free action (see the section on Laws of Nature) and of 'could have done otherwise' (see the section before this one), it must now be concluded that compatibilism is itself implausible. Compatibilism, after all, is basically claiming that talk of acting freely simply means one's actions being determined by one's desires, or by those desires with which one can identify.[2] And yet we usually hold that people are able to resist their desires (including ones they can identify with), and are free to think again. Further, compatibilism is claiming that those who say that a president or prime minister could have adopted different principles simply mean that in other circumstances they *would* have adopted such principles. But this account appears actually to ignore the character of the person concerned, and their capacity to make choices accordingly, and to do so without the circumstances being different.

3. Problems for determinism

This being so, the remaining options are hard determinism and indeterminism. But hard determinism has to be regarded as problematic, as we have seen, in view of its rejection of there being degrees of moral responsibility, and indeed of anyone ever being morally responsible at all. Indeed it could be argued that belief in human agency and responsibility is more secure and more basic than any grounds we might have for endorsing determinism, and thus for rejecting these beliefs.

In any case, determinism (whether hard or soft) faces a further problem. If it were true, then it ought standardly to be possible to learn what we are each going to do by remarking our current desires and discovering it from those. While this can occasionally be done (when we are adopting a spectator's perspective about ourselves), characteristically we find out what we are going to do not on this inductive basis, but by making up our minds, that is, by taking decisions; being active persons (or agents), we cannot standardly or in general adopt a spectator's perspective about our own actions and course in life.[3] So, unless the belief that we shape the future by deciding it is illusory, this fact about predicting our own future actions conflicts importantly with determinism, and thus with both its soft and its hard varieties.

Here is yet a further problem. The determinist has to hold that her own belief in determinism is held unavoidably, just as any contrary belief would have been; so it cannot have been adopted rationally or for good reasons. She can only hold that her belief is rational if she exempts herself from the scope of determinism, and suppose that others would be rational in becoming determinists if they are exempted from its scope as well (in which case it is far from universally true). This reasoning does not show determinism to be false, but does show that it cannot be rationally believed,[4] and thus suffices to undermine the case in its favour.

4. Non-deterministic freedom

It is time to reflect on whether we can make sense of human freedom on an indeterministic basis. In earlier sections of this chapter, we have come across kinds of indeterminism that regard freely chosen action as entirely uncaused (such as Sartre's variety), kinds that make provision for such action to be explicable by the agent's reasons (such as Lucas's and Ward's versions) and kinds that represent the agent as the cause of such action, without her choices being causally determined (Reid's version, recently championed by O'Connor). So far, the first of these versions has been found implausible, while the second and third kinds seem much more plausible, and are compatible with each other.

But can human freedom, thus understood, be reconciled with Darwinism and with our evolutionary heritage? Mary Midgley, drawing on Darwin's own work rather than the interpretations of neo-Darwinists such as Dawkins, has recently argued that the kind of evolutionary inheritance that Darwinism leads us to expect is just what would be needed for capacities for freedom of choice to develop. We tend to think of conflicts on the model of tensions between duty and desire, but in fact our animal ancestors were already experiencing conflicting drives, in the form of clashing instincts between (say) mating and flight from predators. Thus some migratory birds are observed to have conflicts between continuing to nurture late-season offspring and abandoning them to join in a mass migration, while mammals may well be torn between drinking to satisfy thirst and feeding their young.[5] It would be in awareness of such conflicts, and attempts to form goals, plans or priorities, that possibilities for freedom originate, given the need to integrate conflicting drives, whether among non-humans or among human beings. For 'Unlike machines, which typically have a single, fixed function, evolved organisms have a plurality of aims, held together flexibly in a complex but versatile system. It is only this second, complex arrangement that could make our type of freedom possible at all'.[6]

While non-human animals cannot be supposed to have a concept of the future (other than of the immediate scene of action), their behaviour often suggests intelligent responses to the world as they perceive it. Besides, the behaviour of domestic animals suggests that some of their activities are enjoyed, and that others are adopted despite contrary instincts, sometimes as a result of training. While the point cannot be argued here, it seems far from absurd to withhold from non-human animals talk of voluntary action and even of choices, even though the great majority lack the self-awareness and sense of the future possessed by a majority of human beings, and also probably by species such as chimpanzees, gorillas, dolphins and whales.

The development of awareness of oneself and of one's own future adds to the possibilities, particularly when language makes it possible to conceptualize different options and thus different futures, and language is taught in a social setting in which numerous words (many of them verbs) are available for actions one can perform and moves one can make. Language also enables us to retrieve through memory information and messages from the past. At the same time the concept of oneself as an ongoing agent facilitates the formation of intentions and plans. To all this Midgley adds the impacts of a range of inherited motives. The sociability that human inherit facilitates affection and enduring relationships, the ability to understand other individuals' feelings and perspectives and the ability to put oneself in their place; and this brings with it a growing grasp of different values, each supplying reasons for one or another pursuit.[7]

All this makes possible the envisaging of many different ways forward, and also the ability to reflect on them and deliberate between then. Not all actions will be either rational or voluntary, for many will be instinctual and others will be performed either under duress and/or because of social pressures, or in face of inadequate information or awareness of one's circumstances. Hence Aristotle's distinctions between voluntary actions and ones affected by coercion or by ignorance here become relevant (although they may have relevance to the behaviour of animals as well). Once different options can be envisaged, choices can begin; and with the making of recurrent choices in relatively stable social settings, traits of character can begin to emerge. In due course, agents even become capable of shaping the kind of agents that they want to be; but they can be regarded as free agents long before that stage is reached.

In the previous section, Darwin's own worry was mentioned that if our thoughts are determined by our evolutionary inheritance, then they may be valueless (because of being inevitable), or no more valuable than the thoughts of a monkey.[8] But since Darwin seems not to have persisted in holding this conclusion, he must have envisaged the possibility that, rather than our thoughts all being determined to be as they are, our evolutionary heritage empowers us to think and behave in accordance with choices and with values. If Darwinism is understood as deterministic (with all animal and human behaviour being produced by the pressures of natural selection), it undermines its own credibility. But if it is understood in a non-deterministic form, then its credibility remains intact,[9] and at the same time it can provide for the development of human discretion and self-determination, or for what has traditionally been called 'free will'.

Darwin further contributed to this kind of interpretation by maintaining that natural selection is not the only factor behind the evolutionary process.[10]

Midgley is among those who have discussed what further factors there might be,[11] mentioning the self-organization of species and cooperation within and among species as possibilities. But there is no need to seek to resolve that matter here. The key point is that Darwinism does not say, and need not say, that natural selection determines our thoughts and actions. As we have seen, we can hold instead that our evolutionary inheritance makes it possible for our behaviour, and some of our thoughts (such as intentions and decisions) as well, to be shaped by ourselves. And as Midgley says, the mere fact that my thoughts and actions are sometimes predictable does not make me unfree, as long as those thoughts and actions are predictable from reasons and motives of my own.[12]

Since this is a book on ethics, it should be added that Midgley uses the same developmental narrative to explain the origins of morality. Conscious, deliberate choices depend on awareness of a plurality of values, and awareness of values (or reasons for action) in a social setting generates a need (shared among participants in early societies) for goals and principles suited to social existence. So does an awareness of relationships and the loyalties that go with them. Hence Midgley's story of the emergence of freedom concerns not only free will as a prerequisite of morality, but also the emergence of morality itself.[13]

For Midgley, determinism has no contribution to make to this understanding of the evolution of choice, and would probably render it incoherent.[14] This view makes sense because the powers of discretion and of self-determination imply and depend on there being in some situations more than one possible choice, decision or action available to agents. If no more than one future were ever possible in a given situation, then the very idea of these powers would be illusory, and it would be difficult to explain how they could ever develop.

Just which version of indeterminism is preferable cannot altogether be resolved here. Versions that represent human freedom as unconstrained and actions as uncaused should clearly be rejected, since actions have causes in the sense of necessary conditions, and are constrained by material circumstances. What needs to be resisted is the view that for all actions there are causally sufficient conditions. Maybe we should, with Lucas, van Inwagen and Ward, simply hold that actions are to be explained by their agents' reasons, rather than by causal determinants; or maybe we should hold, with Reid and O'Connor, that actions are caused by agents, but that agents' choices are not causally determined (as long as our understanding of causes allows us to hold this view: see Elizabeth Anscombe's account of causation[15]). Or, as previously mentioned, we could combine these two views. Whichever option we adopt, we can consistently hold that agents are often responsible for their actions, to some degree or other.

Aristotle's view that voluntary actions have their origins within the agent makes it at least likely that he would have agreed. And even if his view is premature that actions initiated by agents with adequate knowledge are always voluntary (for there may be unusual circumstances, as when agents have been drugged or hypnotized), this view remains cogent for occasions when there are no such unusual circumstances, or, in other words, for most of the time.

Any of these views allows us to adhere to the third of the three stances presented at the beginning of this section, the stance of indeterminism, also widely known as 'libertarianism'. In adopting this stance, we are importantly enabled to affirm that a key presupposition of ethical discourse (the ability of agents to do otherwise) is sometimes in place, and that on these occasions the future is open.

Study questions

1. Is belief in determinism consistent with belief in the freedom of the will?
2. To what extent are agents responsible for their characters?

Notes

1 Peter van Inwagen, *An Essay on Free Will*, Oxford: Clarendon Press, 1983, p. 8.

2 Harry G. Frankfurt, 'Freedom of the Will and the Concept of a Person', *Journal of Philosophy*, 68, 1971, pp. 5–20; reprinted in Gary Watson (ed.), *Free Will*, Oxford: Oxford University Press, 1982, pp. 81–95. See also Joseph Keim Campbell, *Free Will*, Polity: Cambridge, 2011.

3 R. S. Downie and Elizabeth Telfer, *Respect for Persons*, London: Allen and Unwin, 1969, pp. 101–2.

4 J. R. Lucas, 'Freedom and Prediction', *Proceedings of the Aristotelian Society, Supplementary Volume* XLI, 1967, pp. 163–72, at pp. 171–2.

5 Mary Midgley, *The Ethical Primate: Humans, Freedom and Morality*, London and New York: Routledge, 1994, pp. 160–1.

6 Ibid., p. 164.

7 Ibid., pp. 161–3 and 103–4.

8 Charles Darwin, letter to William Graham, Down, 3 July 1881, in Francis Darwin (ed.), *The Life and Letters of Charles Darwin Including an Autobiographical Chapter*, London: John Murray, 1887, 1, pp. 315–16.

9 Robin Attfield, 'Darwin's Doubt, Non-deterministic Darwinism and the Cognitive Science of Religion', *Philosophy*, 85.4, 2010, pp. 465–83.

10 See Simon Blackburn, 'I Rather Think I Am A Darwinian', *Philosophy*, 71, 1996, pp. 605–16.

11 Midgley, *The Ethical Primate*, pp. 126–7.

12 Ibid., p. 164.

13 Ibid., pp. 3, 133–4, 136, and in particular at pp. 175–9. See also Midgley, 'The Origin of Ethics', in Peter Singer (ed.), *A Companion to Ethics*, Oxford and Cambridge, MA: Blackwell, 1991, pp. 3–13.

14 Midgley, *The Ethical Primate*, p. 150.

15 G. E. M. Anscombe, 'Causality and Determination', in Anscombe, *Metaphysics and the Philosophy of Mind*, Oxford: Blackwell, 1981, pp. 133–47. See also G. E. M. Anscombe, 'Soft Determinism', in Gilbert Ryle, *Contemporary Aspects of Philosophy*, Stocksfield: Oriel Press, 1976, pp. 148–60.

References

Anscombe, G. E. M., 'Soft Determinism', in Gilbert Ryle, *Contemporary Aspects of Philosophy*, Stocksfield: Oriel Press, 1976, pp. 148–60.

—, 'Causality and Determination', in G. E. M. Anscombe, *Metaphysics and the Philosophy of Mind*, Oxford: Blackwell, 1981, pp. 133–47.

Attfield, Robin, 'Darwin's Doubt, Non-deterministic Darwinism and the Cognitive Science of Religion', *Philosophy*, 85.4, 2010, pp. 465–83.

Blackburn, Simon, 'I Rather Think I Am A Darwinian', *Philosophy*, 71, 1996, pp. 605–16.

Campbell, Joseph Keim, *Free Will*, Polity: Cambridge. 2011.

Darwin, Francis (ed.), *The Life and Letters of Charles Darwin Including an Autobiographical Chapter*, London: John Murray, 1887.

Downie, R. S. and Elizabeth Telfer, *Respect for Persons*, London: Allen & Unwin, 1969.

Frankfurt, Harry G., 'Freedom of the Will and the Concept of a Person', *Journal of Philosophy*, 68, 1971, pp. 5–20.

—, 'Freedom of the Will and the Concept of a Person', reprinted in Gary Watson (ed.), *Free Will*, Oxford: Oxford University Press, 1982, pp. 81–95.

Lucas, J. R., 'Freedom and Prediction', *Proceedings of the Aristotelian Society, Supplementary Volume* XLI, 1967, pp. 163–72.

Midgley, Mary, 'The Origin of Ethics', in Peter Singer (ed.), *A Companion to Ethics*, Oxford and Cambridge, MA: Blackwell, 1991, pp. 3–13.

—, *The Ethical Primate: Humans, Freedom and Morality*, London and New York: Routledge, 1994

van Inwagen, Peter, *An Essay on Free Will*, Oxford: Clarendon Press, 1983.

Index